This Is Ethical Theory

This Is Ethical Theory

JAN NARVESON

OPEN COURT

Chicago and La Salle, Illinois

To order books from Open Court, call 1-800-815-2280 or visit
www.opencourtbooks.com.

Open Court Publishing Company is a division of Carus Publishing Company.

© 2009 by Carus Publishing Company

First printing 2009

Printed and bound in the United States of America.

Library of Congress Cataloging-in-Publication Data

Narveson, Jan, 1936-
    This is ethical theory / Jan Narveson.
      p. cm.
    Includes bibliographical references (p.   ) and index.
    ISBN 978-0-8126-9646-2 (trade paper : alk. paper)
    1. Ethics. I. Title.
BJ1012.N35 2009
    171--dc22

                                       2009015858

Contents

Preface   ix

Introduction: Ethical Theorizing   1

PART 1: Metaethics   17

     What Is Metaethics?   19
     Metaethical Intuitionism   32
     Other Intuitionisms   51
     Emotivism and Prescriptivism   62
     Reviving Naturalism   91
     Morals   111

PART 2: Normative Morals: A Review of the Popular Theories   135

     Introduction   137
     Moral Relativism, Again   138
     Egoism   143
     Virtue   148
     Religious Ethics   151
     Conscience   156
     Convention   158
     Legalism: Law and Morals   160
     The "Natural" Law   163
     Elitisms   164
     Innate Moral Reason   166

Kant's Categorical Imperative 167
Bureaucratic Ethics: Rigorism 170
Particularism, Again 172
Sentiment 174
Utilitarianism 175
'Consequentialism'/'Nonconsequentialism'—A Note
   on a Bogus Distinction 183
Rawls 185

PART 3: Normative Morality: A Theory 195

Introduction: The Defining Features 197
The "Social Contract" Approach to Moral Theory 200
Prisoner's Dilemma 204
The Assurance Problem 206
Morality's Contribution to a Solution 206
Rational Morality as the Best Mutual Agreement 208
Nielsen's Critique: Why Should I Be Moral? 210
Alan Gewirth's Argument: Does It Avoid the Social
   Contract? 211
Critique of the Argument 213
The Hobbesian Premise 215
Unpacking the Metaphor of "Signing Up" 216
Negative versus Positive Rights and Duties 217
Counting the Cost 219
The Hobbesian "Law of Nature" 220
What about the Terrorists? 221
Is Morality Rational? The Score Card 222
Morality: The Carrot and the Stick 225
Mutual Aid 226
Charity and the "Social Contract" 228
Moral Complexity 229
Equality and Egalitarianism 230
Arguments for Equality 233
The Two-Variables Fallacy 235
Morals and Politics 236
Virtue, Again 236
Virtues and Rules 239
Fuzzy Edges and Approximate Principles: Rules and
   the Real World 240

Moral Luck   241

The "Existential" Factor   242

Personal Concerns versus Moral Requirements   243

Unchosen Personal Obligations   244

PART 4: Happiness, Living Well, and Doing Well   247

Introduction   249

Human Nature   250

"Realizing" the Self   251

Desire   252

Health as a Model   254

Virtues—One Last Time   255

Accomplishment   257

Meaning   258

A Note on the Religious Life   263

Hedonism   264

Ideals   267

Happiness   268

Challenges   270

A Final Word   271

General Bibliography   273

Index   279

Preface

This is not quite your ordinary introduction to ethical theory, but I hope it is not too far off that model either. People with no previous background in ethical theory can certainly read this book. On the other hand, I certainly intend for people who do have such a background, including many colleagues and other professionals, to read it. I make many novel claims and arguments.

This is neither a history nor a historical introduction, but I frequently refer to various classics. The reader will not fail to notice my interest and affection for those endlessly fascinating writings. In my bibliography I mention a set of those, as well as the many books and papers I have singled out for discussion.

I not only discuss many theories, including all of the historically popular theories, but I also put forth a new theory, the one that seems to me to be the best general account of morals. I distinguish between moral theory in particular and a much more general subject that I call ethics, in the appropriately more general sense that I try to spell out in part 2. That more general subject I do not propose a "theory of," and suppose—in agreement with most of my fellow professional philosophers—that we need not and probably should not have such a theory, except in a sense in which perhaps everyone has one, and in which, anyway, a huge variety can be found.

It remains to thank quite a few people. First, there are my students down through a lifetime of university teaching. So many of these have provided stimulus, inspiration, and the peculiar kind of pleasure that only discourse with young minds can bring. Second, there are many, many people with whom I have discussed many of these matters, and the still more whose works I am familiar with but who did not make it into these pages—the book is much longer than originally intended already. I am especially grateful to David Gauthier, the influence of whose ideas will

x

be, I hope, obvious. Finally, there are my dear and remarkable family, and many good friends, among whom I must single out Mr. James Leger for no end of helpful services and ideas over several decades.

Introduction:
Ethical Theorizing

What It's About

Everybody—well, almost everybody—occasionally thinks or says that something is right or wrong, ought or ought not to be done, is a good or bad thing to do; or that someone is a good or bad person, a "good guy" or a "creep"; or that some way to live is a good or bad one. Almost all of us have a bundle of more or less definite moral beliefs, very likely—say, that killing innocent people or lying is wrong. But almost anyone old enough to be reading this kind of book will also have noticed that every now and then there is serious disagreement between, say, herself and someone else, or among some people you know or have read about, concerning the rights and wrongs of someone's actions or some institution's programs. When that happens, it quite possibly has occurred to you to wonder how such disagreements might be settled in a reasonable way. How do we figure out who's right? And you may also have encountered people—perhaps even yourself—who deny that such issues *can* be settled, perhaps on the ground that ethics is "subjective" or some such dismissive category. If so, books such as this one are written for people like you. For this book is about ethical *theory*. Theorists worry about things like that, and attempt to do something about them.

So what is ethical theory? An old-fashioned view of the matter will have it that the point of ethical theory is to get to the root of the matter—to try to come up with the true general picture of what's going on when we make ethical judgments, along with some sort of general recommended program of conduct. But there are newer fashions, and prominent among them are ones that involve major doubts about the possibility of doing any such thing as getting to the "root of the matter."

1

They ask, "Whose justice? Which rationality?"[1] And they will tell us about the "failure of the Enlightenment" and that "there is no absolute standpoint from which we can arrive at absolute moral truths."[2] The variety of positions about such things among professional philosophers is quite disconcerting, indeed. Perhaps it attests to the plausibility of the contention that there is no "truth" to be found. We will have to consider that idea, and we will, presently. But interestingly, among this same set of thinkers, there is likely to be a much smaller degree of disagreement about many concrete issues of the day, and very little indeed about certain very general principles of morality. No one seriously thinks that killing people for fun, for example, is perfectly all right.

I will show that the arguments against the possibility of reasonable views on ethics are muddled and unpersuasive, and even that the Enlightenment view, as it has been called, looks pretty good. But in the course of coming to such conclusions, we will consider the major options in ethical theory, especially as found in the past century or so. This is not just a tour. We will try to assess those various theories as well, and tentatively accept or reject them, perhaps with some modifications. Many of them are more compatible than is usually claimed; but some are not, and I think that some among those contending theories can be shown to be unacceptable.

In the process, we will have to pay a good deal of attention to methodological matters. These have been, and remain, the subject of intense discussion, especially during that same past century or so. Readers who get interested in these sometimes arcane-seeming matters will want to consult some of the literature, a selection of which will be mentioned in the bibliography at the end of this book. All readers will, I hope, nevertheless leave with a sense that there is decent hope for ethical theory after all, as well as an appreciation of its major issues.

Ethical theory is no new thing. Ever since at least Plato (427–347 B.C.)—who himself made some major contributions to the subject—intelligent people have been interested in, and often concerned about, this subject. Sometimes they have done so simply because it is interesting—one never needs more than that, after all, to pursue a subject. But many writers have in addition had a sense that things were not going well in the social world they lived in, and that they could be improved, that there is practical benefit as well as intellectual pleasure to be had from thinking about the sort of issues we'll be getting into here. It's difficult not to agree with them.

---

[1] See Alasdair MacIntyre, *Whose Justice? Which Rationality?* (Notre Dame: Univ. of Notre Dame Press, 1988).

[2] This was said by Dr. Muhammad Legenhausen, in his review of the aforementioned work, at http://www.al-islam.org/al-tawhid/whosejustice/title.htm.

Organizing the Subject

A familiar map of our subject divides it into two parts, known as "metaethics" and "normative ethics" or sometimes "substantive ethics." With some reservations, we'll accept that division here. A further division is between normative ethics as a general, theoretical subject, and normative ethics in the sense of inquiries into quite specific moral issues and questions. It is especially this last subject that we will *not* be much concerned with in this book, although we will discuss the relation between abstract and general theorizing about normative ethics and its hands-on application.

For much of the twentieth century, a view prevailed that philosophical ethics can only be concerned with the first of this pair, which now goes by the name "metaethics." And it is certainly an important one—indeed, it is the paradigmatic task of the philosopher. Metaethics is concerned especially with *meaning*: just what *are* we talking about when we talk about ethical matters? And it is concerned with logical matters: just how do we go from one sort of claim to another, especially if one of them is an ethical claim and the other not? Saying this brings up what have become deep and sometimes highly technical issues about language. One of my theoretical guidelines in this inquiry is that it is misguided to think that a subject like ethics can turn on subtle and technical distinctions in semantic theory. We are looking for something that should, I think, be accessible to any normally intelligent person. This is not just a prejudice—there are special reasons for thinking that, as we will see later on.

Meanwhile, however, the other general division, "normative" ethics, is intended to cover the propounding, elaboration, and development of ethical claims themselves—not just statements about what other statements *mean*, but claims that some of those statements are true, or at any rate plausible, or acceptable. Metaethics includes as a major one of its tasks that of deciding which of those terms, 'true', 'acceptable', or maybe something else, is the best one to use for this purpose. But whichever, the normative theorist hopes to show us that, indeed, some kinds of actions really are right, others wrong, what sorts of things we ought and ought not to do, which kinds of people *are* good people and which are, by comparison, bad, in the respects in which ethics is concerned with goodness and badness. Or, that in some cases the matter may be difficult or even impossible to decide.

A further distinction can also be made here, as well: between the *general theory* of normative ethics, with which this book will be concerned, and *applied* ethics, with which it will deal scarcely at all. Applied ethics gets down to quite concrete and specific issues, such as whether in vitro fertilization is morally acceptable. A general theory of normative ethics would provide the major premises of discussions about such issues, but the actual application to such things requires further, detailed knowledge, which is well beyond the province of a book on theory such as this.

A major thesis of this book will be that there is an extremely important distinction within ethics, between what I shall call 'ethics' more generally, and a narrower subject that I will designate by the fairly old-fashioned word 'morals' or 'morality.' The need for and importance of a distinction of that kind will be argued for. Some of the historically famous muddles of ethics are due, I think, to the failure to make that distinction. And some of the historically famous writers on ethics, on the other hand, have been fairly well aware of it, and made brilliant contributions to the subject in the course of doing so.

It remains to say that the division between metaethics as concerned narrowly with meaning and normative ethics as concerned with making ethical pronouncements themselves is misleading and unsatisfactory. There's a good deal more to it than that, as will be seen. But while there is, the division as such is not wrong or confused—just inadequate.

I won't go further than this by way of introduction, for each of my topics must be explained as I go along. What I will do, however, is say some more about general questions of how to proceed in this rather special and fascinating subject.

Is There Something Special about Ethics?

We live in a world of various kinds of objects, some of which we put to many uses, others of which we see, or bump into, daily. Still, few of us go around with physical theories in our heads. We've heard of the law of gravity, perhaps, though we have little notion of how it works or precisely what it says. We more or less settle for a crude understanding that could be summarized as "things fall," a familiar fact of experience. By contrast, however, a great many people do have some "moral laws" *in their heads*. They've learned them in their youth, and they have stuck there ever since. Moreover, those rules have effect. People frequently do refrain from certain actions because they think those actions would be wrong, and they often cite some general rules or maxims in support of their judgments. In this respect, it seems that ethics stands in considerable contrast to physics, or more generally, to science. Claims that somebody acted wrongly (or rightly) seem to be made on the basis of antecedently held general beliefs, rather than being made in the way that our usual factual claims are made. "The post office is right down the street" is not said on the basis of some sort of theory held by the speaker, but on the basis of information about that particular fact. You do have to have some idea what a post office is if you are to answer someone's query about its location, but that idea needn't amount to much, and especially, it needn't amount to a generalization or a rule.

Naively speaking, we have a great deal of information about the world on the basis of ordinary perception. We see the lightning strike the barn because our eyes are open and there it was—not because we know anything about how lightning works. Philosophers have raised difficulties about the "empiricist" theory of knowledge, and yet they can hardly deny that we all find out a great many things by seeing and hearing. There might be some antecedent "theory" involved—no doubt the concept of a "material object" is not one that we can easily analyze in terms of sense perceptions, if at all, and we do make daily use of a vocabulary of what philosophers call "material object" terms. Yet if we tried to state the alleged theory, we'd be very hard put to do it. We can assert with confidence that things don't just disappear in thin air (except certain kinds of things, now and then), and that the bed I sleep on will still be there supporting my body as I sleep, and a thousand other things. But do these amount to a "theory"?

Moral judgments are different. The claim that some particular action is wrong requires some sort of a reason for its support. We don't formulate the generalization that murder is wrong from having observed many cases of murder, noted in each case that it is wrong, and concluded that murder is wrong. The generalization is antecedent to the "fact": *this* murder is wrong *because it's murder*, and murder is a *kind* of action that is wrong.

David Hume asks us to

Take any action allow'd to be vicious: Willful murder, for instance. Examine it in all lights, and see if you can find that matter of fact, or real existence, which you call vice. In whichever way you take it, you find only certain passions, motives, volitions and thoughts. There is no other matter of fact in the case. The vice entirely escapes you, till you turn your reflection into your own breast, and find a sentiment of disapprobation, which arises in you, towards this action.[3]

That actions of that kind are to be disapproved of is something the onlooker already "knows"—or if he does not, then observing another one isn't likely to make much difference. Hume says that the difference lies in "our own breasts." He means this in a sense that would distinguish it

---

[3] David Hume, *A Treatise of Human Nature*, edited by L. A. Selby-Bigge. (Oxford: Oxford Univ. Press, 1955), bk. III, part I, sec. I, 468–69.

from the usual cases of perception. "Breasts" are not "eyes": it is not my "own eyes" that *cause* the trees to look green, even though if I had no eyes I would not be able to have the experience I have when I see them. Hume's point is that you can observe anything there may be to observe about the events in which the murder consists, but the classification of it as murder involves more than a summary of information received. It involves also, he says, a *reaction* on our part—not just more information. And it is pretty difficult to deny Hume's claim. (Not impossible. In philosophy, it's hard to think of anything, however apparently obvious, that is not seriously questioned or denied by someone out there.)

Is it the other way around too? Do I need to react with some kind of interest, perhaps with approval or disapproval, before I can see anything? No. Always, I will see something because I am looking in that direction, and often I am looking in that direction because I am interested in something, or even because I approve or disapprove of something. But in the first place, I might not be looking *out of interest* for or at something: I might just be taking in the passing scene. And in the second, whether I have the "reaction" of seeing blue, or whatever else I see, is not *due to* my looking, but to the fact that there is something there causing my perceptions. One can't just *decide* to see something: one simply sees it.

But do we *decide* to approve or disapprove of something? Often not, to be sure. Our upbringings, likely, will be such that a reaction of that kind might be quite spontaneous. But, for one thing, very often we do have to think before deciding how to react. And for another, we can always ask whether a given reaction was reasonable, well taken. It might be that we come, after further thought, to think that we reacted inappropriately. No such thing can be said about a typical case of seeing blue. You do, or you don't, and that's it.

Fact and Value

All this suggests, at least, that there is some kind of a general distinction of *fact* and *value*. As we shall see, the word 'value' in this last sentence has to be taken in a very general way, for theorists may insist that it covers at least three very different things: value, taken generally; *obligation* or perhaps *duty*; and *virtue*, taken as an aspect of *character*. All sorts of things can be good or bad—implements, the weather, works of art, governments, as well as moral actions and their effects; but only acts can be morally right or wrong, obligatory or forbidden; and only character can be morally virtuous or vicious (though virtue concepts apply widely in nonmoral contexts as well). We will be discussing those distinctions more carefully later on, but I think it nevertheless true that we can recognize that all of these fall on one side of a line, and that it has another side—the realm, as we might put it, of *fact*. (But facts too come at various levels: are gravity, or the forces that hold the parts of an atom together, or the "big bang" to be reckoned as facts, along with the blueness of the sky? For present purposes, I am taking it that the answer is in the affirmative.)

We can also see that there are canons of science. Scientific investigation and theorizing can be done well or badly; and scientists value their activity, and its results. Still, when you take a theory, however strongly supported, elegant, or whatever, and then ask whether we ought to do something about some situation where this theory might be applicable in the construction of devices or artifacts, we cross the line over into the territory of ethics. That it was possible to build an atomic bomb was a major result of science; but whether it ought to be used was obviously quite another matter, about which physics as such says nothing at all.

To try to identify this fundamental distinction between fact and value— if indeed there is one —has been a major preoccupation of ethical theory. But another and much narrower one has been the other two subjects, obligation and virtue. The latter two will, in fact, be much more prominent in this book than the former. We would scarcely have a subject of *ethics* if it were not so. We would, however, have a subject of *aesthetics*, for example, and it is important to raise the question of how the two, among many other domains in which we use the vocabulary of good and bad, better and worse, are related, if at all. We will be doing some of that, too.

Is the distinction of fact and value fundamental and generic? Or are values really just one special department, as it were, of facts? To put it another way: are values *some facts among others*? Or, are they *not facts at all*? This sort of question has been a preoccupation of ethical theory for a very long time, and will be a major concern in the next many pages. Later, we will even look at a contribution to the subject by St. Thomas Aquinas (thirteenth century). But it was a special concern—some would say, a mania—of twentieth-century philosophy. Getting somehow straight about it is a sort of Holy Grail of moral philosophy. We will be very much concerned with it in this book.

The "Foundations" of Ethics

Historically, many ethical thinkers would say that they were interested in identifying the "foundations" of ethics. (W. D. Ross's second book is called just that.[4]) In recent decades, however, many philosophers have

---

[4] W. D. Ross, *The Foundations of Ethics* (Oxford: Oxford Univ. Press, 1930).

insisted that there are no such things, or at least that we don't need any. "Antifoundationalism" has become one of the familiar ideas in philosophy. Is it a good one? A classic quip has it that "A philosopher is someone who, when he gets into trouble, makes a distinction."[5] It is really a major insight into our field. Something puzzles us; we form a question about it. But perhaps something is wrong with the question. Further analysis may divide it into two or more questions each of which has an answer, and the appearance of puzzlement in the original question then, perhaps, disappears. Or at least, we have a better idea how to proceed. So let's make some of the needed distinctions.

A first question is: Foundations of *what?* A major thesis of this book will be that there is a rather special branch of ethics, which has sometimes been called *morals*. Hume's *Inquiry concerning the Principles of Morals* and Kant's famous *Foundations of the Metaphysics of Morals* are about that subject, and neither of them, as such, has anything to say about aesthetics, for example. What's more, I want to suggest that the view called "antifoundationalism" has a good deal to be said for it in aesthetics, but much less to be said for it in strictly *moral* philosophy. Is there some general feature in common to all beautiful things, which *makes* them beautiful? No. But is there some general feature in common to all wrong acts that makes them wrong? Yes—so I shall argue. A recent writer, Jonathan Dancy, addressing this matter, says, "It is odd that nobody has spent much time on principles of aesthetics . . . unless there is some significant difference between moral and aesthetic valuations."[6] To this there are two responses: one, that some (possibly misguided) people *do* claim to find principles of aesthetics—witness the well-known (except apparently to Dancy) American (that's probably why) classic by DeWitt H. Parker, *Principles of Aesthetics*.[7] But the other response is—yes, there *is* a striking difference between the two, which will be developed and emphasized in the ensuing pages. We will see both that and why there is such a difference.

Next, we must ask, What is a "foundation"? What are we talking about here? Here we can distinguish four different (though related) things which might reasonably be so called:

(1) *Meaning:* One could identify the foundations of a subject with a general analysis of what the subject *is*—of what it means, then, to say that something belongs to that subject. In this sense the "foundations" are its

---

[5] Alas, I don't know who said this first. I wish it had been myself!

[6] Jonathan Dancy, in a review of a recent book, *Times Literary Supplement*, Dec. 1, 2006, p. 32.

[7] Consider for example, the semi-classic *The Principles of Aesthetics* by Dewitt H. Parker (New York: Appleton-Century-Crofts, 1946).

cognitive location—precisely where it is in the firmament of things and ideas. That is the subject of *metaethics*, with which we will be concerned very soon.

(2) *Explanation:* Why do we have such a thing as morals at all? This would further divide into two subquestions:

(a) *"Moral psychology"*: what is it about people that enables them to have such a thing as moral ideas, moral principles, moral qualms and questionings?—and

(b) Why do we need or want morals? What's the *point*? Or is there any—maybe we're just born that way?

(3) Are there some features of things or actions that are the *basic* ones that *make* those things good or those actions right or wrong?

Here we need to make yet a finer distinction. Some philosophers, notably Dancy, hold that there are no *rules* in morals—no general statements of the familiar kind such as "killing innocent people is wrong" that are both *truths*, and *basic* in the sense that they identify the general and fundamental wrong-making feature of certain broad kinds of acts. Yet Dancy is far from denying that we can explain, in any given case, what makes that particular action right or wrong. Antifoundationalism is not the view that there are literally *no* features of acts to which we can point by way of good and relevant explanation of their moral status. It is, rather, a denial that we can give a meaningful but broad account of what makes *all* wrong acts wrong, say, or at any rate come up with a short list—perhaps just a half-dozen or so—of the really fundamental principles (as in the famous theory of Sir W. D. Ross, or for that matter as suggested by codes like the Ten Commandments) such that all acts will be right or wrong by virtue of their relation to those general rules. In this book, I shall be taking sides with the foundationalists, but with important qualifications that may help to explain why *foundations* seem to be different things from *justifications*. Are they really different? We will have to consider the matter.

(4) Finally, there are the *basic principles* (if any) of morality itself: the most fundamental of the general truths in which we say such-and-such kind of acts are right, so-and-so are wrong, and so on. Again, this may well follow on the heels of the right answers to the previous questions. That, indeed, is what moral philosophers hope (I think). Certainly it is what I hope (and think)! But whether that is so—and many deny it—this last sense of "foundations" is that the basic principles are the foundations on which the less basic ones are built. For example, if we ought not to harm people, and breaking their limbs harms them, then we ought not to break their limbs. Or, if all people are to be treated with respect, then women should be. And so on.

An important temptation, and a very common confusion among students, pundits on public affairs, and so on, is to confuse the job of definition, as in (1), with the job of finding the basic moral criterion or criteria (3) and with the basic principles themselves (4). We will see, in the next section, why that is a confusion. Nevertheless, however, these four should go together. If we are clear about meaning, that should at least suggest where we should be looking for answers to the other questions. If we are clear about what these basic ideas mean, then we should be able to get some sense of why we want or need morals. And that in turn should help suggest what makes something right or wrong. If we know that, though, then surely we should be not far from having a fair idea what the general principles of morals should be like. It will be a virtue of a theory that the answers to these questions harmonize with each other.

Intuitions

The main relevant sense of 'foundations' in which it is possible to ask whether the subject *has* such things is, then, the one identified in sense (3) above. But closely related to that matter is a major issue of *method* in ethics. No one who becomes interested in this subject, very likely, will fail to come to it equipped with many moral opinions or beliefs. (Let us, for the moment, simply *tag* things like the strong sense that killing innocent people is wrong with the word 'belief,' leaving for later the question whether that is exactly the right category for ethical claims.) In this respect, ethics is again distinctive. Few of us come to chemistry preequipped with a body of chemical lore: we expect to learn a good deal that is very new, and often very surprising, in such a well-developed and highly technical field. But will the moral philosopher be equipping us with brand new and surprising doctrines? It is tempting to answer this with a simple negative.

Well, maybe that is too fast. For quite possibly there have been some who, immersing themselves in the writings of philosophers, have been persuaded very far away from the beliefs they acquired in childhood, say. That is unusual but not impossible. On the other hand, the new views are unlikely to be highly technical or esoteric. Moreover, such a reaction is rare, and there is room to question whether persons having such reactions have perhaps gone, so to say, seriously off the rails. At any rate, the point is that an encounter with philosophy that doesn't leave a considerable number of one's prephilosophical moral views intact would be very surprising, unexpected. Which is to say, to be sure, that it never happens.

But some philosophers have gone considerably further than merely recognizing that this would be surprising. For they have also suggested that at least a good many of these beliefs are something like *data* or *constraints* on our investigation. Thus, if someone concludes that lying, on perfectly normal occasions to quite normal people, is a matter of complete moral indifference, these philosophers will take the fact of reaching that conclusion as conclusive evidence that the philosopher in question has *gone wrong*. Their reasoning is something like this:

(1) In a good argument, the premises have to be *more* plausible than the conclusions inferred from them. If something crazy follows logically from p, then we logically conclude that there must be something seriously wrong with p.

(2) But how can anything be *more plausible* than that (say) *murder is wrong?*

(3) Therefore, arguments claiming that it isn't, if they are logically valid, can be dismissed without further investigation. If the arguments aren't even valid, that's another matter. But validity is a matter of the premises actually implying the conclusion, and thus either the conclusion must be accepted, or one or more premises rejected. The idea here is that, under the circumstances, it must always be the latter.

But this raises the question of why we should accept (2)? Are we really entitled to be so convinced of something whose reasons we professedly do not understand—viz., claims about right and wrong—that we can just reject arguments purporting to show that they are in error after all? Why?

The answer to this question will be among the most important methodological moves in ethical theory. One idea about this has come from a school that we might call "official" intuitionism. That idea is that when we affirm ethical claims, we are giving voice to ideas that are *logically primitive*. For example, G. E. Moore argued that 'good' names or designates a unique, simple, "nonnatural property."[8] We will explore his view in more detail later, but for the present, we can see that this, if it is true, would explain why ethical statements could be uttered with great confidence despite ignorance of their foundations. For in a sense, they wouldn't *have* any foundations. Like seeing yellow, sensing goodness would be something that just happened, and statements about it would be deliverances or expressions of this basic experience about which, from the human point of view, no more *could* be said. Like the proposition that this thing looks yellow, it would be an ultimate, final, unquestionable truth.

---

[8] G. E. Moore, *Principia Ethica* (Cambridge: Cambridge Univ. Press, 1903), sec. 15. Moore never uses the exact phrase. He says, "there is a simple, indefinable, unanalysable object of thought by reference to which it must be defined" and, later in the same paragraph, "this unique property . . ."

Official intuitionism is widely rejected today—and for very good reason, I shall suggest. Yet many philosophers continue to regard firmly held preanalytic ethical beliefs as having the status of *evidence* in and of themselves—of being deliverances that we just can't reject, and so as putting limits or constraints on ethical theorizing. Are they right about this?

We shall, at this point, say only this much more about the issue. Firstly, anyone tempted to say this will have a severe problem if there is serious disagreement among different persons. If Jones sees yellow where I see blue, that's bad. If you see right where I see wrong, that's similarly bad. Whom do we believe? My tendency to believe my own view is unsurprising, but obviously Jones could view it as sheer bias, and I can see his point. There is also the problem that we ourselves might change. Today we think that x is wrong, but next week, suddenly, it appears right. Those can't both be unquestionable truths, since one denies the other. So, now what? Indeed, philosophers of this persuasion agree that the main work of moral philosophy is to render our various judgments consistent with each other. And with the facts, if there should chance to be any possibility of conflict with them . . .

Secondly, we may take the pervasiveness of certain ethical beliefs—if such they be—to supply evidence for something, *without* crediting them as direct prima facie evidence for their own truth. Perhaps we shall find good reason, once we got into the matter, why it is unsurprising that so many people affirm these things, but that this reason is considerably removed from the front burner where our ethical affirmations occur. I passionately exclaim, "That's wrong!" But our careful philosopher says, "Yes, it's understandable that you say this, and moreover, there's pretty good reason for you to say it—but even when you're right, all of that can be explained by a more basic theory, and so it should not be taken as having fundamental status in the field." For the present, then, the point is that there are ways of handling intuitions that continue to take them seriously, yet allow for the possibility that further and deeper explanations might be correct accounts of the subject.

Free Will

In introductory philosophy courses professors often discuss the topic of responsibility and free will. This important and interesting concept has been presupposed but not analyzed in this book, so far. In part, responsibility is something we can and should teach and learn. If people cannot be somehow held responsible for their actions, moral principles can have no force, no bite.

Nevertheless, it is worth noting that general philosophical worries about the freedom of the will have no interest for moral philosophy in particular. It does matter, and very much, whether people are sometimes not capable of doing what we think they should do, for it will then be unreasonable to require them to do those things. But that they often are thus capable is, I take it, obvious. It is also something that a general, metaphysical denial of free will cannot genuinely deny in any *interesting* way. What matters for morals is the difference between being unable to do x (as when tied to a tree, say) and being somehow able to do so, however that is to be accounted for. If every event really does have a cause or causes, so that even the most responsible actions are nevertheless accountable in causal terms, so be it.

That it cannot make a genuine difference to morals whether this is so or not is evident on reflection. Consider the man who says, "We are never responsible." Is he going to go on to say, "therefore, we ought not to punish this criminal"? His saying that we 'ought' not to implies that we have some sort of choice in the matter. But—didn't he just get through saying that we don't? If so, his advice makes no sense on his own view.

But it makes no sense anyway. Whether we accept or reject certain moral assessments makes a difference to our behavior; and obviously people sometimes succeed in learning to make such distinctions, while those who do not are a menace to others and to themselves. Thus general worries about free will, however fascinating, must be purely academic.

I emphasized the word 'interesting' above. The philosophical determinist claims that nobody ever has any real choice whatever, about anything. Yet, in all likelihood, when presented with the cookie platter at the party, he chooses one from among others, knowing perfectly well that it's his choice. On the other hand, when pushed downstairs, he does not deliberate whether to fall or not—that is not a matter of choice, though perhaps he has some limited options to reduce damage on his way down. In between these two extremes we have the very important cases such as Aristotle mentions: there's a violent storm, and the captain orders all the extra baggage thrown overboard, for the ship may not survive the storm if he does not.[9] Literally, the captain has his choice. But given the purposes of the trip, people's interest in remaining alive and getting to where they are going, or if not, then at least getting wherever they do end up in one piece rather than to the sea bottom, he has in that sense no choice.

It is easy to overreact to the challenge of determinism, as in the example about criminal punishment. To think that we are unjustified in cor-

---

[9] Aristotle, *Nichomachean Ethics*, bk. III, ch. 1.

rectional activity on the ground that the rapist, say, "could not help" what he did, and then proceed to let him free because of this lack of justification, would be to choose an absurdly dangerous course of action for the community. A different kind of overreaction consists in supposing that determinism doesn't hold good after all—that somehow, causality breaks down when it comes to human action. This idea has several problems, not the least of which is that it is very close to unintelligible. However, more important than that, perhaps, is that it is misguided. Causality is, or at any rate is necessarily related to, regularity: when causality breaks down, the connection between antecedent and consequent conditions is random. Let's see how this affects matters.

Take any course of deliberation leading to decision, and then to action. We consider what our options are, we assess them in light of our various values and powers, and we select some option on the ground that it will either likely be best, or at least as good as any other, and we then act. But suppose that having decided that x is best, I to my surprise find myself doing y, some completely irrelevant and counterproductive act. Backing up a bit, suppose I consider this and that aspect of various options, noting that x seems to offer the best prospects of success and to do the most good; and then, having considered that, to my astonishment I find myself deciding in favor of z, which has nothing going for it at all. Would these strange goings-on testify to my having free will? Or would they, instead, suggest temporary insanity, or short circuits in my nervous system? Obviously the latter. The idea that what we call "free choice" in human affairs has anything whatever to do with general metaphysical causality is simply off the rails—absurd.

On the other hand, freedom in the sense that people out there aren't determined to prevent you doing what you want is another matter entirely, and very relevant indeed. John Stuart Mill makes this distinction in his *Essay on Liberty* at the outset: "The subject of this essay is not the so-called "liberty of the will," but civil, or social liberty: the nature and limits of the power which can be legitimately exercised by society over the individual."[10] He was right to throw cold water on the former, and right to address the latter. That's what we will do in this book as well.

There are certain features that theories must have if they are to be any good. Theories aim at truth, and they aim to explain things. If they are to accomplish this, they must, in the first place, be *clear*. We have to be able to understand what they claim, rather than being smothered in impressive-sounding but perhaps meaningless terminology. And they have to be *coherent*. We—we mere people, as we might put it—are often not

---

10 John Stuart Mill, *Essay on Liberty*—opening sentence.

coherent. We change our minds, we are vague, we forget relevant things, and so on. But if we are going to claim that such-and-such is the right *theory* of our subject, no such defects are allowed. If one part of our theory contradicts another part, then it's back to the drawing board for the theorist. And there has to be reason to think it true. Theories are to explain, and how can we have an explanation that's *false*? There is considerable discussion, as we will see, whether ethical claims are "true" in the usual sense of the word. But here our point is that a theory claiming that they cannot be true or that they are true in some *special* way, must itself be true in the *ordinary* way—that the premises to which we appeal really do correspond to the way things are out there. There are "error theorists" who hold that what we typically say in the way of ethical pronouncements has elements that are necessarily and always false, though somehow they are helpful. On the face of it, error theorists have a major job awaiting them: to show how error can nevertheless be combined with reliable ethical truth. But we will get to that.

I take all the above to be pretty obvious, and will not belabor them further here. It will at least appear that at various points, some familiar ethical theories run afoul of one or another of the above. In the course of our discussions, the claim that they do so fail will be explained and, hopefully, established in a convincing manner. With that in mind, we turn to our first sort of theories, the metaethical ones.

Metaethics

What Is Metaethics?

The idea of metaethics is to step back, as it were, from the concrete detail of the many moral issues that we might be concerned about and to try to get a view of what these issues all have in common, what makes them "ethical" or "moral" issues at all, and in general, of what their logical character might be. Note that it's what the *issues* have in common that we seek—*not*, as yet, what the *principles* of morals all have in common, apart from all being about the same subject.

For this purpose, we must set aside the specifics and consider what is in common to ethical judgments generally—including false ones. So instead of looking at the claim that, say, 'telling Mrs. Jones that you enjoyed her party when you really didn't is wrong [or: right],' or even 'killing innocent people is wrong,' we consider instead all sentences of the general form, '_____ is wrong [or right].' We will use the letters x, y, and z to designate the subject position in such sentences: read 'x is wrong' as '_____ is wrong' where 'x' crisply replaces the subject of the sentence, leaving us with the predicates, 'is right' or 'is wrong.' And then we will ask, "What does the predicate 'right' do in this sentence, as distinct from any other expression that might be used to characterize its subject?" In general, then, we ask how we are to understand the expressions 'right' and 'wrong,' 'good' and 'bad,' and so on. That will be our way of asking, what do they mean? There are also the expressions 'moral' and 'morally,' and 'ethical' and 'ethically' themselves. Which department or aspect of our activities do those terms refer to?

When we pick on the words 'right' and 'wrong,' we rely on a sense that these are suitable for the purpose of understanding ethics. But there can clearly be nonethical uses of these terms: 'the right cufflink' wouldn't be a good example of an ethical expression, and on the other hand, many other terms figure in ethical talk, such as those mentioned at the outset. Is 'creep' an ethical term? It sometimes is. But right and wrong are nevertheless wholly suitable choices, and hopefully working on them and some closely related ones (especially 'good') will enable us to get quite a way without serious distortion.

What philosophers are especially interested in is: how do we show that a given ethical claim is to be accepted or not? What constitutes proof and reasons in ethics? Or does anything? Are reason and proof even possible in ethics? It is often said that ethics is in some very important and basic way a "matter of opinion"—that ethics isn't at all like science, where we have publicly accepted ways of proceeding and standards of evidence and the like. Do we have any such things in ethics? That is one of the major questions before us.

Meaning and Definition

Meaning is not the same as *definition*: definitions are *explanations* of meanings—normally, verbal explanations. So, definitions attempt to state, in words, what some other words mean (though it is often possible to assist the process of definitions by providing examples, pointing: this is called "ostension." We'll say a good deal more about that shortly.)

What has meanings? Answer: words, at least. Some might want to say "concepts"; but it is more appropriate to say that concepts *are* meanings than that they *have* meanings. The word 'chair,' for example, conveys the idea, or concept, of chair—that is, of whatever it is that makes something a chair—a "chair-thing." We let capitals starting with 'F' stand in for the *concept* of F-things; if we need more in a given case, we use further letters, G and H.

To be sure, however, we also ascribe meaning to other things besides words: a meaningful glance, a meaningless gesture, the meaning of some work of art, or for that matter the "meaning of life." Nevertheless, linguistic meaning is paradigmatic, and it is especially relevant to inquire into it in abstract investigations such as this. But it is important to be aware of the possibility that the words we are especially interested in in ethical theory have meaning in a different way than, for example, the many words which do designate various kinds of objects or events or relations or situations. Such awareness was a major preoccupation of thinkers about these matters in the twentieth century.

Among the major problems of analysis is the fact that meaning is somehow a psychological phenomenon. People mean things by what they say, and the meaning is somehow part of their *intentional* make-up: we "mean" this or that when we say such-and-such, and we do so in the sense that we want, and intend, to convey something by using those elements of speech. But this makes meaning sound too protestant, so to say. In fact, the things we call "words" are by no means simply up to individuals. Humpty Dumpty claimed that words mean whatever he jolly well wanted them to mean, and that's that. But on that dispensation, there's no reason anyone else would understand him—in which case, what's the point? Meanings have to be social, not just individual, to work. But they have to be both, of course: a meaning cannot really be "social," or anything, if there is not the intentional aspect, the "meaning *to me*" that is, as we might put it, the bottom line. This divergence is recognized in a useful distinction: between meaning in the sense of what the words already do mean in the linguistic community where the word has its home, and meaning as *conferred* on a word by a speaker at a time. This last is called "stipulation": "for present purposes, I will use word W to mean 'F' . . ." Within fairly severe limits, stipulation can function usefully. (The limits will be discussed below.) Meanwhile, notice that stipulation is also social, and functions in an environment of preestablished language: the speaker is able to attach this meaning to this word, successfully, only because his audience understands a common language with him including the set of expressions needed to make clear that one is stipulating, and also the set of words in which one explains the stipulated meaning.

Whose Words?

When words in common usage are the subject, then it is the words of standard speakers of the language—those whose native tongue it is, those who speak that language in everyday life. This certainly applies to words like 'good' and 'right,' which, at least in various cognates, are familiar to all. It's a natural thought that inquiry into right and wrong would be promoted by inquiring into the meanings of the words 'right' and 'wrong.'

A caution: it isn't that there is a different inquiry in each language that people speak. Words are normally translatable, especially insofar as they convey cognitively transmissible meanings. If we can explain the meaning of some word, the explanation will work equally well for any sound that is used to convey that meaning, in whatever language. Since I write in English, we concentrate on the vocabulary of English; but our results, if good, will also be good for any language containing a vocabulary that does the same things. And it is reasonable to suppose that every language contains words more or less like the ones we consider here, though doubtless local variation is instructive.

We now need to make some more distinctions, however. Consider some sentence offered as a definition. What might it be doing? What is it to "define"? All definitions have the purpose of explaining meanings, of course, but they do so in different ways. We can distinguish three here.

Three Sorts of Definitions

1. REPORTIVE DEFINITIONS

A reportive definition is one in which the definition purports to say what those who use the vocabulary in question already mean by it. This can take us to the very difficult further question of what it is for someone to "mean something by" a word, and what it is for a word to be a part of a public language spoken, with mutual understanding, by a great many people. These questions would take us too far afield for us to inquire much into them here. We have to rely on our "linguistic intuition" for much of our consideration here. (More on this below.)

We can distinguish between reportive definitions based on the type of vocabulary they define. Sometimes we inquire into a word in "common" use. Certainly the words 'good' and 'bad', 'right' and 'wrong,' 'ought' and 'ought not' are such—everyone uses them. Definitions of these may be said to analyze "ordinary language" or "ordinary use." But sometimes there is a specialized use. For example, there are vocabularies of expertise in all sorts of disciplines. Besides that, there are subvocabularies of common notions. These definitions would be, then, "technical" definitions.

Can there be "technical" senses, used only by experts? Surely there can. But an important question of ethics is whether there can be any "experts," and a plausible answer is in the negative. What we philosophers may be expert on is the range of theories that have been proposed concerning morals; but 'expert at morals' is a phrase without a clear meaning. We think there are unusually good people, but their goodness isn't much like expertise at anything. In any case, though, experts needn't use ordinary words in an idiosyncratic way—and if they did, it is questionable what relevance their claims would have. They would have to relate their use to ordinary uses of the words in question. At a minimum, they must use words that are intelligible to their fellow experts. Otherwise we will suspect that the supposed specialist is a fraud, offering snake oil instead of the real goods. That is a suspicion to keep in mind in ethical studies, alas.

2. STIPULATIVE DEFINITIONS

Sometimes, though, we are not even trying to report preexisting usage, either ordinary or special. Instead, we might simply declare that we are going to use such-and-such a word to mean so-and-so. The word for this procedure is 'stipulation.' We "stipulate" a meaning when we simply *give* a certain meaning to a certain word that we propose to employ in that way. (For this reason, these have also been called "legislative" definitions: the speaker "legislates" the meaning of the term.) Yet the point of this sort of definition, as of all definition, is to facilitate communication. This you won't do very well if you confusingly specify a meaning for a word that already has a quite different one, and it's even worse if you claim to have stipulated it and then don't stick to your special meaning.

Stipulative definitions cannot, so far as they go, be "true" or "false, "correct" or "incorrect." They can, however, be useful or useless, helpful or unhelpful. But since they are simply given to the words in question, then the question whether they correspond to what is already there doesn't arise. But, of course, once the stipulation is made and we commence using the term in question, we can stick to it or we can deviate. Consistency of use is important in language, for language is used to communicate, and you cannot communicate if each time you use a word you mean something different by it. Heraclitus is persona non grata when it comes to communication. Even he, when he says, "You cannot step into the same river twice," had better mean the same thing by 'river' and 'same' as he did when he said that yesterday!

By contrast, when we are attempting a reportive definition we are trying to define a word that is already in use in the relevant linguistic community: we are trying to say what its users mean by it. This is usually what we try to do in philosophy. In this case, then, our definition can be true or false, correct or incorrect: true or correct if people really do mean by it what your definition says they do, and false or incorrect if they don't. (And then, maddeningly, it can perhaps be close to or far from a truth that we don't seem to be able to quite formulate.)

There may seem a puzzle about this. How can we *not* know what we mean by a word? And if we must know what we mean—because it's *our* meaning, after all—then what's the point of analysis? We'll take up that question in a moment, but first, let's complete our list.

There is one further point of importance about the uses of stipulation. A main use, and perhaps the only good one for present purposes, is to select one from among several meanings that are associated with a given word, and for the purposes of the contexts we are considering, the stipulator announces that he proposes to confine the word to *that* one and exclude the others. Or possibly, he could even adapt some vocabulary so as to help keep the distinct meanings distinct. Perhaps we can then understand several of the others by relating them to this one. In principle, there's nothing wrong with that procedure.

3. THEORETICAL DEFINITIONS

There is one more use of the term 'definition' that is very widely found in science, especially, and more generally in contexts of inquiry. This is where the "definition" doesn't actually define the *term* in any of the previous senses. What it does, rather, is to supply a theory about the *thing* denoted by the word. Take, for example, the familiar scientific dictum, water = H_2O.[1] Water, it turns out (or so we are told by scientists) is composed at the molecular level of two atoms of hydrogen, one of oxygen. Ordinary users of the term 'water' or its equivalent in other languages characteristically know nothing about chemistry or physics, and yet they

---

[1] Not, apparently, exactly true anyway . . .

successfully use the term 'water.' It would be unhelpful to tell some ordinary French person in 1700 that by 'water' we mean 'H_2O'. But it would be helpful to tell him that 'water' is English for the French 'l'eau'.

Analytical versus Ostensive Definitions

We now come to an important distinction of two ways of supplying meaning, or defining, which cuts across the previous distinctions. One is the sort of definition that breaks the meaning down into components. Take the definition, 'bachelor' = 'unmarried man.' This is called an *analytical* definition because it explains the meaning of one word by exhibiting it as a construction from two (or more) other words—in this case, 'unmarried' and 'man.' To be a bachelor is to exemplify both of those features. Many words in the language are susceptible to that sort of definition, in which linguistic wholes are analyzed into structures of more elementary parts.

But many words are not, or at least not easily or obviously. In those cases we will need to do something else—especially, to produce examples that we can point to or clearly cite in such a way as to illustrate the idea that the word is intended to convey. This is called "ostension." It would be helpful to tell a two-year-old girl learning the language that "this"—pointing to some water—is called "water." In so doing we supply a sort of definition. The child does not learn some new fact *about water* when we say, "this is water"; what she learns is that the word we apply to this stuff is the *word* 'water' as opposed to any of the indefinitely many other phonic structures or sets of marks that might have been used for that purpose. We in effect are saying, "this is [a sample of] the sort of stuff we call 'water.'"

The big problem in defining by ostension is getting it right. In typical cases, the word (such as 'water') applies to innumerable particular examples of the kind of thing we are trying to define. How does the learner come to identify just the right set of examples? If I point to the pond near my house and say, "This is Silver Lake," my use of 'this' and perhaps other cues conveys that I am providing a name for this particular body of water, rather than all water in general. Moreover, I am not naming the particular set of molecules that happen to be in the batch of water before us just now, for the lake is a widening of a stream, and its water changes continually. Even so, I can manage, for most hearers, to succeed in establishing 'Silver Lake' as the *name* of the body of water, whatever it is, that exists within this set of banks. (Saying this to a normal speaker also confirms that it is strictly a proper name, since the characteristic color of this body of water is muddy-gray rather than silver.)

Another good example is color terms. If I say, "that is yellow," meaning thereby to convey that that shade of color is what is called by the English word 'yellow,' what is before both of us is not only a hue but an intensity, a level of saturation, a location in space and time, and more. Success at identifying just the batch of reality intended is not entirely easy to come by. That it often does work is an important fact about us and our environments and our language. If we move to the much more difficult notion of 'good,' say, then formidable problems arise, as we will see. Still, some have proposed that some kind of ostensive process is the only one in principle possible for that word. We will be examining that idea in subsequent pages.

Returning to our distinction: if ostension is difficult, we must realize that analytical definitions may not be so easily arrived at either. This is conspicuously true in philosophy. It may seem a surprising thing that we, who use certain words every day, should be at a loss when asked to supply a definition, even when, as it turns out, a definition could be supplied. (Readers of Plato will be familiar with the point.) But this reflects the distinction, previously noted, of meaning and definition. All words have to have meaning in order to be words; but definition is an unnatural act. We use words all the time, but we rarely have occasion to define them. We know what we mean when we use them—in one sense: namely that we know how to use them, at least in familiar contexts. But knowing what we mean in the sense of knowing how to use, is not the same as, nor does it entail, knowing what to say when asked for a definition.

How Do We Test Claims about Meanings?

A definition asserts a synonymy: the term being defined, we claim, means the same as the perhaps more complex phrase that we propose as its definition. How do we test for such claimed equivalences (synonymies) or nonequivalences of meaning? How, in short, do we test whether proposed definitions or analyses of familiar concepts are accurate or off the mark?

According to G. E. Moore, whose *Principia* is one of the modern classics of ethical theory, we evidently must do this by what we may as well call "inspecting concepts." But how do we do that? Are concepts real things that we can "hold before our minds" with a view to scrutinizing their logical structure? And how would we know whether you are "inspecting" the same concept as I?

When we consider meanings, we are considering how words are applied or employed in the circumstances in which they are used by those who use them. We look and, hopefully, see. Inspecting concepts might involve, perhaps, using a procedure of imagining various circumstances and asking what one would say, how one would describe, those cases; plausibly, that is what the terminology of inspecting concepts comes to. It isn't clear where "concepts" figure in all this, but one useful thought here is to identify the "concept" associated with a certain word or use of that word with the patterns that pair the words with a certain identifiable class of situations. 'Cow,' for example, is generally a sort of label. We conjure up a suitable picture and are confident that we have the sort of thing 'cow' is meant to refer to. We can compare our own reaction to real cows, and nonmental pictures, with those of others; if we all react alike, we have a linguistic uniformity of the type we are looking for.

When we ask ourselves what we mean by a given word, we use our imagination: we dream up circumstances in which the word would be appropriate and ask what we would say in those circumstances, for instance, whether the word in question would be used to describe the sort of things we dream up. We are using ourselves as *typical speakers* of the language—not as some kind of special "experts." Recent philosophers call the little reports we get in this way "linguistic intuitions." An "intuition" about the use of a word is a hunch or sense or presentiment as to what it means. It is an actuation of a disposition that has been instilled into us in the course of our use of the language in question. Intuitions in this sense can be wrong—but they're presumably not very likely to be. For if we know how to use a word, we must have a fair idea of what we would say in (at least) familiar kinds of circumstances, and a fair idea of when a word isn't appropriate. We, and the rest of us, engage in behavior that constitutes data for the theorist of meaning.

Let's now attack the question we left hanging above: how can analysis be of any interest, seeing that in some sense we must know what we mean? There is a decent answer, and as usual it requires making a distinction, suggested by the phrase 'in some sense' employed in the previous sentence. The sense in which we *must* know what we mean is that we must be able to pick out the things our word applies to, and know, at least pretty well, that this is the word to use for those and not for other things—else we shall indeed mean nothing. But being able to do that— to recognize an F when we come upon one—is one thing, and to be able to *say*, in *words*, just on the basis of what we recognize as specimens of F, is quite another matter. Sometimes it's pretty easy: 'bachelor' = 'unmarried man.' Anyone would say, "he's not a bachelor—he has a wife!" But with other concepts—'space,' 'being,' 'knowledge,' and to the present point, 'right'—it is quite possible for that achievement to elude us for a long time, or maybe forever. So there is discovery possible here. And therein lies part of the answer to the puzzle of how this sort of philosophy is possible. We can test proposed *definitions* by our shared sense of *meaning*. Our definition will declare that this, that, and the other thing are indeed F. Our sense of meaning will tell us whether those things are the sort of things we mean by 'F.' We can see that we were right or wrong.

In this, to be sure, there will be a danger of warping our linguistic sense to suit our theories. Guarding against that is difficult. But in public academic discourse, there are lots of other theorists out there all ready to apply *their* senses of English or whatever language to the claim at hand. The sort of meanings we are looking for cannot be private property—anybody can play! But words being what they are, we also have the means for confirming or disconfirming hypotheses about what they mean. We see whether someone, confronted with something implied by our proposed definition as being an example, does in fact spontaneously call it by the name we are trying to analyze.

What do we get out of analysis, if successful? The main answer is: clarity. We become able to see that certain things are not examples of the same thing as certain others, that confusion is easy here, and that on the basis of our analytical excursion, perhaps, we can help avoid such confusion in cases where it matters. And in ethics, there are a lot of those, and it may matter a very great deal.

Good and Right

Should we expect to have a similar analysis and the same sort of considerations and constraints operating on all the different evaluative notions? In particular, there seems to be a significant division between value notions, typified by 'good' (and 'bad' and 'better' and 'worse'), on the one hand, and by 'right,' and of course 'wrong' and 'ought' and 'ought not' on the other—but, interestingly, there is no obvious corresponding idea for 'right' that makes it a matter of degree in the way that 'better' and 'worse' obviously function. 'More right' doesn't work; 'more nearly right' more or less works, and that's suggestive. But there is an evident difference here that we mustn't overlook. Accounting for this may provide insight.

It is customary among authors of books of this kind to identify the two by different generic terms: "teleological" and "deontological." Teleology has to do with *ends*; deontology sounds more like *orders*. Often the former category is assimilated to "consequentialism" and contrasted with the other category, still called "deontology." There are said to be "deontic" theories and "consequential" theories, the latter often referred to as "consequentialism." This latter assimilation, I shall show later, is a muddle, and has had deleterious effects on the handling of this subject that are in serious need of correction. It is hoped that this book will do something to allay those effects.

The first thing to point out is that both 'good' and 'right' are used not only in ethics, narrowly speaking, but in a very great range of other things. In fact, as Aristotle observed in the famous opening sentence of his *Nichomachean Ethics,* "Every art and every inquiry, and similarly every action and pursuit, is thought to aim at some good . . ." About this he seems to be correct, broadly speaking. Whenever we do virtually anything at all, we can ask whether we did it well or badly, how well or how badly. The word 'right' is not similarly ubiquitous, but still ranges very much more widely than in ethics in any narrow sense. We can choose the right car, the right book with which to entertain ourselves for the afternoon, the right tool for the job, and so on. This raises two questions, then. First, is there anything in common to *all* these uses? And secondly, how do we identify a "distinctively ethical" use, which is the primary concern of this book?

Let's take up the first question first. Aristotle identifies the context of goodness, in effect, as that of *action* (inquiry and pursuit being kinds of actions). Is this so? It might seem not. We think there are good or bad pictures, and good and bad specimens. Are there good and bad galaxies? Not exactly. But there are good and bad *examples* of galaxies.

Let's see whether we can draw these together. The "action" context is united by *aim*: we are trying to do something or other, and thus the stage is set for succeeding or failing, for doing it well or badly. Aristotle followed up the famous opening clause with another: "and for this reason, the good has rightly been declared to be that at which all things aim." But there he may go off the rails. Is there one ultimate object of all action? That's what he seems to say there, but it doesn't follow. On the face of it, different actions could have different aims. Instead of "the good" there may be only "goods"—though one might also speak of the set, or perhaps the sum, of all the good things, thus imparting a spurious unity to the lot. We will return to that interesting question later. For the present, the point is that the ubiquity of considerations of good/bad in life is quite well accounted for by the fact that we (at least) almost always act in order to bring about something or other. And then the natural suggestion about 'good' is that an action is good when it succeeds, bad when it doesn't. (Reader take note: we have not yet got to the second question, about *ethics.* Where we are at present is that it is intelligible when even some horribly evil action is being performed, that its agent may judge that he has done a "good job of it" in slicing up his victims neatly, for instance, or economically (as in the "final solution to the Jewish problem"). Humans act for a great variety of ends, they appraise their efforts at achieving them, and the words 'good' and 'bad' are the ones you use in so appraising them.

What about the classificatory use mentioned, though? If I say that this is a "good shark," I may mean not that this is a shark that accomplishes its aims, or *our* aims, but rather that it is a good example or specimen of the category 'shark.' Now if we ask, "and what is that good for?" there is a good answer available: for purposes of inquiry we need classificatory labels, words of various kinds, and it helps us along in those endeavors to be able to locate the specimens that exemplify our classificatory purposes well, and the ones that do not. Thus there are good arguments, good analyses, good theories—or bad, in each case. But they all figure in things that some of us are interested in *doing*.

One more very general context in which notions of good and bad are standard fare is, broadly, the *aesthetic*. When we say that some symphony, or some person, or the sunset, is *beautiful*, for example, what has this to do with aims and ends and action? Again there are decent answers to that question. We enjoy such things, we admire them, sometimes we "love" them, and those attitudes and experiences motivate us to create works of art, to go to museums, to cast an appreciative eye on our fellow humans and sometimes to invite some of those humans to lunch, or for that matter to ask their hand in marriage.

Still, this brings up a distinction—a very important, very interesting, and again ubiquitous one. That distinction is again suggested by Aristotle (one of the secondary purposes of this book being to foster appreciation of some of the great thinkers), who says "we do not choose everything for the sake of something else (for at that rate the process would go on to infinity, so that our desire would be empty and vain) . . ." His logic here is impeccable. If we ask, "Why do *this*?" we suppose there will be an answer, "in order to bring about *that*." But in turn, we can ask, "very well: and why should we try to bring about *that*?" Sometimes there will be a further answer of the same general structure, specifying another aim or end. But suppose there was no last answer of that kind, no stopping point? Aristotle says that in that case, action would be "empty and vain."

Why would he think that? There is a good reason, but it requires a distinction. Suppose that we perform action x *only* in order to bring about end E. The force of 'only' here is that we would have *no* reason to do x if it weren't for the bringing about of E. Now suppose that E in turn is a "subordinate" end, and that there is a further end, call it E1, such that the *only* point of achieving E is the hope that it in turn will bring about E1. If now there is literally no last term in this sequence, it seems that Aristotle's dictum is confirmed: there is no reason at all to do any of these things, seeing that none of them are worth doing if they don't bring about this thing—but, hey!—there *is* no "last thing." So what's the point?

Again, it is easy to be misled. Aristotle himself was fishing for the thesis that there is some one general kind of end that underlies all actions, the supreme, final, Last Word about anything at all. It is far from clear that he was right about that, and in any case, it doesn't in fact follow from his argument. What follows is only that for each action or pursuit, there is, somewhere down the track, something that is the "final end" of *that* action or pursuit. None of this shows that there might not be a completely different final end of some quite *other* pursuit.

And in human life, it doesn't take a lot of experience to appreciate the force of this last possibility. We might think a certain movie to be a quite wonderful one, and a certain food to be very delicious—and find it quite impossible to say what they have in common—apart from one thing: both are "in their way satisfying."

That might lead us to say that there is indeed one supreme end of all action: *satisfaction*. But the result would be hollow and formal. One satisfaction seems to be altogether different from another.

Might there be a good that has nothing whatever to do with satisfaction, though? Asking that gets us into the thick of ethical theory, which we will be doing—but later.

First, however, let's pursue the same inquiry in regard to the words 'right' and 'wrong.' When we pronounce something or other to be "right" or "wrong," we are, for one thing, employing terminology that does not suggest matters of *degree*. Is it right? Yes or no. Something in between doesn't fit well with these concepts. Of course, life doesn't care about that and very often we must admit that the terminology isn't as useful as we hoped—we have to resort, after all, to the more flexible and accommodating terminology of better and worse. Insofar as 'right' and 'wrong' *do* useful work, then, it's because the items in question either do fit or they don't, do fill the bill or not. And that suggests a background in which there is something to 'fit' or 'suit': something like a rule or a template for the purpose at hand. In ethics, such talk is frequent. One of the issues in ethical theory, as we will consider later, is whether ethics is a matter of rules. Or is it, instead, a matter of virtues and vices, which behave considerably more like the terminology of value and less like that of right and wrong? In fact, we do use both sorts of vocabulary—obviously, we do not need to choose one set of terms to the exclusion of the other set. However, we will leave all such questions to later pages.

One more note about right and wrong. If an action is wrong, then the implication is that we are *not to do it*. But is there a corresponding opposite implication about right—that if an action is right, then are we *to do it*? There is not. Or rather, there is here a very important ambiguity to be aware of. *Sometimes*, indeed, the implication *is* there. "Is this the right thing to do?" is sometimes the question, "is this what I am to do?" But at other times, that is not so. For we may instead really be asking, "Is this something I *may* do, something that's okay, *permissible*? For it may be

that several things or thousands would be so, though I would need still
to decide which among them I will actually do. In short, sometimes 'right'
means 'required' while at other times it means something more like 'not
wrong' or 'permissible.' And that obvious distinction opens up a very
broad set of issues about ethics—which, again, I must here beg off with
a promise that we will be concerned about those in later pages.

Values, Ethics, and Morals

Instead, let's turn to the second of my two general questions: what is the
"narrowly ethical" sense in which we speak in terms of 'good' and of
'right'? And on this matter, we can see, I believe, the need for another distinction.

The subject matter of Aristotle's *Nichomachean Ethics* provides one
answer to this question: ethics is about *how to live*. It is about what we
should, in the most fundamental way, *do*. A credible, though discussable
answer is that we should do whatever will give us the *best life*, or more
generally, the *good life*. Whether even that is a good answer to that question will, again, be discussed later. But meanwhile, we have to distinguish
that very general question from another, for which there is a word that
has become more or less standard, though it was not in Aristotle's time:
the word is 'moral' (and 'morality,' along with 'immoral' and also 'non-
moral'). Alas, there is no complete uniformity here, for a book about
"moral philosophy" could easily be about both, as indeed this one is.

Well, what is this still narrower sense of these words? There is, again,
a pretty good general answer: morality has, specifically, to do with how
we are to treat, or deal with, or act in relation to, *each other*. The thought
is that we live among other people, and this makes a difference. There
will be considerations of what to do that are drastically affected by the
fact of these other people being around. The famous philosopher
Emmanuel Kant supposed that morality is centrally about *rules for all,*
and he offers a very famous formula for generating the rules in question,
his "Supreme Categorical Imperative." We will be looking at that idea in
particular later on; at present, the point is just that the social factor, as we
might call it, seems to be a very distinctive one. This is true even though
no remotely plausible account of the first subject, the "good life" is going
to leave other people out of the picture—hardly anyone will opt for the
life of the hermit. Nevertheless, the focus seems entirely different when
we address the subject of what *everyone* is required to do, in relation to
and because of the existence of other people in general. (Kant, by the
way, thought this too narrow, conceptually: he supposed that morality
reaches to all *rational beings*. But, of course, the only such beings he and

we know about are fellow humans—though the subject of how other animals fit into the picture soon arises as well. We will, however, say very little about that in the present book, and even less about the possible existence of "rational beings" somehow "higher" than we humans instead of "lower" as most of us think the other animals to be.)

Metaethical Intuitionism

The most obvious thought regarding the meaning of words like 'good' and 'right' would be that they must stand for some or other features or properties or attributes of actions or characters. The view that that is exactly what they do, on all fours with words like 'red,' 'sharp-edged,' 'drunk,' 'bloody-minded,' and a host of others, is called "naturalism." According to naturalism, we can define basic ethical words such as 'good' or 'right' by finding the right set of features, the one that those words are used to stand for. For example, we might suppose that to say that something is "good" is to say that it causes pleasure, or is conducive to evolutionary survival, or some such thing.

The very idea of ethical naturalism was not formulated in so many words until the twentieth century. Did earlier philosophers have metaethical theories? Maybe. Some of the things that some of them say do suggest that, although one can hardly be quite certain. Be that as it may, we can almost say that modern ethical theory began, at the beginning of the twentieth century as it happens, with a famous argument to the effect that naturalism in general is misguided. Never mind which features or properties the theorist would like to define 'good' in terms of—he can just forget it, for it can't be done! The philosopher who argued thus, coining the term 'naturalistic fallacy' in the process, was the Englishman G. E. Moore. Moore's argument about this is remarkably simple—bringing up the distinct possibility that it is *too* simple, a possibility we will pursue shortly. Meanwhile, though, his argument is extremely influential and we must be aware of it. His central claim is that naturalistic theories, as he defines that idea, fail a particular kind of semantic "test"—the *open question test*. That will be the subject of scrutiny in a few pages.

G. E. Moore's *Principia Ethica*, published in 1903, made a major splash (in the world of British philosophy at least). It would not be too much to say that it took the moral theory part of that world by storm. Suddenly, it seems, everyone was persuaded by Moore's arguments; or perhaps equally much, we are told, by his manner, his way of staring in stark disbelief at those who questioned his conclusions.

But he didn't convince everyone. He didn't make nearly the impact in America that he did in his native England, and we may well wonder why that is so. American philosophers, it seems, didn't see the alleged "common sense" of this celebrated defender of common sense. (The Cambridge philosopher C. D. Broad is said to have remarked that when philosophical theories die, their souls go to America!)

Moore's theory has two main parts, a point I emphasize at the outset, because what is mainly remembered about Moore is only one of those two parts. In very brief outline, Moore held, first—the part not sufficiently remembered—that 'good' is the *basic notion in ethics*, all others (especially 'right') being definable by reference to it. And second—the remembered part—he held that this basic notion of goodness is indefinable. This he expounded as a matter of its referring to or designating a "simple" property. Not just a simple one, though. For, third, he held that goodness could not be any natural property at all—that any attempt to identify goodness with any such property commits something known as the "naturalistic fallacy."

In the widely neglected later portions of the book, Moore draws fascinating conclusions about what we would normally call 'ethics' properly speaking, or as he called it, "Ethics in Relation to Conduct" (chapter 5 of the book). We'll look at those a bit more carefully below. Finally, in the concluding chapter, "The Ideal," he asks what things really do have this fundamental quality of goodness. His answers: interpersonal love and (good) aesthetic experience. Those, he thinks, have "by far" the most value, even though a few other things no doubt do too. But this view of the ideal, as he quite explicitly insists, does not "follow" from the apparatus at the beginning. All that he claims to have done is to clear away mistakes, illusions, and fallacies so that we may look with a clearer view at the landscape. When we do, he asserts, that is what we shall find.

And so, the ethical life will consist in pursuing and promoting, roughly speaking, love and art. Some will ask, "Well, those are fine, no doubt: but surely the list is too short. There are many other things of value, too." We will consider that too, below.

Complexes and Simples

We have distinguished two types or methods of definition:

(1) "analytical" definition, e.g. "genus-species." Example: a right triangle is a triangle with a right angle

from

(2) "ostensive" definition. Example: "That is a cow"

With this second kind, one somehow points to or otherwise picks out a sample of the kind of thing the word is to apply to, without presuming to identify the essential components that make things of that kind what they are, and then one simply "tags" or *names* things of that kind by the word in question (making clear to one's intended audience that that is what one is doing). The category of ostension is of fundamental significance in analysis. If analysis reduces complexes to simples, what, then, do we do about the simples? Ostension provides *an* answer: we point. More generally, we somehow locate examples of the simple entities in question, and then we simply *name* them, thus providing meaning without further definition of the linguistic sort.

We are all continually immersed in experience: visual, auditory, and various other sorts of sensory inputs are with us always except when we sleep soundly, and on those occasions "we" may be said to be having no experience at all. And whenever we have experience, we would seem in principle to be in a position to put tags, names, on elements of it capable of being recalled. If we do, though, we have a problem: how do we communicate with others by means of the names we've attached to these items? After all, other people are *other:* they don't have *my* experience, they have *their* experiences. Somehow we interact in ways that enable us to be pretty confident that when Jones calls something "red" he is saying the same thing about it that Smith says when she in turn calls something "red."

Analysis consists in breaking a whole down into its component parts. But simples have no parts, by definition. Therefore, although you can point to things whether they are complex or simple, it would seem that in principle you can *only* "point" to "simples," which by definition cannot be "broken down into parts." Or is this so?

The theory of ostension is no easy matter. Consider Hume's example of the missing shade of blue. We are presented with a spectrum of blues, segmented into, say, a dozen areas, each of which is a uniform hue, but where there is a discernibly greater gap between samples 6 and 7 than between any two other adjacent samples. Hume supposed that we might be able to form a mental image of the missing shade, even though we've never seen one before.[2] Can anyone have a decent idea of blue without seeing *any* samples? Maybe not. But one who has seen all the other samples might be able to fill in the missing shade without having actually seen it. Couldn't we define some words in that sort of way? Presumably we could—but not all. For in the absence of any other color experience, one would have no resources for imagining the missing shades—when they're all missing, we are at an end.

---

[2] Hume, *Treatise of Human Nature.*

That brings up a further need: to distinguish relational and nonrelational components. Being blue is in this sense nonrelational, but being five miles from Toronto's City Hall is relational. It is not clear whether relations counted as "properties" for Moore, but it is hard to see why they shouldn't.

What is it for a word to have a "complex" meaning? Something like this: it is complex when it picks out the things it stands for on the basis of their having at least two distinguishable features (Or, one could say "properties," "characteristics," or "aspects"—we'll treat those as the same; by "distinguishable" is meant, by some means or other; in the normal case, it will be perception: by look or sound or whatever. So the distinguishability of them is what philosophers call "phenomenal" or perhaps "phenomenological"). It isn't just that the word applies to some complex things, but that it applies on the *basis* of the thing's complex features. If it does, then analytical definition is possible.

Our question is whether goodness, or rightness, as the case may be, is like that. And here we have a problem regarding this idea of "features": what is, and what isn't, to count as such a thing? We'll return to that important question in a bit.

Ostension

It is in the "whole-part" sense of 'definition' that Moore denies that 'good' is definable. In this sense, 'indefinable' means 'simple'—but it does not mean 'meaningless'. Simples are defined ostensively (and contextually): we point to examples, we indicate when we are and when we aren't in the presence of the thing or quality in question.

Moore's example is the color yellow: Could we define 'yellow' in terms of physical wavelength? Of course we can, for scientific purposes— but not for philosophical or everyday purposes. For someone had to discover that yellow has such a thing as a wavelength at all—had to formulate and find some theoretical basis for the wave theory of light; and then, someone had to identify that the wavelength of yellow light in particular is whatever it is. Well, how did Professor Abigail, let's say, know what she was discovering if she didn't already know that this bit of color here (the one she's testing) is intended to be designated by the word "yellow"? Plainly 'yellow' was in use long before modern physics.

The point of "ostension" is that it cues a piece of language directly to the world—or rather, to be more precise, to our experience of the world, the world as we see and hear it. That is not so simple a business, as we have already seen. We are, after all, talking to each other: words are public, but experiences are private. So if I am to define a term by pointing, I need to be sure that you have the right idea of which object I intend by my act of pointing; otherwise what I tried to convey will be different from what you pick up, and we would end up using the words differently after all.

Nevertheless, it is hard to resist the force of the argument that eventually all words must be defined by fundamentally ostensive processes. We can only define words in terms of other words if those others words mean something. At the end of the line, there are only those "other" words and the bits of the world they are intended to stand for.

The epistemological philosophy known as empiricism leans heavily on this idea—that in the end our words must be defined ostensively. Empiricism has it that the ultimate ostensions will be sense-experiences, especially "simple" ones such as seeing yellow. Yet there might be other primitive, immediately accessible experiences besides sense experiences, might there not? What about our own thought processes? Locke and Hume apparently agreed that we are immediately aware of those, too. A distinction of that kind is important in ethics as well, for some philosophers have held that pleasure, or more generally feelings, are the only ultimately valuable things, while some others have held that we are immediately aware of things like duties and virtues. We will return to discussions on such matters below.

Definition in Ethical Theory

What is definition for?

Moore claims that the question what 'good' means—or rather, of what goodness is—is the "most fundamental question in ethics." Why? Presumably because he is thinking of definition as actually telling us what our subject is. But is this something we must know before we can do anything in ethics? No!

Of course, we must have a sense of meaningfulness when we use words, a sense of what we're doing when we use particular ones. But as we have seen, we need not be able to define them, and in the case of the fundamental words investigated by philosophers, we usually cannot, anytime soon, anyway. So long as we can use them confidently, it is by no means obvious that we "need" to be able to define them as well. If Moore really thought so, he would have been guilty of confusing *meaning* with *definition* here. We must be able to recognize a use of the word 'good' when we encounter it; but—to repeat—that doesn't mean we have to be able to define it.

Roughly: a word has meaning to a user if that user is able to use it (reliably): if, in that sense, it "means something to" that user. But the user may not be able to *formulate* that meaning in some neat sentence.

Definitions are explications of how a word is used. It's like the difference between knowing how to ride a bicycle and knowing how to write a manual about how to ride bicycles.

Why pursue definition? One very important reason is this. Words in ordinary usage (and many in nonordinary usage as well) tend to get rather vague, and often enough ambiguous as well. 'Good' may be an example: there is ethical good, but there is also good snowmobiling technique, good brandy, good questions. It is possible that the word doesn't mean the same thing in each case. And in some inquiries, it might be that we would tend to confuse one usage with another, and that might get us into trouble. A definition might be handy to ward off such problems, if it is a good one.

Moore holds that 'good' is indefinable. However, we can (and he does) use an expression such as 'the good' to designate all that is good. It refers to the sum of all the good things. If there are two or more of those fundamentally different good things, as he (unsurprisingly) thinks there is, then "defining" that would consist in identifying, listing, pointing out, the various good things.

But this is not "definition" in the usual sense of the word: it's value theory. It is quite misleading to describe the specification of the domain of 'good' as a matter of "definition." We can define the expression 'the good': it refers to the set of all things that are good. But we don't continue to define it when we claim that this or that or the other thing actually is good. This would be to confuse predication, or in the case of 'good,' assessment, that is, characterizing things as really being good or bad or better or worse, and thus, making genuine claims about them, with mere definition—quite a different matter. Definition tells us what we are attributing to something when we call it by the term being defined. But which things have the property being defined is another matter. Grass is green (often); but it might be (and sometimes is) some other color. Knowing which shade is green isn't enough to tell us whether grass is green. Does knowing what 'good' means enable us to know all that is good? No. For that we would need much experience.

If we know what 'good' means by ostension, then the examples used as our paradigms to explain the term would have to be good, by definition. Or would they? Actually, no. Remember the grass, which can turn other colors.

Moore and Naturalism

Moore is famed for having done something very special: namely, refuted, once and for all, a whole large class of ethical theories, which he calls "naturalistic." Or at any rate, he is famed for having convinced almost everyone in the field (at least in England and, roughly, the Eastern seaboard of the U.S.) that these theories, which he calls "naturalistic" theories, are hopeless in principle. We must examine both his celebrated arguments for this negative view, and also his positive theory, known (but not to Moore!) as "intuitionism."

'Ethical naturalism' is a term with a rather specialized meaning. The thesis that Moore claims to refute is the theory that *the word 'good' can be (wholly) defined in "natural" terms*. More broadly, it's that ethical terms, or at least certain allegedly fundamental ones, can be defined entirely in naturalistic terms. More precisely still, it is the theory that when one says that something is V, where 'V' is one of those terms, then what one is saying about it is that it has some or other characteristics each of which is a "natural" characteristic.

This brings up the question what 'natural' means. Alas, the answer turns out not to be so easy. A shot at it is this: the "natural" world consists of all those things which we can either see, hear, feel, touch, smell—that is, which we can detect with the senses; or—and here's where things get tricky—which, at least, we can produce a plausible theory about, based on but not confined to our sense experiences, a theory that can, in turn be tested by making some sort of experiments or observations. Not a very satisfactory characterization, really, but it's all I can manage, and Moore does no better.

Now, Moore also tends to equate naturalism with the view that 'good' has a definition in the "whole-part" sense of 'definition'. But he doesn't really mean that, for he recognizes that there are natural simple "objects," such as the color yellow. So it's more satisfactory to say that naturalism is the view that 'good' (or whatever the basic terms in ethics are) can be defined completely, without leaving anything out, in "natural" terms, whether just one or a lot more than one.

Other Senses of 'Naturalism'

Note too that 'ethical naturalism' does not mean the view that ethics is confined to the "natural world," that we must have no "nonnatural entities."

First: nonnaturalism or "intuitionism" doesn't mean that the fundamentally good things are "nonnatural." Plato and many religious philosophers have held that The Good is really beyond human experience, outside of "nature" altogether. Moore does not hold this. (See the last chapter of *Principia Ethica*, where Moore describes the "Ideal." It consists entirely of quite familiar things: "the pleasures of human intercourse and the enjoyment of beautiful objects." His kind of "nonnaturalism" is strictly metaethical.)

Second: 'naturalism' in this very specialized sense isn't the view that ethics is compatible with the hypothesis that there isn't anything except "natural objects"—in other words, that ultimately physics can account for everything there is. That could be true even though naturalism is false. As we will see, later philosophers typically held just that.

Moore's thesis applies only to what he calls (and what philosophers have generally called) "intrinsic" value. This is to be distinguished from "extrinsic" value. What's the difference?

1. *Intrinsic* value is value "as an end" rather than "as a means." The idea is that what has the value in question has it without depending on a relation (causal, usually) to anything outside it. It is good simply because of what it is, not because of its connection to something else, distinct from it. Thus, if something is good only because of what it brings about, then it is not intrinsically good. The thing that is good in that way, however, could be very complex, presumably—a great symphony, for example. (But see the refinement below.)

2. *Extrinsic* value is usually characterized as what is valuable as a means to something else, and as such is easy to define: to have value as a means is to be capable of, or efficacious in, bringing about something else that has value. In the end, perhaps after several links, this would have to be value as an end, in other words, intrinsic value. So intrinsic value is basic value: it's at the end of the epistemic line here, that which makes the whole thing go around, as it were. (Aristotle, you may recall, proceeds that way. He holds that happiness or "eudaemonia" is the only ultimate end; all of ethics is thus concerned with the business of finding the best means to that ultimate end.)

An extremely important point to make about intrinsic value is that there is nothing whatever to prevent *weighing* of extrinsic against intrinsic values. It is misleading to talk that way, to be sure: for since the "value" of extrinsic value always comes from the intrinsic value to which it is a means, when we weigh one against the other, we are always, ultimately, weighing some intrinsic values against others. As a reasonably obvious example: the taste of the martini I sip at a certain time is an intrinsic value, but I might easily judge that it is more important to attend a certain meeting, even though it will bore me, than to continue to dwell on this pleasure.

Another point, perhaps only slightly less important, is that there is no reason why what has extrinsic value might not also have intrinsic value while it's at it. I walk to my office at the university. That is essentially a means to the end of getting there. It is also a means to health, according to my doctor. But also, I enjoy walking (usually), and often take walks simply because I do so. The means we employ to various ends often themselves have value apart from their value as means. That is fortunate, for it much increases the value of life. It would be sad if the means we choose to various ends were themselves devoid of the intrinsic kind of value. And it can happen that the means take over: even when they aren't successful as means, we keep on choosing them because they have become enjoyable in themselves.

This last way of putting it brings up a longstanding issue in value theory. Are enjoyable activities enjoyable in themselves, or is what really has the intrinsic value the enjoyment they bring? It is difficult to resist the latter alternative, for few of us are unacquainted with the unhappy development that what we have enjoyed for long somehow ceases to bring enjoyment. Our tastes change or perhaps we get too tired, or whatever; but it does happen, so often that, as I say, few lives are without this experience. And so that calls for a refinement.

A Refinement: Inherent/Instrumental Value

To complicate life but add depth to our inquiry, we should note here a further distinction, due (so far as I know) to the American philosopher C. I. Lewis[3]: between "inherent" and "instrumental." Consider something with typical instrumental value, such, indeed, as an instrument. A violin is valuable because (and if) when suitably played on, it yields a beautiful sound. More precisely, the playing of that violin, when done expertly, produces that sound. But what about that sound itself? How is it valuable? Is sound, even when beautiful, to be classified as "intrinsically" good? Or should we instead say that it is something further, something that is a direct function of the sound, that is fundamentally good—say, the beauty of that beautiful sound, as distinct from the sound itself? Lewis thought there was a direct experience of value at the end of the line, and that the shimmering violin sound wasn't quite the end of the line itself.

Is he right? We will return to that matter later when we consider Hedonism. Meanwhile, we should agree also that Moore's "intrinsic value" is to be identified with the ultimate value identified in Lewis's refined distinction, rather than the "inherent" value of the many things that directly inspire the response of enjoyment, admiration, or pleasure. (And this is confirmed in Moore's work, where his favored exam-

---

[3] C. I. Lewis (1883–1964) See his *An Analysis of Knowledge and Valuation* (La Salle, IL: Open Court, 1946), ch. 12.

ples of intrinsic value include personal affection and the enjoyment of beauty.[4])

The "Naturalistic Fallacy"

Moore accuses all previous philosophers (more or less) of committing what he claims is a fallacy—the "naturalistic" fallacy. Trying to pin down this supposed fallacy is not easy. The general idea goes like this: it is the "fallacy" of, in effect, trying to get from facts to values by logic alone. Karl Popper has put it thus: "It is impossible to derive a sentence stating a norm or a decision from a sentence stating a fact."[5] This general claim has been extremely influential in twentieth-century ethical theorizing. It may be said to have been the major impetus to the theorizing of this century. It was once all but universally accepted and is now very widely denied. That is puzzling. Await further . . .

Why does he think this is a fallacy? Well, if the word 'good' cannot be defined in any natural terms, then you couldn't infer from some sentence making only "natural" claims that something was good or bad: for good and bad would be nonnatural properties. But how does he know that? The sense that the "naturalistic fallacy" is a fallacy has to come before a theory to explain why it is. So, why does he suppose there is a naturalistic fallacy? Mainly because of one, extremely interesting, extremely influential argument: the so-called *open question test*.

The Open Question Test

Moore provides what is evidently intended to be a general test for proposed definitions of ethical terms. A definition, in general, asserts an equivalence of meaning: it says that the meaning of one word or expression, or sentence, is the same as that of another expression. We will write this as follows: 'F' = 'G'. Here the '=' sign indicates identity of meaning. So the statement <'F' = 'G'> says that the words that 'F' stands for have the same meaning as the ones that 'G' stands for.

We are talking here about an equivalence of *meaning*. Such an equivalence must be distinguished, sharply for present purposes, from another sort of equivalence, which philosophers now call an *extensional equiva-*

---

[4] Moore, *Principia Ethica*, ch. 6, "The Ideal."

[5] Karl Popper, *The Open Society and its Enemies*, 5th ed., vol. 1 (Princeton: Princeton Univ. Press, 1966), 64.

lence. In such an equivalence, the claim is only that *everything which exemplifies the left-hand concept also exemplifies the right-hand one, and vice versa*: so, "x is F if and only if x is G" asserts such an equivalence between the notion of F and that of G. But it does not assert meaning equivalence.

A famous[6] example of an extensional equivalence that is clearly not a meaning equivalence is this one:

K: *something is a creature with a heart if and only if it is also a creature with kidneys.*

Details apart (such as creatures with only one kidney, say), K is true; yet obviously we could imagine something with one of these organs and not the other. They are clearly two different things. On the other hand, someone is a bachelor if and only if he is an unmarried male of marriageable age. Being a bachelor isn't a clear distinct thing from being an unmarried male: it is absolutely the same thing, 'bachelor' being in effect a shorter expression for the same thing.

Having made this clarification, we now see that if the two halves of a proposed definition do have the same meaning, then the statement 'F = G' has, it seems, the same meaning as 'F = F'. For after all, we may substitute identicals for identicals. '2 = 2' means the same as '1 + 1 = 2'; for '1+1' and '2' are different expressions standing for the same number (namely, 2). (That may sound rather odd. That it does so, we'll see, is quite important.)

So, suppose someone offers a definition of 'good,' claiming that

(1) 'good' = 'F'

in other words, that

(1*) The statement 'X is good' is identical in meaning with the statement 'X is F'

Therefore

(2) Statements of the form, 'F is good' would have the same meaning as statements of the form 'good is good.'

Similarly,

---

[6] It comes, so far as I know, from the famed logician and philosopher W. V . O. Quine.

(2*) 'A thing which is F is a thing which is good' [or: an F-thing is a good thing] is equivalent in meaning to 'a good thing is a good thing'

And

(2**) 'If x is F, then x is good' = 'if x is good, then x is good.'

Now actually, statements of the forms displayed in the right-hand members of the identities asserted in (2), (2*), and (2**)—'F is F' or 'good is good' or 'if x is good, then x is good'—are in a sense devoid of meaning. They don't exactly *say* anything at all: no matter what the world is like, A is A, and good is good. Even if there were no good things, it would still be true that good = good.

(3) Some definitions of 'good' might seem to work, because they really define 'good' in terms of other words that are already defined in terms of 'good,' such as 'desirable'. But, the argument proceeds, for any given proposed definition in which 'F' is not already synonymous with 'good' (for example, 'desirable'), the proposed definition will fail the test; that is to say, the two sentences, 'Fs are good' and 'good things are good' will not be found identical in meaning. In fact, 'Fs are good' will be found to be meaningful (significant).

We can express this alternatively by saying that the question, "Are Fs good?" will be found to be a logically open question—a question which conceivably could be answered either yes or no. But the questions, 'Are Fs F'?, or 'Is good good?' are clearly not "open"—it would make no sense whatever to say 'no'. In short,

(4) *For all proposed 'naturalistic' definitions of 'good,' sentences of type (1*) are not true: all such definitions are erroneous. So ethical naturalism is false.*

Note that Moore has not proved that no naturalistic definitions can work, and therefore that the naturalistic fallacy is a fallacy. Claim (4) does not *follow* from (3). What do we need to complete the argument? As it stands, it seems to be "inductive"; that is, we try a bunch of definitions, test each one in the way indicated, find that it fails, and reject it. After testing a lot of them, and in particular those that might seem most promising, and finding that none of them work, we might conclude that all will fail. But , after all, we don't know for sure that the next one won't work. Induction is not deduction: we can't pass with certainty from premises about particular cases to conclusions about all cases, so long as there are an indefinite number of cases that we haven't actually looked at. There will always be this indefinite number of further cases—language is open-ended.

The Naturalistic Fallacy and Ethical Reasoning

If we accept the 'naturalistic fallacy,' then we accept that ethical arguments cannot look like this:

(1) x has natural properties F1, F2 . . . Fn

Therefore

(2) x is (intrinsically) good

Must we, similarly, reject the following:

(1) *action* x would have natural properties: F1, F2, . . . Fn

Therefore

(2) action x is right [or, the right thing to do]?

What follows is that one or the other of two things is true. One possibility is that rightness has the same resistance to definition as goodness. Moore, however, does not think that. He thinks that the other possibility is true: we can reduce rightness to goodness. According to Moore, 'right' means 'conducive to maximum good'. But if he is right about goodness, it is indefinable in natural terms; so if Moore is right, then rightness is not fully definable in such terms either. Clearly, if we are on track so far, then there is going to be quite a problem establishing any ethical claims. For if we can't appeal to any "natural" facts, what, after all, can we appeal to?

Moore's result appears to be extremely important, as it was thought to be in his day—devastating, a bombshell. But is it? I devote the next many pages to discussing the argument, its implications, and the alternatives.

From Nonnaturalism to Intuitionism?

Since the argument seems to show that we cannot base our ethics on natural facts, the inference Moore draws is that we have to appeal to "nonnatural facts": evaluative "facts" about basically good or bad things, not reducible to any natural features these things have. His argument was evidently something like this:

(1): Naturalism is false

The burden of his preceding arguments is that statements about what is basically or fundamentally good do not attribute any natural properties to their objects. So we come to

(2): There are only two possibilities: namely, either 'good' is meaningless or 'good' means something "nonnatural."

(3): 'Good' is not meaningless.

Plainly, Moore thinks, we must accept (3). Obviously 'good' means something. We all use it all the time, and how could we do that if it were meaningless? Thus we arrive at

(4) Conclusion: intuitionism is true.

So, we are stuck with (4): goodness must be a very special quality, radically different in kind from anything else in the world. (In chapter 3 of *Principia Ethica*, Moore goes to great lengths to argue that goodness is not, for example, pleasure, nor is it "what we desire." In chapter 4 he argues that it is also not something "metaphysical.")

Important note: Remember, this all applies only to the notion of "intrinsic" value, value "as an end" rather than "as a means."

Ethical Intuitionism

If Moore's conclusion is accepted, we are stuck with a theory known as "intuitionism." (Now, however, this term needs to be qualified: "metaphysical" intuitionism. The newer sort, "methodological" intuitionism, will be discussed later.) This is the name philosophers gave to theories holding that we cannot find out certain things by empirical means, that is, by observation and sense experience, but must instead find them out by "nonempirical observation." Ethical intuitionism holds that fundamental ethical values must be "intuited": we cannot account for them by analysis into anything else.

Obviously, a very important question now would be: just how are we supposed to do this? Moore, unfortunately, doesn't say. Indeed, he does

not even seem to be very interested in it. Having concluded that goodness is this sort of a property, he seems content to let the rest take care
of itself. We will see that that is a mistake.

Intuitionism and Objectivity

The idea of intuitionism is that what we intuit is the presence or absence
in various things of genuine ("real") properties, properties that are *there*
independently of whether we happen to think they are. They may be
peculiar—"nonnatural" —but nevertheless, such is the idea; they are real
parts of the world.

Philosophers have long disputed whether ethics is in this sense
"objective" or how it is if it is. But I think it quite clear that Moore thought
his theory did preserve this idea of objectivity—that he came down on
the "objective" side as against "subjectivism." But, does it? I think we can
raise serious doubts about that claim.

The term 'objective' is used in several ways. For instance, that which
someone is aiming at or striving to achieve is often said to be the person's "objective." But what we have in mind here is rather different.
When a person is said to be "objective," for instance, in the carrying on
of an inquiry or investigation, then an idea of not being biased, especially
by her own emotions or interests, is prominent. One thinks of such a person as being impartial, for instance.

We can distinguish three components in this cluster of ideas.

(1) The impartial person equally balances the claims of all parties: she
doesn't attach greater weight to her own, for instance, or those of people
she happens to like. This is equality of assessment.

(2) If we are objective, then you and I, say, will *agree*, at least if we
both look carefully and under the same conditions. The objective is that
which secures such agreement. This is objectivity as intersubjective cor-
respondence, unanimity of distinct minds.

(3) The objective person is guided by the facts themselves. The idea
is that there is a truth "out there" which she is trying (with some success)
to grasp: her decisions are prompted by this independently existing thing
rather than by such factors as her own "subjective" inclinations or pre-
sentiments.

In the special sense we are concerned with here, the idea of the
"independently existing thing" is foremost. Consider the idea of a material object, such as a planet or a mountain. Such things do not, we think,
disappear when we cease looking at them or thinking about them. They
are "there," whatever we may think. Their existence is a matter of fact,
totally independent of ourselves. It is this last idea to which Moore is try-

ing to lay claim. Does he successfully capture this idea? There are good reasons for thinking that he does not—that, in fact, the objectivity of good claimed by his theory is in principle impossible, and, in a sense, something of a delusion.

First, Moore says that this "property" of goodness is objective in my third sense. It is simply there, whatever you or anyone may think. But how are we to be sure that it is if we are in doubt, in any particular case? Suppose, especially, that you and I each "look" at something or other and you "find" it to be good, while I find it to be bad. What, then, do we do? Moore, alas, can give us only one piece of advice: "look" again!

Notice that 'look' has quotation marks around it in the preceding sentence. That is because intuiting goodness cannot literally be looking, since we do that with our eyes and what we detect with those are natural qualities (namely colors), not "nonnatural" ones. And it is not at all obvious that we are going to reach agreement in any particular case just because we open our "value-seekers" and "look" again. Why won't we just have the same reaction we had before? You claim it is good; I deny it; and there seems nothing we can really do about it. I can't claim that you weren't really "looking," for I haven't the least idea how to tell whether you were or not. I will claim that you weren't in view of the fact that you continue to disagree with me. And you in turn will say exactly the same thing, only with 'you' and 'me' reversed. In large part, this, I think, is because we don't know anything about the sort of thing we're supposed to be "looking" for. But it is a main point of Moore's theory that it can't tell us anything useful about this, for remember, goodness is supposed to be a simple property, on his view. You can't take it apart, because it doesn't have any parts.

Second: as regards the "equal weighting" idea, it should be pointed out that there seems to be no inherent reason why a totally simple quality should adhere in equal "degrees" to anything in particular.

Further reflection on that matter turns out to reveal a very interesting problem. It's rather subtle, but I hope most readers will be able to follow it.

The "Two-Pictures" Problem

Consider a type of case that has been much discussed in the literature of ethics, including, later (and remarkably unsatisfactorily) by Moore himself.[7] There are, let us say, two paintings hanging on a wall, side

---

[7] Moore, "The Conception of Intrinsic Value," in *Philosophical Studies* (London: Routledge, 1922), essay 8.

by side. The paintings are identical in appearance: you could not tell one from the other just by looking at them. Now: could one of these paintings look *better* than the other one? Could one of them be a *better painting?*

As a matter of aesthetics, there is a factor we must set aside. One of them could be a perfect copy of the other, and we might think that the original—if only we knew which it was—is better just because it is original. However, its originality is not a visual property, and we are here only asking whether one of them looks better. The one that was historically original may be more valuable in some other respect, to be sure—as a collector's item, say. But it wouldn't look better—it can't, for by hypothesis these two pictures are indistinguishable.

There may not actually be any absolutely indistinguishable pictures, but this is irrelevant, isn't it? Anyway, consider two successive imprints coming off a printing press, say, or two successive playings of the same digital recording of something. Surely it would be nonsense to say that the playing that occurred at 5:00 was better than the one that occurred at 5:15? After all, it's absolutely the same music we are hearing—the same performance, same everything.

But what does Moore's theory say? According to it, goodness is a "simple" quality. In this respect it is like simple color (to which, in fact, Moore himself compares it). Now consider two identical billiard balls: same size, same shape, same weight, equally smooth in surface, and so on. In fact, suppose there is absolutely no difference between them—except for one thing: one of them is blue, the other red. Perfectly possible, right? But if goodness itself were another simple quality, then why couldn't two things that were alike in absolutely all perceptible respects nevertheless differ in that one of them was good, the other bad?

This may strike you as a rather esoteric problem. But it and matters related to it are crucial to our understanding of ethics, as I shall often be observing as we go on. It's decidedly worth thinking about.

Supervenience

The problem about the two pictures brings into focus an important feature of evaluative language: that talk about goodness (and also rightness, justice, and so on) always, so to speak, rides piggyback on other aspects of things. That is to say, in the terminology that has come to be adopted, goodness is "supervenient" on the other characteristics of what has it. If something is good, it is always appropriate to try to figure out what it is about the thing in question that *makes* it good. And when we say this sort of thing, we mean, what properties—what "natural" properties, that is—

the thing has in virtue of which, or on account of which, we think it good. This drink is good because it's refreshing, or because it tastes a certain way, or because it has certain useful effects on us, and so on. There always has to be some explanation, in terms of the features or characteristics or relations of what is evaluated, why that particular thing has the value it does. (Note that we are discussing here evaluations of particulars; it is not obviously true that there has to be, or even, as Moore insists, that there can be, "explanations" of why very basic qualities or types of thing are good or bad.)

The goodness of particular things, then, always points beyond itself, as a matter of its logic. Why is this so? That's the question. And the trouble with Moore's theory is that it seems to be unable to answer it. If goodness is just another quality, why shouldn't it go off on its own, as it were, independently of other, "natural" qualities?

Motivation

This is not the end of the story regarding intuitionism. What is arguably the main stumbling block for intuitionism is its bearing on practice. Namely: does it have any? If goodness is literally just another simple property, why should we *care* whether anything is good? But we *do* care—don't we?

To put it another way, the word 'good' and related ethical words such as 'right' and 'ought' are such that the questions whether we ought to do x, whether y was the right thing to do, whether such-and-such would be a good thing to aim at, are questions about things that matter to us. It is, we think, important that we do what is right and avoid what is wrong.

How important? We do indeed meet people who, at times, seem to pay little attention to moral obligation. Those people are to worry about, morally speaking. But in the first place, we aren't only talking about morals here. People value lots of things, and in valuing them they show that those things matter to them. If they don't value morality, that raises further special problems, but we'll table those until we get to the specifically moral sphere.

There is another question: isn't there something odd about agreeing that x is the very thing one ought to be doing, yet expressing utter indifference to whether it is done? There is something wrong with such attitudes, to be sure; but there is also an air of oddness. What was the *point* of deciding whether x was the right thing to do if, all along, you simply didn't care whether you did the "right" thing or not? Indeed, can we understand someone to have even addressed the question we all have in mind when he asks whether he ought to do x, if the answer will simply make no difference whatever to his behavior?

Moore, interestingly, himself caricatures one sort of naturalist as follows: "Do, pray, act so, because the word 'good' is generally used to denote actions of this nature! Such is the substance of their teaching."[8] His point, surely, is that one may not care whether the word 'good' does denote them—nothing about what we ought to do can follow from a mere fact like that. But when we are talking about moral goodness, it is, Moore is evidently assuming, obvious that the goodness of something cannot be a matter of indifference. We must in some way or to some degree want (at least, other things being equal) to do what would bring about x, if we agree that x is indeed good.

How can an intuitionist theory account for this? I am rather inclined to think that it simply can't. Proponents of this sort of theory tend to gloss over this problem, or to insist that there's really nothing odd at all, however immoral they may be, about people who are indifferent to moral qualities. That large question is one we'll be pursuing considerably later. It especially animated the move to emotivism, the next sort of general theory we'll be looking at.

A Note on Moore's Ethics

Meanwhile, you may wonder what this all has to do with ethics. I sympathize. As a matter of fact, Moore's ethics, in the usual sense of the term in which we expect an ethics to tell us what we ought to do, doesn't come out in the usual selections from Moore in anthologies. Indeed, modern philosophers pay scant attention to what Moore himself thought was most important in his work, namely, his actual ethics.

In *Principia Ethica*, Moore held that there was only one indefinable term in ethics, namely 'good' (or more precisely, good and bad). But what about right and wrong? At that time, Moore held that the notion of 'right' *is* definable. To say that an act, x, is right is, Moore thought, to say nothing more nor less than that x would bring about, or cause, more of what is intrinsically good than would any other action open to the agent. This view, that the rightness of an action is a matter of the good it causes, is called in the trade "consequentialism." The historically most influential form of consequentialism is utilitarianism, about which we will be saying more later. But the historical utilitarians were hedonists: they thought that

---

[8] Moore, *Principia Ethica*, 12.

the good was pleasure, or at least happiness. Moore's theory differs from theirs, in a sense, in being more general. However, we have here gone well beyond our topic, metaethics. We will return to issues raised by Moore's *ethical* theory later.

Other Intuitionisms

Which concept is "the fundamental concept of ethics"? Or is there more than one? (That view is known as "ethical pluralism"). Moore claims that that fundamental concept is goodness (which he maddeningly calls 'good') but this view is actually in a minority among philosophers who have professed some kind of intuitionism. One of them was Moore's own teacher, Henry Sidgwick. Two others were H. A. Prichard and W. D. (Sir William David) Ross, who was one of the most respected and influential ethical theorists in England in the earlier part of the twentieth century and also a classical scholar, famed for his translation of the works of Aristotle.

Sidgwick

Sidgwick considered and rejected various theories of ethics, for good and familiar reasons. He then concludes that a proposition of the form 'x ought to be done' cannot be further analyzed: it is simply a "deliverance of practical reason." But he thinks that there aren't millions or even dozens of such deliverances. Instead, he comes up with just three "Self-evident Principles" of practical thinking. They are:

Principle I. Universalizability: If x is right for one person in given circumstances, it must also be right for any other person in such circumstances. (Or: if it is right for A to do x and wrong for B to do x, then there must be some relevant difference between A and B other than that they are simply different persons.) This is essentially the requirement that morality is a matter of principles, general rules rather than arbitrary fiat or whim. Is that part of the very meaning of 'right'? We'll consider that later.

Principle II. Prudence: one ought to aim at one's own long-term happiness, one moment of one's life having the same "weight" as any other moment.

Principle III. Rational benevolence: I ought to aim at the good of all persons, impartially considered.

This involves two parts: (1) "the self-evident principle that *the good of any one individual is of no more importance, from the point of view (if I may say so) of the Universe, than the good of any other*[9]*;* and (2) I ought to aim at maximum absolute good—that is to say, the fact that something is, *absolutely,* good is *a sufficient reason* for me to try to bring it about.

We might question this notion of "absolute good" —or good "from the point of view of the Universe." Egoists might deny that there is any such thing. Alternatively, we might question the other part—we might deny that there is any obligation to promote "absolute good." But if we accept the notion of impersonal, absolute good, then we must surely agree with the first part of the principle.

If we accept both parts, and accept it as the supreme of these three principles (or anyway, superior to principle II), then we have utilitarianism, which makes precisely the promotion of maximum good for everyone the sole criterion of morality. This was in fact Sidgwick's conclusion.

Philosophical Intuitionism

Sidgwick's use of the term 'intuitionism' refers to the method of refining our commonsense views about right and wrong until we reach solid axioms that can be accepted without qualification. In his view none of the moral beliefs of common sense will serve as such axioms. When we look at them carefully, Sidgwick holds, we reach the principle of utility as the underlying foundation of them all.

It should be noted that Sidgwick's use of 'intuitionism' is fundamentally the same as its application to more modern and more ancient writers. But there is a difference in a subordinate sense of the term 'intuitionist': namely, whether one accepts several basic principles, or on the other hand, just one—the difference between ethical "pluralism" and ethical "monism." Sidgwick is distinguished from such intuitionists as Butler in holding that there is ultimately just one basic principle of morality—the principle of rational benevolence, or pure utilitarianism when that is combined with his view about ultimate good. (It is true that he holds that there are three self-evident principles, as we noted above. But the first of these is purely formal, for it does not say which features may relevantly distinguish one person from another for ethical purposes; it therefore says nothing until some principle supplying those features is given. And the second principle isn't exactly an axiom of morality, but rather of prudence.)

---

[9] Henry Sidgwick, *The Methods of Ethics,* 7th ed. (Cambridge: Cambridge Univ. Press, 1906), 498.

Sidgwick's claim that all commonsense ethical principles reduce, under analysis, to the principle of utility has been hotly disputed in recent times. We defer discussion on that to part 2.

Sidgwick, as we have seen, thinks that 'ought' or 'right' is essentially an indefinable notion. But he doesn't think that 'good' is indefinable:

> It would seem then, that if we interpret the notion of 'good' in relation to 'desire,' we must identify it not with the actually desired, but rather with the desirable:—meaning by 'desirable' not necessarily what ought to be desired, but what would be desired, with strength proportioned to the degree of desirability, if it were judged attainable by voluntary action, supposing the desirer to possess a perfect forecast, emotional as well as intellectual, of the state of attainment or fruition.[10]

If we ask what is good in this sense, then, Sidgwick comes down in favor of hedonism, or more precisely, the view that the only intrinsically good things are desirable states of consciousness. He admits that we do sometimes desire other things than to feel certain ways or have certain experiences, but he thinks that to do so would be found, on reflection, to be essentially irrational. And thus he ends up with a view of the good essentially the same as J. S. Mill's.

Here's where the dualism comes in, then. If it is irrational to desire things other than states of consciousness, then why is it rational to desire states of *other people's* consciousness? For after all, one does not feel or experience those, any more than one feels what it is like to be a Buddhist stone carving: their states of consciousness are not part of *my* consciousness—so how can I desire them intrinsically?

Prichard

Another influential intuitionist was H. A. Prichard of Oxford (1871–1947). His famous article, "Does Moral Philosophy Rest on a Mistake?" is widely anthologized.[11] The relation between his view and the other two is quite interesting, for our purposes.

Ross takes the more familiar view that what we "intuit" in ethics are certain general rules or principles, such as that we ought to keep our promises, to refrain from deliberately harming others, to tell the truth,

---

[10] Sidgwick, *Th Methods of Ethics*, 110–11.

[11] H. A. Prichard, "Does Moral Philosophy Rest on a Mistake?" in *20th Century Ethical Theory*, ed. Steven M. Cahn and Joram G. Haber (Englewood Cliffs, NJ: Prentice-Hall, 1995), 37ff. It and other interesting papers are found in his *Moral Obligation: Essays and Lectures* (Oxford: Oxford Univ. Press, 1963). The essay mentioned is on 1–17.

and to return favors. Prichard, on the other hand, seems to have thought (the matter is obscure) that what we intuit is the rightness or wrongness of particular acts. Prichard is thus considered an "act intuitionist"; Ross, by contrast, is called a "rule intuitionist."[12] I should caution the student that it is quite a tricky scholarly question whether Prichard (or Dancy) is correctly so labeled.

Ross's Intuitionism: "Prima Facie" versus "Sans Phrase" Rightness

Ross's interest for ethical theorists is that he claimed that Moore was wrong about rightness being definable in terms of productiveness of good consequences. In fact, he held that 'right' could not be defined at all. His view about rightness was exactly like Moore's view about goodness. Rightness must also be "intuited."

The view that a number of distinct moral principles are self-evidently true has, besides the sort of epistemological obscurities we have been and will be discussing, a major logical problem. Consider any general ethical rule, such as that lying is wrong. But is lying *always* wrong? A very few people (Kant, apparently) have thought so—or rather, have thought that they thought so. But most of us do not, nor in the end does Kant. Most of us think that, in various unusual circumstances, it may be right to tell a lie. To take the Kantian example, suppose that a murderer comes to the door seeking his victim, and you know just where the victim is. The murderer asks you where he is. Should you tell him the truth—at the expense of the poor fellow's life? Certainly not!

How are we to describe the situation? For we do think that lying is wrong, after all—and we have a point. Perhaps Ross's most important contribution to ethical theory was his handling of this problem. He makes a distinction between what he called "prima facie" and "sans phrase" obligation. When we say such things as that lying is wrong, what we are doing is looking at a certain aspect of action, and judging that that aspect is morally objectionable. Any case of lying, insofar as it is such a case, is to be avoided, so far as it goes. However, particular actions don't just have one or two morally significant aspects, but many. We have to look at the other ones, too. And some of those may come under a quite opposite moral rule. For instance, it is right to save lives. But in the case of our murderer at the door, if you tell the truth, someone loses his life, whereas

---

[12] A contemporary writer who appears to take such a view is Jonathan Dancy. See his *Moral Reasons* (Oxford: Blackwell, 1993).

if you lie, his life is saved. What we have here, then, is two normally consistent ethical rules that, in certain cases, come into conflict. In such cases, we could not act on both rules, if those rules were regarded as exceptionless. But, Ross suggests, they are not. Rather, we must, when they conflict, weigh the one against the other, and decide which is more "stringent," that is, which of the two rival duties is more of a duty.

Our duty "sans phrase," that is, our duty simpliciter, or without qualification, is, according to Ross, to do what has, in the circumstances, the greatest moral "requiredness" or stringency in those circumstances. In complex cases—and so many are, after all—this will not be easy. We must size up the case, looking for all the morally significant aspects; then weigh those aspects against each other and see what we ought to do, all things considered. If there are a lot of those "all things" to consider, we may have quite a job on our hands.

Particularism

It was this latter feature that Prichard emphasizes in his intuitionism. Prichard's view seems to be that there are no rules for the making of a judgment of duty in the particular case. He claims that the sense of obligation is absolutely "immediate" and cannot be arrived at by an argument. Rather, "if we do doubt whether there is really an obligation to originate A in a situation B, the remedy lies not in any process of general thinking, but in getting face to face with a particular instance of the situation B, and then directly appreciating the obligation to originate A in that situation."[13]

The view that moral obligation attaches to particular acts, as such, is called "particularism." Or so it is said, but the view is prima facie unbelievable. I can have a conviction that just in these circumstances I ought to do so-and-so. But as Henry Sidgwick points out, I can certainly be confronted with another example, in all respects alike, and if I then have a quite different conviction about that one, I can be called to account. What's the difference? The fact that John is John and Bob is Bob is not enough to justify saying that John should do x in these circumstances, but Bob should do y. Perhaps John is capable of doing it and Bob isn't— that would be relevant. There could be any number of other relevant factors that might differentiate the two cases. But if nothing at all of a general kind is found, then it is surely nonsense to say that Bob has a moral obligation to do y while John has no moral obligation to do y.

---

[13] Prichard, "Does Moral Philosophy Rest on a Mistake?" 47.

Something's wrong. Prichard, it should be noted, uses familiar examples—keeping *this* promise, for instance. He leans on something general about the case to make his convictions plausible.

Prichard's arguments don't clearly exemplify this popular characterization of it. For notice that he talks of a "particular instance of the situation B." But if by 'particular' he meant, literally, particular, then one instance of situation B is one particular and another instance is another particular. Yet it is in virtue of their both being of the "particular kind B" that we have, he thinks, the duty to do the thing or not. It is, in fact, doubtful that anyone has ever literally been an act-intuitionist in the sense in which 'act' refers, literally, to 'particular act'. Surely the claim that in case 1 of a certain situation it is our duty to do x, while yet in case 2, absolutely identical with case 1 in every possible respect, we ought to do not-x, that is, x is wrong—is not credible—is just nonsense. And that's an important point about how evaluative language works.

Part 3 of this book amounts to a general theory of the complex issue of rules in morals.

Who's Right?

Rival intuitionists, as we see, have claimed that we "intuit" very different things. Moore holds that we intuit what is good and bad, but calculate, so to speak, what is right and wrong. Sidgwick, Ross, and Prichard hold that we intuit what is right and wrong. But Sidgwick believes we intuit highly abstract rather formal principles, and that these principles lead us to the principle of utility, whereas Prichard thinks we intuit specific obligations in particular cases, while Ross believes that we intuit several concrete general principles—only they are overridable, prima facie principles rather than rigorous or "strict" principles.

How are we to decide who is right? What they have in common is the belief that there are fundamental unanalyzable moral "properties" of an evaluative kind, properties that must be just "apprehended" (or not!); we can give no further reason for their attribution to acts or objects. Certain moral judgments, in either case, are absolutely fundamental, "self-evident." Our question is whether any such view is plausible in either case. Is there any reason to think that one or the other or both of these views is wrong?

There is, indeed. But as between them, it is Prichard and Ross who are wrong, and Moore whose view makes more sense. However, precisely what they are wrong about is not so easy to say, though very important to try to get at. What I think Prichard and Ross are wrong about is their apparent belief that no *rationale* can be given for holding that certain kinds of things are right, others wrong. In that respect, Sidgwick has the better of it. And Moore thinks he is improving on Sidgwick. However, at bottom, all intuitionists must and do fail in the same fundamental respect. In the end, they claim that some really fundamental truth of ethics is true because it corresponds to some sort of indefinable "reality"—but one that cannot be explained, and so, cannot be rationally defended against someone who differs on that matter.

What, really, is their claim? If their claim is only that when one has a sense that one ought to do something, one's sense is a kind of peculiar felt urgency or "mustness" that cannot itself be "analyzed," they might be right. What intuitionism has going for it is mostly this, which is a *phenomenological* observation. But that wouldn't prove what they seem to be maintaining, namely that there are fundamental judgments of right or wrong that are incapable of being rationally supported or refuted, where by 'rationally' is meant that accountable, analyzable reasons can be given for or against them in terms of other considerations that rationally support certain moral judgments. I might intuit that the person before me is none other than my long lost friend Johann, and I might be right. But if I am, it isn't because I have intuited it; it's because the person in question, upon investigation, turns out to be Johann after all.

Intuitionists have some tendency to claim that intuitions are nevertheless "rational." But this would appear to be just hype, or window-dressing: if you can't give a *reason for* something, other than the lame shrug-off that it is self-evident, then what you are maintaining is not that it is rational, but that it is *non*rational.

I will later argue that there are *no* judgments of moral right or wrong that are "fundamental" in the sense claimed by Sidgwick, Ross, and Prichard. *All* moral claims, I will insist, must be supported by considerations that do not themselves consist in or presuppose claims about rightness or wrongness. That is a tall conceptual order, and one not widely accepted even now. In saying this, I pick up a gauntlet that has been, so to say, thrown down by Ross and Prichard. They say, either about all moral judgments or at least about certain fundamental ones, that you can't establish these moral judgments by further, nonmoral, reasons. I will argue that we can, and that moreover, we must.

In this respect, Moore (that is, the Moore of *Principia Ethica*, which is what we are considering—he changed his mind later[14]) is in my camp, not theirs: Moore thinks that all particular judgments of right and wrong are judgments that can be supported by claims about what is good or bad (not morally good or bad, but just good or bad—"intrinsically" good or bad, in the end). And he thought that the general judgment, "It is right to

---

[14] See G. E. Moore's little book, *Ethics* (Oxford: Hutchinson Univ. Library, 1912).

do what maximizes the total sum of value in the world" is true by definition, so that it didn't need a further "moral intuition" either. For Moore,
in fact, there are no *moral* intuitions.

It was this last matter that he eventually changed his mind about.
Hastings Rashdall[15] and W. D. Ross persuaded him that the judgment that
"we ought to maximize good" is not an "analytic" truth, that is, a proposition true solely by virtue of the meanings of its component terms. (See
Moore's later book *Ethics*.[16]) I will later argue not only that Moore should
not have changed his mind, but also that he was wrong in his characterization of what our general ultimate duty is. Stay tuned!

A Different Sense of 'Intuitionism': 'Methodological' versus 'Theoretical'

Much later in the past century, a quite different sense came to be attached
to the term 'intuitionism.' In this new sense, an "intuition" is simply a
prephilosophical moral belief or judgment, but no assumptions are made
about the exact logical or metaphysical constitution of that judgment. In
this new sense, it is not claimed that moral judgments are judgments about
the presence or absence of funny unanalyzable qualities. In principle, no
claim at all, they held, needed to be made about that, one way or the
other. What was claimed, instead, is that it is the job of ethical theory to
"make sense of" our pretheoretical (prephilosophical) moral beliefs. The
theory we come up with should systematize these beliefs. Some of them,
after all, may conflict with others of them, and if we try to put them all
together, we might find that some seem to stick out like sore thumbs,
while others fit together nicely into a harmonious whole. Then we might,
as philosophers, discard some of the sore thumbs. However, we can't, on
this view, discard them all. To do so would be to throw out the baby with
the bath water. On this view of ethical theory, our overall theory must preserve the truth of a lot of our prereflective judgments: if a theory conflicts
with what we basically just believe, then the theory must go!

A parallel with epistemology is pressed in this connection. How do
we know that there is an external world? How do we evaluate scientific
theories telling us that the world contains various exotic entities, such as
molecules and atoms, that are responsible for all the phenomena of our
experience? Very generally, the answers must appeal to our experience
itself. A theory that conflicts drastically, and at the relevant points, with
our experience will be rejected on that very account.

---

[15] Hastings Rashdall, *The Theory of Good and Evil* (Oxford: Clarendon Press, 1907).
[16] Moore, *Ethics*.

Philosophers differ about the character of our experience. Early in this century, it was popular to suppose that our ultimate appeal is to "sense data," such as seen red or blue, tickles, sensations of heat or cold, and many more. Others insisted that we see trees and mountains, not just "sensory qualities." A scientific theory purporting to show that there are no trees would be laughed out of court. Those, we say, pointing at some trees, are what we mean by the word 'trees' and to deny that the world contains any of those things is just crazy.

Moore's moral theory is a bit like the sense-datum theory: we intuit thousands of little value-facts, but we must put them together somehow to make up overall moral judgments which might, any of them, be wrong. Ross, on the other hand, thinks that we see, so to speak, "moral trees": that is, we "see" that lying is wrong, helping people in need is right, and other "moral facts" of that kind. A moral theory purporting to show that these general judgments are all wet would be for that very reason unbelievable; such judgments are not up for revision.

We will discuss methodological intuitionism later, when we encounter more of it in practice. Meanwhile, however, we should notice that Ross and Prichard also subscribe to it. They may have felt that their theoretical intuitionism entails methodological intuitionism. (It doesn't, in fact. Why couldn't rightness be a funny nonnatural quality, which we have always been wrong about in the past, so that all of our regular ethical beliefs are actually false?) The two types are compatible, but neither, in principle, actually entails the other.

(I should add that I am actually somewhat doubtful about this. It seems to me that if you insist that some of our pretheoretical moral beliefs must be true, come what may, then you must think that no theory can really explain them; in which case how could you regard them as anything but unanalyzable truths? However, we needn't settle this here.)[17]

Evaluating Theoretical Intuitionism: For

What should we think of intuitionisms of the Moore-Ross-Prichard type? Let's do a brief run-down of where we are at this stage in our inquiry. I

---

[17] In "Outline of a Decision Procedure for Ethics," John Rawls presents a kind of methodological intuitionism, without actually calling it that. In his later work he continues to claim to be using a methodological metatheory of that general type. The essay is reprinted in *20th Century Ethical Theory*, ed. Steven M. Cahn and Joram G. Haber (Englewood Cliffs, NJ: Prentice-Hall, 1995). It was originally published in *Philosophical Review* 60, no. 2 (April 1951): 177–97.

shall divide it into reasons for and against, throwing in some doubts and comments as we go.[18] We start with the reasons *for*.

What is the source of such plausibility as these antinaturalisms have? Mainly Moore's open question test: there seems no contradiction or difficulty in the idea of Jones agreeing that x has F, where 'F' designates some empirically observable property or complex of properties, yet denying that x was good (Moore) or right (Ross) or ought to be done (Prichard). Claims of that type seem always to be in some fundamental sense deniable or debatable. Question: Is this due to a problem in principle or is it only because we haven't tried hard enough or haven't looked in the right direction? The argument, while interesting and important, is hardly sufficient to establish intuitionism.

Moore thinks that propositions about fundamental goods are "self-evident," but denies that any statements about duties are so, other than the perhaps analytic truth that we ought to do what is on the whole best. Ross and Prichard hold that some propositions about duties are self-evident. As a claim about how they seem to people who believe them, this claim has some plausibility. It is sometimes called 'phenomenological plausibility'—a fancy phrase meaning that if we just think about it, that's how they seem—how they "present themselves to consciousness," to put it in old-fashioned terms.

This would seem to make them not "deniable," in some sense. Is it deniable that the sum of the angles of a plane triangle is 180°? Supposing otherwise can readily be shown to lead to contradictions—and it's pretty hard to beat that for proof. But again, it's not clear how much it proves. Why couldn't things that don't "present themselves to our consciousness as unanalyzable" nevertheless turn out to be analyzable? And mightn't things that do "present themselves to consciousness" be mistaken nevertheless? Don't some people hold certain mistaken moral views, but hold them so firmly as to be unshakable? We do not lack for fanatics in our world.

Sidgwick and Ross both compare moral intuitions to mathematical ones. But there is a problem with this. Mathematical intuitions are such that their denials seem to make no sense at all. It would be nice if this were true of moral ones too—but unfortunately, it seems not to be. We have too good an idea what someone is saying who denies a moral axiom—or at least, too good an idea what to expect. And at the very least, we must be extremely careful to distinguish purely formal "axioms" that don't actually say that anything in particular is right or wrong, and

---

[18] See P. F. Strawson, "Ethical Intuitionism" in *20th Century Ethical Theory*, ed. Steven M. Cahn and Joram G. Haber (Englewood Cliffs, NJ: Prentice-Hall, 1995) for more interesting discussion.

substantive ones that do—but which, as I say, seem quite possible to deny consistently. But we'll resume that later.

Evaluating Theoretical Intuitionism: Against

Here are some of the main problems with intuitionism.

1. *The Metaphysical Question.* Are there any "nonnatural qualities"? Stevenson remarks, "I recollect no Platonic Idea, nor do I know what to try to recollect. I find no indefinable property nor do I know what to look for."[19] We should emphasize this last point: the reason we can't find these "qualities" is that they are mysterious—we simply don't know what we are supposed to be looking for, so no wonder we don't find them! Merely reiterating moral truths won't do: the fact that we are sure that murder is wrong does not prove that its being so consists in the fact that murder has a unique nonnatural property of wrongness.

How does one even define such qualities? Moore spent much perplexed effort trying to identify the "natural" qualities, and therefore at least to give us a negative understanding of 'nonnatural' ones. But he has a terrible time trying and never succeeded even to his own satisfaction, let alone anyone else's.

2. *The Epistemological Question.* How can we have ethical knowledge if intuitionism is the right account of what this knowledge consists of? It in effect invokes a perceptual model, but it is (to put it mildly) questionable that we have a perceptual "faculty" for these things—in contrast to color, say. It's true that many people have a "sense" of right and wrong—indeed, we would hope that everyone does. But is this 'sense' literally a *sense*, like seeing or hearing? (People have talked of the "still small voice" of conscience. But we cannot identify moral truths with the deliverances of still small voices, or for that matter, deep, resonant voices such as those of actors playing the part of God! Clearly, too, the theoretical intuitionist scenario, with its peculiar "perceptions" of peculiar "qualities," leads up to a particularly serious issue: how would one ever resolve a disagreement about such things? This factor will loom very large in our later deliberations.

3. *The "Practical" Question.* Looming over the entire intuitional enterprise is a problem that many philosophers have regarded as fatal to the entire idea of intuitionism in its "theoretical" versions. Suppose we were

---

[19] Charles Stevenson, "The Emotive Meaning of Ethical Terms," in *Facts and Values* (New Haven, CT: Yale Univ. Press, 1963), 30. Originally published in *Mind*, New Series 46, no. 181 (Jan. 1937): 14–31.

to grant that there are these funny unanalyzable qualities—well, so what? Why should we do anything about them? Who cares about nonnatural qualities? Why should I lift a finger to bring something into existence that would have such a quality? How can the perception that I ought not to murder people plausibly be thought to have anything to do with the possession by murderers or victims of unique, unanalyzable properties? Intuitionists are content simply to assume that these properties are relevant, and indeed calling them moral strongly suggests that they are supposed to be. But you don't prove that a theory has a certain implication simply by asserting that it does. Patrick Nowell-Smith, in a lovely discussion of intuitionism on this point, observes, "Learning about 'values' or 'duties' might well be as exciting as learning about spiral nebulae or waterspouts. But what if I am not interested?"[20]

Emotivism and Prescriptivism

It may come as a surprise to the modern student to hear that intuitionism was so popular among moral philosophers, at least in Britain, after Moore's work that we may regard it as having been for some decades the dominant view. But it is a view that grates against the modern temperament. Meanwhile, philosophers in other fields were probing in the general direction of what has since been known as positivism, and also, less popularly but more accurately, as radical empiricism.

Positivism

The positivists maintained that all statements may be divided into two sorts: (1) analytic, and (2) synthetic. The idea is that the former were simply true by definition and were fundamentally linguistic; the latter, on the other hand, are empirical: establishable or refutable by observations. Thus, for example, 'all sisters have siblings' is analytic; 'all sisters are nervous wrecks' is empirical (and presumably false!). Denying that there were any a priori truths that were not of type (1) was one of the positivists' principal preoccupations—even though it was not so easy to square all this with a large class of what certainly seem to be truths, namely those of mathematics, in which they were keenly interested, and which seemed obviously not empirical, yet almost equally obviously not just definitional.

---

[20] Patrick Nowell-Smith, *Ethics* (Harmondworth: Penguin, 1954), chapter on Intuitionism.

Meanwhile, what about ethics? The positivists, like everyone else, were persuaded by Moore's idea of the "naturalistic fallacy." They too rejected what Moore called naturalism. On the other hand, their general world view was certainly naturalistic. So they were strongly disinclined to have anything to do with "nonnatural properties." What to do? The first strong entry into the field was by A. J. Ayer, whose *Language, Truth and Logic*[21] (1936) was a brash young-man's manifesto of positivism. Ayer put forth the view that we don't have to decide whether the propositions of ethics are analytic or synthetic, for we can instead hold that, despite appearances, they really are not "propositions" at all. They make no statements, either of fact or anything else. What do they do instead? They *express* attitudes, emotions. The term 'emotivism' was coined to apply to this type of theory.

Subjectivism in General

Emotivism is a theory of a general type that is called "subjectivist." This deserves a few words first. Subjectivism could be expressed, in the vernacular, as the view that "it's all in your head!" More precisely, and as applied to ethics, it's the view that when we say that something is right or wrong, what we are doing involves, in some essential way, aspects of the speaker, rather than being exclusively about the act, or whatever, which that speaker is at least ostensibly speaking about. A recent writer defines 'subjective' thus:

> "F-ness is subjective" = "Whether something is F constitutively depends at least in part on the psychological attitude or response that observers have or would have toward that thing."[22]

Two things matter here. The first is the choice of the terms 'attitude' or 'response.' When we make observations of external objects, the observations are in us, not in the things observed; they are, then, 'subjective' unless we distinguish between the kind of subjective response that consists in perception of something, and the kind that consists in having an "attitude toward" it. The latter is needed for claims that evaluations are specifically and interestingly subjective.

The second point that matters is 'constitutively'; F is not subjective if it merely *causes* certain states of our minds. The states of mind have to

---

[21] A. J Ayer, "Critique of Ethics," in *Language, Truth and Logic* (London: Gollancz, 1936).

[22] Michael Huemer, *Ethical Intuitionism* (London: Palgrave Macmillan, 2005), 2.

be logically essential to F in order for F to be subjective. Whenever we say *anything*, the "subject"—that's us, after all—is "involved." But often the subject is no part of the subject matter of the speech. When we describe the properties of mountains—apart from their aesthetic "properties"—nothing we say need involve knowledge of the person doing the describing, unless what she says is unclear or the like. To say that talk about a given subject matter or in a given domain is "subjective," on the other hand, is to say that we simply cannot understand what is being said about the matters in question without some understanding of the speaker of the claims in question.

People value things. It is obviously impossible for values not to be "subjective" in that sense: no subjects, no values. But is what valuers attribute to the things they value subjective, insofar as what they attribute to them are *values*, rather than something else? Let us see.

"Naive" subjectivism in the philosophical literature is a species of the kind of naturalism that Moore supposes he has refuted. This theory holds that when someone says that something, x, is good, what he's really talking *about* is himself, or at any rate about a relation between himself and x. For example, it might be held that 'x is right,' spoken by person A, really means 'A approves of x'; and that 'x is good' really means 'A likes x'. If I say, 'x is right', then all I'm really saying is "I approve of x."

Words like 'really' have to be inserted in the naive subjectivist account, because on the face of it what we are talking about isn't ourselves, but x. Of course, it is true that when we say 'p' we imply that we think that p. But the point of our utterance is not to state that fact. If I say that the moon is about 240,000 miles from the earth, I imply that I *think* the moon is about that far from the earth. But while I imply that, still, what I am talking *about* is the relative position of the earth and the moon—not the current state of my mind—and the relation I am attributing to them obtains entirely independently of my own mind or anyone else's. So, what about values? Are they subjective in a more important way?

Disagreement

But whatever the surface facts may be, analysis shows some major problems with the naive account. These are the kinds of accounts that come under the gun of Moore's naturalistic fallacy arguments.[23] But Stevenson adds a pointed argument that is, in my judgment, very strong—and long

---

[23] See also Paul Edwards, "Naive Subjectivism," in *The Logic of Moral Discourse* (New York: Free Press, 1955), 49–66.

thought to be decisive.[24] Suppose we have two people, A and B, who disagree about the merits of something. A says it's good; B says it's bad. They disagree. But can naive subjectivism explain this? It has a terrible problem. Consider: Logic tells us that one statement, p, denies another statement, q, only if they cannot both be true. That's a truth of logic. One statement, p, is inconsistent with another, q, only if p implies the denial of q. But consider the statements (1) 'A likes x,' and (2) 'B dislikes x'. Clearly (1) and (2) are not inconsistent. On the contrary: both may be true, and in the hypothetical example both are true—especially on the naively subjectivist theory, which after all actually equates 'it's good' with 'I like it.' Something has gone wrong. What started out as a disagreement has been turned into something quite else—two apparently *logically unrelated* statements: 'A likes x'; 'B dislikes x.' A could like it and B like it, or dislike it, or either could like it when the other disliked it. No problem, logically, about any of these possibilities. But plainly it can't be the case both that the thing being evaluated is good and yet that it is bad—so long as we are really evaluating the same thing, in the same respect.

So, where do we go from here? Remember, the point is not that people cannot arrive at opposite views. They do it all the time. The question is whether both can be right. Emotivism denies that both can be right by denying that both are actually saying something that can have the logical relation to others that is required for truth or falsity to be in question at all.

Stevenson

Here we turn to the work of Charles Stevenson, a distinguished American philosopher who became the standard-bearer of emotivism, holding to that theory in one form or another for the rest of his long life. His seminal paper, "The Emotive Meaning of Ethical Terms"[25] will be our main source for discussion.

Although he doesn't put it that way, one thing that Stevenson's work does is to point the way to an open question argument *against* intuitionism. Let's go back to that theory for a moment. Its principal argument against naturalism, remember, is the open-question test. But we may now distinguish two versions of the open-question test, which I shall call the general theory (GT) and the special theory (ST).

---

[24] Historical note: he was far from the first to see this; Moore, Sidgwick, and Hastings Rashdall were all aware of it.

[25] Stevenson "The Emotive Meaning of Ethical Term," as cited in note 28.

According to the general theory, the open-question test is essentially inductive: We try naturalistic analysis X, find it won't do, then try naturalistic analysis Y, find it won't do, then Z—it doesn't do either—and eventually we give up, concluding that none of them will work. On this view, though, the test is not theoretically conclusive. Maybe the week after next, we'll find one that will do after all.

But what if we could find some property that we know ethical statements have and natural statements lack? A property, moreover, that showed us why naturalistic statements would never pass the open question test? That would be what we might call the "special theory" (ST). It would say: All ethical statements have property P; all naturalistic definitions fail because all would lack property P. Is there such a property? Much reflection suggested to Stevenson (guided, one might note as an historical aside, by the writings of David Hume) that there is such a property. He called it "magnetism." The idea is that ethical statements affect us. If we agree that something is good or that it is right, then this belief will be reflected in our actions. Goodness or rightness, and all the other "positive" evaluative notions "attract" us; badness, wrongness, and evil "repel" us. Or we might say that these supposed "properties" are such that they seem to "push" us into doing things. Or perhaps "pull": they reach out and "grab" us.

Let's try to be a bit less metaphorical. Suppose that Jones believes that doing actions of type x is morally obligatory. An occasion comes along when Jones could perform x—he clearly realizes that now is the time to do so. What do we expect? Given his professed belief that x is obligatory, we clearly expect him to do x. Moreover, we would expect him to favor other people's doing it (a point that will loom large later in these pages).

We can put this as follows: Arguments of the form

(1) x is right; therefore

(2) "Do x!"

seem to be valid. From the premise that something is right or good or morally required, we infer something like, "Do it!"

Historical Note on Practical Reasoning

Aristotle noticed and discussed this type of reasoning. Here is his example (slightly rewritten): "Dry food is good; this is dry food; therefore—crunch!"[26] (As I put it.) The idea I mean to convey by using "crunch!" is

---

[26] Aristotle, *Nichomachean Ethics*, tr. W. D. Ross, bk. VII, ch. iii: "The one opinion is

that the speaker proceeds to eat the food in question. The conclusion of "practical syllogisms," as Aristotle called them—that which our assembling of the premises is intended to lead to—is an *action*—not a proposition *about* action. Strictly speaking, he would have needed a few more premises in the selected example, such as that one is hungry now and the food in question doesn't belong to someone else and that it won't poison you while it's at it and so on. And also, the conclusion is often not an action right now, but rather, a decision to do some appropriate thing when the time comes. But the point remains: in evaluating, reason influences what we *do*. Moreover, it does it because underlying the process is a *desire*—something we *want*.

For the moment, let's just say that the property of ethical statements that arguably defeats naturalistic theories is "grab" or, as Stevenson calls it, "magnetism." For consider any mere matter of fact. One might say that mere recognizing the truth of that matter of fact isn't, of itself, enough to get one to act. The person who simply recognizes the facts but does nothing about them—doesn't even feel like doing anything about them— is not the person who thinks that something is right or wrong. There is no contradiction in observing cold-blooded killing and then not doing or feeling anything about it. But there is something like a contradiction in calling it wrong and yet not feeling anything or being inclined to do anything at all about it.

So: the special-theory version of the open-question test is whether the metaethical theory in question can account for "push" or "grab." It accounts for it if the theory makes it clear that one could not accept an ethical statement and yet fail to have the relevant attitude or perform (or at least be disposed to perform) the relevant actions.

Well, then—what about Moore's own theory? His intuitionism apparently claims that this is a good inference:

(1) x has a unique, nonnatural quality, H ("that one . . .")

Therefore

(2) x is good (Moore) [or right (Ross)]

---

universal, the other is concerned with the particular facts, and here we come to something within the sphere of perception; when a single opinion results from the two, the soul must in one type of case affirm the conclusion, while in the case of opinions concerned with production it must immediately act (e.g. if 'everything sweet ought to be tasted', and 'this is sweet', in the sense of being one of the particular sweet things, the man who can act and is not prevented must at the same time actually act accordingly).

But would any such thing really be a good argument? Well, suppose Jones says, "Oh, I agree that x is H, all right; but I don't see that x is good!" [or, right]? Do we have any sense of inconsistency here? I don't think so![27]

Now let's apply the special-theory test. If the "magnetism" version of the subjectivist theory is where the action really is, then it would go like this. Let H be the very property, whatever it is, that Ross, say, would identify with rightness. Now consider arguments of this sort:

Premise: Action x has the following unique, nonnatural property, H.

Conclusion: Do x!

That doesn't look too good either. In the case of Moore, we would have to reformulate the argument a little. Let's let x be an action that would bring about something that has the unique, nonnatural quality Moore supposedly identified with goodness—call it 'J'. Then the argument would be the same: Couldn't someone be quite uninterested in J-ness? After all, *all we are told* about J is that it is a "unique, nonnatural quality." Moore's *claim* is that this quality is identical with goodness. But if it is, then anything we would say about a claim that x is good would also be sayable about a claim that x is J. And this quite evidently is just not so.

Would Moore accept that his view would have to commit him to the validity of some such argument? There is some evidence that he should. For he does seem to think that a good test of consistency here would be provided by a reaction of indifference to the information that x has the proposed property F, whatever it may be. Remember, he made fun of the naturalist as follows: "Do, pray, act so, because the word 'good' is generally used to denote actions of this nature!" His point, surely, is that one may not care whether the word 'good' does denote them—nothing about what we ought to do can follow from a mere fact like that. But if so, then he must think that the recognition that x is good would be incompatible with indifference. We must *want* (other things being equal, anyway), or more generally be at least somewhat inclined to do, what would bring about x if we agree that x is indeed good.

But then, as we have seen, one may not care whether x is H, if all we know about H is that it is a "unique, nonnatural quality." "Do, pray, act so, because the word 'good' denotes a unique, nonnatural quality!" is basically no more impressive than Moore's caricature sentence. If so, then intuitionism is hopeless, since it maintains that goodness is (nothing more nor less than) a nonnatural property. We can surely be indifferent to the

---

[27] Again, see the Nowell-Smith selection, "Intuitionism."

presence of *any* such property, so long as it is not attached to anything we care about—to anything that we, in fact, value.

If we were to add that it is a unique, nonnatural quality that we happen to be awfully and uniquely interested in, that would solve one problem—now the conclusion would follow. But, as so often, it does so only at the cost of making the premise incomprehensible or too controversial to be of any use. (I could just *stipulate* that you simply love martinis, no doubt . . . but what if you *don't?!*)

J. L. Mackie advances a celebrated argument against objectivism in morals—what he calls the "Argument from Queerness."[28] How, we ask, can it follow from the fact that something has a certain property that we somehow must do something? The property that could do that would seem to be magical—"queer," as he put it. This suggested 'queerness' of the notion of "moral properties" perhaps stems especially from the aspect of 'magnetism'. How could it follow from something's having some property that we must do something, unless we posited something in the agent to respond to it in some way, such as an interest or attitude? The human organism's sheer perceptual and cognitive apparatus, that is to say, is not enough to get us moving: we must, in addition, have emotional propensities, desires, and interests, to supply what would otherwise be completely missing, namely motivation to act.[29] As Aristotle so lucidly puts it, "Intellect of itself moves nothing."[30]

Stevenson's Emotivism—A New Reaction to the Naturalistic Fallacy

We have already seen that it's essential to any theory trying to incorporate the right sort of reference to attitudes and motivations that the speaker not be claimed to be simply *stating* that she has the attitude in question. That would be to make a (true or false) descriptive statement, which the emotivists staunchly deny ethical sentences are. Emotivists pro-

---

[28] J. L. Mackie, *Ethics: Inventing Right and Wrong* (Viking Press, 1977).

[29] Readers wanting to follow this up still further will want to see the arguments of, for example, E. J. Bond in *Reason and Value* (Cambridge: Cambridge Univ. Press, 1983). Bond claims to deny that goodness has anything to do with desire. Yet he agrees that if one becomes persuaded that something is good, then one must also favor it or want it. Interesting! See also Panayot Butchvarov, *Skepticism in Ethics* (Bloomington, IN: Indiana Univ. Press, 1989), an attempt to defend a broadly Moore-like kind of intutionism—with, so far as I can see, the same problem.

[30] *Nichomachean Ethics*, bk. VI., ch. 2: " Intellect itself, however, moves nothing, but only the intellect which aims at an end and is practical . . . choice is either desiderative reason or ratiocinative desire, and such an origin of action is a man."

pose to take care of this problem, by saying that when people say that x is good , then what they are doing is verbally *expressing* their attitudes toward x. The attitudes in question are variously characterized as attitudes of "approval," of "favoring," or even as "liking" (or disapproval, disfavoring, and so on).

It is an important feature of this theory that it disclaims any intention of producing a verbal equivalent of such sentences as "that was a good thing to do." 'X is good,' they agree, does not *mean* 'I like x'. It does, however, imply it, in the sense that when one does something that expresses an attitude, what you do would not in fact express that if you didn't have that attitude.

Or wouldn't it? Well, you could be faking it, or acting in a play. So the emotivist would have to add that one is evaluating insofar as the expression of the value-claim in question is sincere. (We will also have to add that the speaker is addressing the item from her own point of view. Of course, I can say "this is good for Charlie" and have no such attitude myself.)

Emotive Meaning?

The emotivist claim is that the word 'good' and other evaluative words have a different *kind* of meaning—"emotive" as opposed to "cognitive" meaning. It expresses one's liking of x without asserting it. Strictly, then, the sentence "x is wrong!" isn't literally a statement at all. Its surface grammatical form belies its true linguistic status, which is really pragmatic rather than semantic, to use some recent terminology for these matters. (Semantics has to do with the reference of words to the world: denoting or designating properties, for instance. Pragmatics relates the use of a word to the actions of the speaker—to what she is doing with words, such as stating facts or asking questions or giving directions—or expressing attitudes.)

Whether this theory makes good sense of the linguistic facts is an important question. But if it does, then notice how it avoids Moore's proposed dilemma. Since naturalism is false, he says, then either statements about good are meaningless, or they mean nonnatural qualities. Stevenson avoids this dilemma by holding that statements about good are meaningful, but they have a different *kind* of meaning than statements about pineapples or planets. Some words in our language are used in such a way that what they do is not to designate qualities, but rather to express attitudes and emotions. So there is a third alternative, and we are not compelled to go for one of Moore's two.

Note that there is no exact correlation between vocabulary and linguistic function. Consider the difference between "John loves Mary," and

"Mary, I love you!" when said by John to Mary. Both sentences may be said to inform us of a certain fact, namely that John loves Mary. But the two sentences don't "feel" the same. The second seems to have an emotional ring to it that the first does not. Mary is less likely to be impressed by the first utterance as compared with the second. (But if she's decent at inference, and interested in John, maybe she'd settle for it!)

Stevenson merely says that the emotive use is the "characteristic" or "typical" use of 'good.' Thus he quite agrees that we very often use such sentences at least in part to make factual claims. In context, my saying "Jones is a better goalie than Smith" may well make the claim that Jones has fewer goals-against on his record than Smith. But, says Stevenson, the word 'good,' if used in its typical sense, would never just be equivalent to any factual claim.

Logic

Emotivists challenge naturalism with its inability to account for disagreement. But does emotivism itself account for it either? That depends a bit on what is meant by 'account for.' Consider: "'Do it!"; "No, don't!'" Are the two speakers envisaged there contradicting each other? Do they disagree? We would surely say that they are, and do. But the disagreement in question is not obviously the same as what is involved in, "'Yes, it is!'" "No, it's not!'"; the first pair contains no propositions.

But though it doesn't, there is something else, stable in propositions, that does capture the desired sense of conflict. In the case of the conflicting imperative sentences in our first pair, what captures it is this: If the first order is complied with, then the second is necessarily not. If one does it, then it is not the case that one does not do it. If emotivism is roughly correct about the relation between evaluations and actions, then the sense of conflict is accounted for by pointing out that positive evaluations imply actions such that if they are done, then the ones implied by the corresponding negative evaluations are not. If I eat x, then I necessarily have not refrained from eating x. More generally, interpersonal practical conflict has the structure that if party A does what she wants to do, then party B thereby does not. A's proposed course of action *conflicts* with B's in the simple sense that both cannot be done, fulfilled, realized. And this is surely what emotivists were getting at.

If that is right, then one might ask whether emotivism is really necessary to fix things up. For after all, "I like it!"; "well, I don't!"—disagree in just the same way. The actions that would be taken or are being recommended by A are ones that will be avoided by B: if we follow A's course, we don't follow B's. Nor is this incidental: necessarily, doing is incompatible with not doing.

The question surely arises, why we need any more than that? For practice is what we are talking about: evaluating is connected with deciding, choosing, doing. It is not inert.

Metaethics Only—Blanshard's Objections

It's vital to keep in mind that emotivism, like intuitionism, is intended only to be a metaethical theory—to tell us what people are saying (or doing) *when* they make moral judgments, but not to tell us which of their ethical judgments *are* correct and which incorrect. We must especially appreciate, for example, that emotivism is definitely *not* the theory that *whatever a person approves of is right*—not even that whatever he approves of is "right *for him*."

Since this last is an important matter, note that there are two quite different meanings we can attach to the expression 'for him' in such sentences as 'x is right for him':

(a) it can mean that x is right *according to* him

(b) or it can mean that x is the right thing *for him to do,* as opposed to someone else—that the person whose actions are being appraised as right are *that* person's actions, in those circumstances, rather than someone else's. (Of course, the same thing might be right for the others, too; but the point of using the qualifier 'for him' is to pick out that individual from the others and identify him, rather than others, as the subject of the judgment, whatever may be true of the rest.)

Meaning (a) is, trivially, the right option to attribute to emotivism, while (b), which is decidedly nontrivial, definitely is not. Emotivists do not say that whatever a person thinks is right for himself to do also *is* right for that person to do. That would be to enter into the ethical fray, as it were, and take sides, rather than to stand on the sidelines and explain what's going on.

Note also that there is no reason why we can't have attitudes about such things as past or future actions of others or ourselves. That answers a supposed problem with emotivism urged by Brand Blanshard.[31] By way

---

[31] Brand Blanshard, "The New Subjectivism in Ethics," in *20th Century Ethical Theory*, ed. Steven M. Cahn and Joram G. Haber (Englewood Cliffs, NJ: Prentice-Hall, 1995), 183–88. Originally published in *Philosophy and Phenomenological Research* 9 (1949).

of criticizing the emotive theory, he says that if goodness and badness "lie in attitudes only, and are brought into being by them"—then emotivism can't account for the wrongness of past actions or actions where the speaker is not present. But the theory says no such thing. It denies that there *is any* such quality as goodness or badness, so of course it denies that such qualities are *brought into being* by my or anyone's attitudes. And on the other hand, the qualities in objects that elicit such attitudes are indeed merely natural qualities, such as the sufferings of Blanshard's trapped rabbit; such attitudes may be elicited by the thought of actions taking place in however distant a past or future we can imagine, or by Moore's remote possible worlds, for that matter. And if we think suffering bad as such, for example, then we will think it bad in all cases, whether we know about them or not, and whether they are past, present, or future.

Objective versus Subjective Rightness

Blanshard points to a distinction we all make, between acts that are "objectively right" and those that are only "subjectively right." We think that there is always some thing (or set of things) that is (or are) objectively right in that situation. "But of course we often don't find it. We do acts that we think are the right ones, but we are mistaken; and then our act is only subjectively right." Blanshard tells us "the new subjectivism would abolish this difference at a stroke."[32]

But why would it? For example, suppose that I approve of telling the truth—I think that lying is wrong. However, I also think that in special cases, lying might still be justified, for example, in the case where a small lie would spare someone unnecessary pain. For that reason, I tell what I thought was a "small lie" to Martha on occasion X. Unfortunately, it turns out that the lie was not a small one in her view, and far from sparing her unnecessary pain, it actually ended up causing her more. I would then plead that I thought I had done the right thing, but I would also admit that I really had not. I acted in ignorance, doing what I thought was right when it really wasn't. But emotivism doesn't make me think that my act was right after all, just because I approved of it at the time. For I turned out to be approving something that wasn't actually happening; what actually did happen was something I do not approve of.

Nevertheless, Blanshard's article does go some way toward making a criticism that really must be taken seriously. We'll get to that in a bit.

---

[32] Blanshard, 187.

Emotivism and Truth: Stevenson and the Tarski Paradigm

Emotivism is widely said to hold that ethical sentences are really devoid of truth value; since they state nothing, they are neither true nor false. The category of truth just doesn't apply to them. This seems, on the face of it, an embarrassing implication. It is an apparent implication so obvious-seeming that many include that as a defining feature of the theory. However, life is not so simple! This time, the problem lies in the ancient and puzzling subject of the nature of truth. Stevenson, considerably later, addressed himself to this matter of "ethical truth" in a most interesting way.[33] He held that truth is to be understood along the lines of what has been called "the semantic theory," due in essentials to the Polish logician Alfred Tarski. That theory emphasizes an important equivalence, which came to be known as the "Tarski paradigm": Where p may be any statement whatever, then

'p' is true if and only if p

Thus, 'snow is white' is true if and only if snow is white; 'diamonds are hard' is true if and only if diamonds are hard. In like manner, surely, 'lying is wrong' is true if and only if lying is wrong. The predicate 'is true' saves one the trouble of repeating statements, but adds nothing to the statement itself. A statement, to put it another way, is simply a set of truth conditions as it stands.

Well, it's pretty hard to knock that. And it prompts Stevenson to argue that we can be perfectly happy ascribing truth values to evaluative sentences after all, even if evaluative sentences are the sort of thing he claims they are. But will this really work? For comparison, consider the case where 'p' is the sentence, 'Hooray for Slonimski!'. Now suppose we say, following the semantic paradigm,

'Hooray for Slonimski!' is true *if and only if hooray for Slonimski!*

Well, equivalence ('if and only if') asserts sameness of truth value. But what about the case where the sentence has no truth value? And surely sentences of the form 'Do x!' don't have a truth value? Surely 'Please pass the juice!' isn't *true?* Nor "Hooray for Slonimski!"? Of course, these sentences aren't false, either. But that's just the point. Invoking the Tarskian theory in this way doesn't seem to cast much light on the worry people were trying to get at when they wondered

---

[33] Stevenson, "Retrospective Comments," in *Facts and Values.*

about ethical truth, given emotivism. So it isn't clear quite where we go from here.[34]

One possible place to go, though, deserves mention. Consider, again, the sentence 'Hooray for Slonimski!' It's not "true"—yet it may be appropriate, well-taken, justified, called for. Similarly, ethical ratings—'right,' 'appalling!', 'unfair', and so on may also be taken to be so. There will still be the question of how we know that these utterances *are* called for, appropriate, and so on; and so the question will arise whether sentences of the form 'it is appropriate to congratulate Smith on this effort' can be said to be true in the usual sense of the term (whatever that is!). If we say 'yes,' does that commit us to anything strange? We will have to consider this more closely.

Questions about "Emotive Meaning"

We need now to ask, just what is it that the thesis of emotivism really says? In saying that the use of value terms "expresses" our emotions or attitudes, it seems to be referring us, somehow, to certain psychological states, states of mind. Now, in saying that a descriptive statement is different from an emotive one, these theorists seem to be marking a distinction among the kinds of thing in one's mind that are available to be "expressed." To "express" is to "press out"—the idea is that we have these things in our minds and, for some reason, we want to get them out into public view, or at least to the view of a certain other person or persons, our audience. Now, *all* sentences "express," but they express different mental states: descriptive sentences express beliefs, whereas others express, say, attitudes or emotions. The emotive theory has it that evaluative sentences are to be classed among these latter. Well, beliefs can easily enough be said to be true or false. But attitudes? Not so obviously, at least.

We often talk of "evaluative beliefs": "Sheila believes that justice isn't being done to the Inuit," for example. Naturally most evaluative sentences do have the subject-predicate structure typical of descriptive sentences. On the face of it, then, emotivism is fighting something of an uphill semantic battle when it insists that despite these appearances, ethical claims are really to be classed with the emotive rather than the cognitive ones.

Consider that when a statement is made, one that we agree is a candidate for truth or falsity, then it becomes appropriate to speak of

---

[34] J. O. Urmson, *The Emotive Theory of Ethics* (Oxford: Hutchinson Univ. Library, 1968), offers a book-length discussion of emotivism.

evidence: the question, "Why do you think that is so?" is in order, and we would expect to be given something that we can in turn appraise for its bearing on what has been said, whether it tells in favor or against the truth of the sentence uttered. But if what is uttered is an expression of "attitude," things seem to be different. The question, "Why do you have a headache?" is not in order if what is meant is, "What is the point of your having a headache?" Headaches have causes, but not reasons. "Why do you believe that so-and-so?," on the other hand, is a reasonable question. It calls for justification, defense, via the supplying of appropriate reasons or evidence. We don't, usually, care very much what caused you to have a certain belief, but we do care whether you have good reasons for it. But it seems clear that no such thing applies to headaches. Are the "attitudes" which ethical sentences perhaps express more like headaches, then, or are they like beliefs?

That's our question. The evidence is mixed.

Which Noncognitive States?

Emotivists hold that ethical sentences express some states of mind other than strictly cognitive ones. But which among the many noncognitive states are they supposed to express? The term 'emotivist' vaguely, and perhaps misleadingly, suggests that the states in question are emotional. But that is surely mistaken, if the term 'emotion' is taken in any very narrow sense. People can and do get emotional about moral matters, to be sure—but also about lots of other matters. Yet they also often do not; it's surely clear that they need not. In deliberating about what to do in an ethically touchy situation, emotion may not come into it much or at all. We might quite calmly consider the whole thing, for instance, and indeed, we are often well advised to—emotions, as is well known, can color or bias one's thinking and lead to foolish or impulsive, and certainly to biased, decisions.

Moral Emotions? "Value Emotions"?

We asked, in effect, which noncognitive states are associated with value judgments and value claims generally. But for our purposes, we also want to know which of them are unique to moral utterances. And that's the rub. It's surely not possible to find any emotions that are unique to morals. We do sometimes speak of having a "feeling of obligation," and so on—but the question is, which feeling is that? How do we identify it? Emotivism may seem to imply that there is one particular set of emotions that we can, without begging the question, pick out to identify with moral claims. But that seems implausible, at least. Imagine that we have meters and screens on which we can graph our emotions. Would it be possible, some day, to find the unique profile of a *moral* emotion that distinguishes it from all other emotions? Not likely!

More likely, we know what obligation is first, and thus we know when a feeling we have is a feeling of obligation rather than some other "feeling." 'Bob got very upset with Barbara because he thought she was deceiving him' makes sense—if, as is usually reasonable, we assume that Bob doesn't like being deceived. But his perception of the wrongness of the deception is what drives his negative reaction, not vice versa. It's not that he thinks deception is wrong *because* he feels upset about it; it's that he's upset with her because he thinks deceiving people (at any rate, in the sort of circumstances in which he thought he was deceived) is wrong. And if Bob thinks about it and decides either that she was not deceiving him after all, or that although she was, she was actually justified in doing so, then his emotional reaction will cool down.

Emotivism, Intuitionism, and Reason(s) in Ethics

I hinted that Blanshard was edging up to an important criticism of emotivism. In fact, the criticism in question is not only applicable to emotivism, for intuitionism—which seems to be Blanshard's view—turns out to have what is really the same problem. The problem is this: if ethical claims are essentially expressions of attitudes or emotions of some sort, then how can we ever be rational about ethics? What account of reasons in ethics, if any, can the emotivist give us? And in the absence of any such account, how can anybody ever provide evidence for, argue in favor of, some ethical viewpoint? How would anyone ever be persuaded of any ethical belief she didn't already hold?

The same problem, essentially, applies to intuitions. Just calling those things by another name isn't going to solve the problem: a *fundamental* intuition is precisely one that cannot be justified by analyzing it and giving good reasons for it. But if so, then when someone else disagrees, there is no basis for resolving the disagreement. This is bad news, and it is extremely bad news for morals in particular. Morality is important. We shouldn't have to leave it in the realm of the undecidable. For moral problems to be difficult is one thing. But for them to be in principle beyond the reach of rational discussion is far worse.

We may also focus on this point more specifically by asking this question: Suppose we found some sort of reason, R, such that given R, it would follow that certain emotions, E, were *appropriate*—most especially, those emotions that had a bearing on one's doing the action whose rightness was in question. In other words, suppose that we could find a reason that was connected with some practical attitude such that if R, then E. But then the question would arise whether what was special to ethics was not E, but rather, R. This would be even more important if what mattered about E, in turn, was its relation to a certain action, x. For if we could say that (1) R → E, and (2) E → x, then it would seem that by transitivity, (3) R → x. E would seem to drop out of the picture, as it were. What would really matter is just R, in the end. Or at least, that would seem to be the logical situation of emotivism. (I leave it to the reader to apply the same point to intuitionism.)

Stevenson seemed to think that "reasons" in ethics were not independently establishable. He thought, it seems, that whenever we have a reason in ethics, what we really have is just *another attitude*. A "reason" for specific attitude E1 is simply another attitude, E2. We might say, as many have, "on the emotivist view, there really aren't any reasons for action at all."

But to do so would be unfair. The question, in effect, is whether there really are any reasons for action at all, and therefore, whether there are any "moral reasons" at all. But the emotivist could maintain that of course there are fundamental reasons for action; however, those reasons are all of an emotional sort. But there is also another and much more important point to make about all this that specifically affects *morals* and not evaluations generally.

Why might Stevenson have supposed this? The reason, I am sure, is this: to have a reason for action is to *favor* the action in question, to be inclined toward doing it. (And how else could one act at all?) But 'favoring' and 'toward' are words that suggest an emotion-like condition. Certainly they are distinct from sheer cognitive states, which are utterly neutral so far as action is concerned—except, perhaps, other cognitive "actions"—does the person who is interested in the differential calculus have a different sort of attitude, a different emotional relation to that branch of knowledge, than most of us who yawn at the very thought? It surely seems so.

What has been forgotten in all this, or at least not born clearly in mind, is that morality isn't private. It's about what people *in general* are to do. What makes us think of emotivism as a matter of rams butting their heads together instead of rational people trying to solve serious problems is that insofar as *I* have some attitude, nothing at all seems to follow about what *you* should do. Yet what you as well as I should do is of the essence here—it's what morality is all about. If emotions are to play any kind of serious role in morals, it has to be shown that there are *interpersonal* ramifications to them that significantly affect the situation.

Jones letting off steam is a poor model for morality, on the face of it, if morality is seriously supposed to lay down plausible rules for the conduct of people in general—and not just Jones. Something has been left out!

What has been left out, in short, must be the basis of appeal to Smith of the emotions of Jones. Is there anything about Jones's emotions, or of their expression, to raise any serious prospect of such appeal?

There would seem to be three possibilities:

1. It might be posited that we humans are just built in such a way that each other's feelings matter to us. We're all siblings under the skin, say. Or we follow Hume and suppose that there is at least a "particle of the dove" along with the wolf and the serpent, in every one of us. If that is right, then one person's *expressing* his or her emotions to another runs a decent chance of eliciting a response from that other person.

2. A different idea is that emotions and their expression play a *strategic* role. If I show that I am getting excited about x, you get the information that I'm likely to do various things about x that you wouldn't otherwise have reason to expect me to do. And if the things I would do would impact on you in some way that matters *to you*, then you have reason to get involved. So both emotion and its expression become relevant, at least in some cases. Then the question is whether it would be *enough* cases. We'll put that on the table for further discussion below.

3. A third idea is that there is some sort of logical alchemy that transfers my emotions to you and vice versa. I attribute this idea to Hare (who would undoubtedly object), whose ideas will be examined just below.

Once we assemble these, it is hard to resist the conclusion that the second view is the right one. The first view no doubt has something to be said for it, but it seems at most a very weak hypothesis. And if it's very weak, it's hard to see how it could account for the importance we attach to moral considerations. Scarcely enough sentiment to move my little finger *really isn't enough*. On the other hand, people's emotions do have crucial connections with their trains of action, and those in turn are of great interest to whoever might happen to be standing on the rails at the time. Given the sort of focus of morals, which is highly general, the point is that there is an excellent chance of the latter, so far as people near us are concerned. Even for those more distant, there is also a not insignificant chance, especially in the modern world.

If this is right, though, then it is also clear that emotivism's central idea, that the utterance of ethical sentences is importantly different from the making of statements, may be beside the point. But to see this, let's first look at some further developments.

Other Noncognitivisms: Multifunctionalism

Among many other philosophers of broadly noncognitivist persuasion, I single out for mention two in particular. One is P. H. Nowell-Smith (see his *Ethics*, Penguin Books, 1954). Nowell-Smith is a multifunctionalist, holding that we do lots of different things with ethical words, expressing attitudes, issuing orders, confirming arrangements, and so on. Nowell-Smith, and many others who took a similar line in the near postwar era, take their general guide from Wittgenstein and J. L. Austin, who held that we do many things with language, and that to understand the use of language is to understand patterns of action—in Wittgenstein's words, "forms of life." An example: when the minister says, "I now pronounce you man and wife!" he is not exactly stating a fact; nor is he merely expressing his feelings about anything in particular; nor is he ordering anybody around. He is, in Austin's felicitous phrase, doing things with words.

It's not clear, though, that all these other functions are of much interest. (Shortly we will consider an interesting idea about promising as a way of getting from "is" to "ought.") Is the idea that ethics is just hopelessly ambiguous—that there simply is nothing in common to all ethical claims, other than, perhaps, the word 'ethical'? Or is it perhaps that there is a distinctive function that is, say, "moralizing"? That strikes me as implausible. Or in any sense in which it is plausible, it would seem to rest on a prior understanding of what morality is. Given that, we could then understand how various uses of language might have a bearing on morals. But that's very different from claiming that we can understand what morality is in light of those uses of words. To "moralize" is to express views about moral matters. They aren't seen to be moral by virtue of being the subject of moralizing.

R. M. Hare and Prescriptivism

R. M. Hare was for a long time the standard-bearer of a theory he called "universal prescriptivism." According to Hare, a fundamental truth about moral language is that it entails prescriptions. We have already seen Moore's implicit recognition of this aspect of morality, in implying that we expect moral claims to issue in such sentences as: "Do, pray, act so!" Hare proposes that we must take this quite literally: any moral statement, in his view, must entail some or other sentence of the form "Do x!" directed at someone. In fact, his "universalism" says that in principle, it fundamentally addresses such a sentence to *everyone*. The addressing is strictly notional since we cannot in fact do any such thing—the communications problems are, even in the twenty-first century, insurmountable!

We'll consider the thesis about universality a little later. Meanwhile, the question is whether Hare is right about the prescriptive function. When anyone says that a certain action is right, or good, or just, and most distinctively when we say that someone ought to do something, are we in effect telling someone, or perhaps everyone, to do something? This is an important and interesting question, and in my view one of the most basic questions about the semantics of ethical language. And I must report that, after many years, I am still inclined to think that Hare is basically right. But the word 'basically,' unfortunately, must be taken pretty seriously.

For one thing, it isn't always obvious what, if anything, a certain ethical judgment tells us, or anyone, to do. For instance, if I say, "Caesar ought not to have crossed the Rubicon," I would have to be a bit daft if I thought I was literally telling that general, who has been dead for 2,000 years or so, to do something other than what he has already done. We must say something like this: that in a situation of that type, if we were addressing someone of Caesar's characteristics and in Caesar's position, and think (say) that he ought not to cross, then in effect we are addressing a directive to any such person not to cross. 'Caesar, don't do it!' is the natural directive to associate with 'Caesar ought not to cross'; putting it in past tense means that the question as addressed to him in particular is no longer a practical one but only academic, in view of its being uttered now; but we are also saying that the thing we would, appropriately with our general judgment, have uttered at the time, had we been in a position to, is that piece of negative advice.

The crucial point is that there is no problem in understanding how a directive would issue from the ethical judgment in question in whatever circumstances may be appropriate for issuing a directive. And there is also no problem in appreciating that 'ought' statements are practical, that is, that they do concern action, and are about the general question, what to do.

The big issue in this respect would, as we noted before regarding emotivism, be this: when is a directive *ethical*, or better yet, *moral?* Hare does not suppose that whenever anyone, A, tells someone else, B, to do something, x, then A's statement 'B, do x!' is a moral statement. Sometimes it is, sometimes it isn't. One interesting question about ethics is whether there are any types of decisions that could not even possibly be moral. But we all agree that there are lots that are not, at the time and in the circumstances, moral statements. Recommending a good restaurant, suggesting an iron to use for a certain play in golf, showing how to make a computer do a certain task, and so on, are all examples where sentences containing imperatives or having imperative force are plainly not, as they stand, about what's morally right or wrong. So what's the difference? Where does everything else leave off and ethics begin?

Universality

That's where Hare's universalism comes into the picture. Hare does suppose that he can answer the question that has just been raised. Moral judgments and principles are distinguished by being, or in principle are to be derived or derivable from, prescriptions that are addressed to *everybody*. So when I say, "Sally, you ought to do x," I am intending that as a moral prescription only if I suppose that there is some universal principle ("Everybody, in circumstances C, do y!") such that Sally's doing x in these circumstances is a particular case of doing y in C. For instance, "Sally, you ought to mail that letter!" would be a moral directive to her if I suppose that there is a general prescription such as "Everyone, be grateful to those who have benefited you!" and Sally's mailing this letter now would be an appropriate expression of gratitude to a benefactor.

The question of universality and a property that Hare calls "universalizability" is going to loom very large as we go along. It was Kant, especially, who opened up this aspect of moral theory, and Hare can be seen (and saw himself as) as, in part, a modern-day Kant. We have also seen that Moore's intuitionism has a problem (the two-pictures problem) that also relates to or is an example of this same general feature. Because we will be considering this aspect of ethics very carefully later on, I only mention it here.

Prescriptions and Logic

The important question of how there can be reasons and reasoning in ethics was raised above in the aspect of a possible criticism of emotivism. It is important, then, to appreciate that there is a logic of prescriptions, that is, that prescriptions can have logical relations to each other and to other propositions. Hare, in *The Language of Morals*, gives some examples. Here's one:

Premise one: Bring all of these boxes over there!

Premise two: Z is one of these boxes

Conclusion: Bring Z over there![35]

Here's another:

Premise one: Fish or cut bait!

---

[35] R. M. Hare, *The Language of Morals* (Oxford: Oxford Univ Press, 1952), 28.

Premise two: Don't fish!

Conclusion: Cut bait!

In each of these cases, it is surely perfectly appropriate to say that the conclusion follows from the two premises, indeed follows logically. But how, we may ask, can this be so if prescriptions can be neither true nor false? One reasonable answer is that a prescription is either asserted or denied. Whoever asserts the premises, we can say, thereby asserts, and is logically committed to asserting, the conclusion, on pain of inconsistency.

Further, we can say that an imperative is either "obeyed," or "conformed to," or not. Hare talks of an imperative being "assented to" or not, and holds that to assent to an imperative is to act on it. Or rather, it is to be disposed to act on it. If I accept a directive to do x, then I shall, at some appropriate time, do x. My assent is now, but my action is at the appropriate time. And if the time comes and I don't do it? Then I must either have forgotten, or think that relevant circumstances have changed, or, if none of those, then it would seem that I have changed my mind—withdrawn my assent. What I can't do is say, "well, so what?" That is, I can't say, "I *agree* that one ought to do actions of type F on occasions of type C, and this is an occasion of type C—but, so what? I can't see any reason why I should do act F now." Someone who said this would have to be viewed as inconsistent.

To think that 'ought' sentences entail imperatives is therefore to think that whoever accepts such a sentence also must be ready to act accordingly. The general point here is that the imperativist view makes sense of the idea of our actions being consistent with our moral beliefs. Hare believes that we can't otherwise make sense of the "practicality" of ethics. Ethics is about what we are or are not to do. How could this be so if an act's being right or wrong, say, or it's being the case that we ought to do it or ought not to do it, had no such implication? Can I believe that I ought, now, to help this suffering person over here, and yet walk right by? Some have thought so. It's a major point—to which, again, we shall return—pausing here only to note that frankly, I think Hare must be right about this.[36]

Is Universal Prescriptivism the Answer?

In Hare's early work, when he professed to be a sort of existentialist, he had the idea that our moral principles simply are what we are willing to

---

[36] For contrast, see Philippa Foot, "Moral Beliefs," in *20th Century Ethical Theory*, ed. Steven M. Cahn and Joram G. Haber (Englewood Cliffs, NJ: Prentice-Hall, 1995), 365–77. I discuss her view below, pp. 91–94.

universalize. But what exactly does that mean, and why should it make any difference?

The answer to the first question, in *The Language of Morals*, seems to have been simply a willingness to tell everybody to do the thing in question, whatever it is. Of course, different people would be willing to universalize quite different things, one would think, and so universal prescriptivism, so far, doesn't look very promising if it is supposed to do something to construct a plausible universal moral theory—the same for everyone. Well, so what? Why shouldn't each person have his own morals? There is a short answer to this: why on earth should anyone else care about it, in that case? You say, "Everyone ought to do x!" I say, "Count me out, pal!" And then what?

Hare seems to have supposed that when we will something universally, that means willing it in all future possible circumstances and cases, and this fact is supposed to do something for us. But—*what* is it supposed to do? In his second book, *Freedom and Reason*, Hare's insistence that no prescription can be entailed by a descriptive statement (his version of the naturalistic fallacy principle) shows some signs of strain. In the first place, he tells us that *descriptive* predicates are all, as they stand, universalizable. This is on the ground that if I say that x is red, then I am also saying that if y is exactly like x, then y too is red. The respect in which it has to be exactly like x in order for this to follow is color, which in this case is red. I take it to be a tautology that if x is red and x exactly resembles y in respect of color, then y too is red—what else could 'red' mean? 'Red' is a "universal"—that is, it applies to an indefinite number of instances. But nevertheless, it does not follow that if x is like y in some *other* respect, then y is like x in the particular respect in question. Things are still what they are, and not other things. Logic doesn't spread predicates around the world.

But value is different. If I say that x is valuable in some way, and then accept that y is exactly like x in all *other* respects, then I have to agree that y is also valuable in the same way and to the same degree that x is. And that is interesting. Descriptive predicates do not have that feature.

It is odd that Hare wants to say what he does about descriptive predicates, then. This is especially so in view of the fact that prescriptivism gives us an interesting explanation, or at least a partial explanation, of this odd behavior of evaluative predicates. What offers some hope of explanation is the fact, as prescriptivism maintains, that value predicates aren't really predicates at all. When I evaluate something, I am just expressing my negative or positive feelings about it, and recommending to others that they do this or that regarding those things; I am not adding another feature to the list of features that the thing already has. This being so, it is not surprising that if two things are exactly alike in all respects, I would have to evaluate them alike: my attitude toward them is a function of what those things are like—of what their properties are. So identity of properties dictates identity of attitude, it would seem. Or at least, a different one would seem to be unintelligible: "There is, I agree, no difference at all between this one and that one—I couldn't tell which was which if you played the shell game on me—and yet this one is good, that one bad!" does not make sense. If the emotive/prescriptive analysis of evaluation is right, we can see why it does not.

But what is it about the identical cases with differing prescriptions that "doesn't make sense"? It does seem logically possible to have a different attitude toward one instance of a certain set of qualities and another, identical instance of those qualities, doesn't it? (This is like the little school girl in *The Lavender Hill Mob*[37] who when the mobster says, "we need to exchange this model for that one, but they're just the same," insists on not making the exchange "because *that* one is *mine!*") Is it that we think that attitudes not based on any qualitative differences are unreasonable? Or is there really an "analytic truth" kicking around here? That is: is it a "linguistic fact" that if x is just like y, then if x is good, y too must be good? Or not? And if it were, why would that be interesting?

Perhaps we need to dig a bit deeper.

In Hare's later book, *Freedom and Reason*,[38] he still wants to be something of an existentialist. Even the Nazi can be consistent, but he is so at a high price. For instance, the Nazi is committed to exterminating the Jews. So suppose that he, the Nazi, turns out, to his surprise, to be a Jew? Then he is committed to putting himself in the gas chamber, or turning himself into people who will perform that service for him. Okay—but he might even accept that. "If I turn out to be Jewish, then let me too be put in the gas chamber!" is something that we can imagine someone being fanatical enough to accept. (He's unlikely to think that there is any real possibility of his being such, and we suspect that if he considered the possibility an appreciable probability instead, that would sway him.)

Hare argues that moral claims entail universal claims of this sort: "No matter who I am, all persons should be treated in way x." But in *Freedom and Reason*, there is a subtle change. Hare distinguishes between prescribing (1) that everyone, including myself, be treated in such-and-such a way whatever situation I might be in—"even if I were in your shoes"— and (2) that one would continue to prescribe this even if one were not

---

[37] *The Lavender Hill Mob*, a delightful movie starring Alec Guinness, Stanley Holloway, Marjorie Fielding, and other notables (1951), was a favorite in college film circuits back in the author's undergraduate days.

[38] R. M. Hare, *Freedom and Reason* (Oxford: Oxford Univ.Press: 1963).

only in the other person's shoes, but had the other person's feelings, beliefs, and memories—in short, that one were the other person.[39] This interesting move, however, puts him on the road to the ultimate development of this position, which comes out in his still later book *Moral Thinking*.[40] There we read that we must distinguish between,

(1) I now prefer with strength S that if I were in that situation x should happen rather than not;
(2) If I were in that situation, I would prefer with strength S that x should happen rather than not.

According to Hare, "Confusion between these statements, or pairs like them, is very common. . . . What I am claiming is not that these propositions are identical, but that I cannot know that (2), and what that would be like, without (1) being true, and that this is a conceptual truth."[41]

Hare evidently thinks that this makes a big difference. For he thinks, plausibly enough, that everyone who, right now, claims to think, for instance, that if I were a rabbit, I should be shot and served up for dinner by humans, is such that if he *were* actually a rabbit, he would prescribe no such thing. People's prescriptions are driven by their interests or wants; and it now turns out everybody's wants are to count, and count how? Equally: that is, the desires of each person will have to be compared and weighed up, and the right thing to do will turn out to be the thing that is prescribed by the weighted sum of all desires.

In other words, Hare reaches the conclusion that utilitarianism is an analytic moral truth! That is astonishing, especially in view of Hare's long-standing insistence that we can't derive real moral judgments from tautologies. What has gone wrong?

Plenty, I think. Most significantly, this: It simply is not true that when I prescribe that all persons, or all organisms, or whatever, are to be treated in manner x, I must suppose it to be some kind of fundamental mistake on my part if I don't accept that organism O has to be willing to prescribe this too, or that its desire has to be weighed in along with mine on some basis of equal weight for equal strength of desire. I may not care how organism O feels about it. The fact that this goose doesn't want to be eaten simply doesn't count, as far as I am concerned, against my eating it anyway.

---

[39] Hare, *Freedom and Reason*, 126.
[40] R. M. Hare, *Moral Thinking* (Oxford: Oxford Univ. Press, 1977).
[41] Hare, *Moral Thinking*, 95–96.

Now, consider the claim that "I will that, if I am organism O, then I am to be treated in way x." Well, the fact is that I am not organism O. This being so, why should the fact that the organism in question doesn't like the idea matter at all to me? If I think my house might burn down, I am motivated to take out insurance. But if I know that creatures like y are likely to be eaten by creatures like z, then the fact that I am not and never will be a y makes it quite irrational for me to try to guard against the consequences of my being so. Forget it!

In short, if your wants, and yours and yours and yours, are to "count" for moral purposes, it's going to have to be for a much better reason than what has been provided by Hare. And it's quite unlikely, I think, that they are going to count in the way that utilitarianism says they are to count: namely, equally weighty given equal strengths of desires. That just isn't how it's going to work. Scarcely any of us are built that way—to put it mildly.

Still, the prescriptions and commitments we make do matter. We turn next to an extremely famous essay arguing that certain of them matter so crucially that they take us right across the "is-ought gap."

The argument was advanced by John Searle in his 1964 paper "How to Derive 'Ought' from 'Is'."[42] Searle's thesis has the great advantage of being spelled out in a clear series of steps. Let's pause to have a careful look at this interesting argument. It is set forth in precisely five sentences, each of which is claimed to follow from its predecessor; so we have four steps to get from the first sentence to the fifth. Here are the five numbered sentences:

(1) Jones uttered the words, 'I promise to pay you, Smith, $5'.
(2) Jones promised to pay Smith $5.
(3) Jones placed himself under an obligation to pay Smith $5.
(4) Jones is under an obligation to pay Smith $5.
(5) Jones ought to pay Smith $5.

The argument, as promised, goes from 'is' to 'ought'. Is it valid? Does the conclusion in fact follow from its premises?

Note that at each step, certain further conditions are required. For instance, it could be false that uttering the words mentioned in (1) was, on that occasion, an act of promising. They might instead have been uttered in the course of a dramatic presentation, or they might have meant something wholly different in the language Jones was actually speaking (in Shrdluvian, say, they actually mean 'Where on earth are the

---

[42] Searle, "How to Derive 'Ought' from 'Is'."

eggs, Maisie?'). And the step (3) → (4) requires, importantly, some such premise as "other things are equal." (This is for reasons that Ross brought home to us: in some circumstances, we ought not to keep our promises, even though we did make those promises.) Similarly, as Searle says, the step (4) → (5) may require such a clause. That depends on a certain ambiguity in the expression 'is under an obligation to'. Sometimes this means 'is obligated to,' and other times it means, in effect, that there is one source of obligation that bears on us—but possibly, merely one among others. Whether we need such a clause here depends on how we used this notion in (4).

But no matter. It matters that the "other things" called for by these 'other things being equal' clauses are themselves norms—ethical items. Some have thought that this undoes the whole project. Clearly we could not get to (5) without such clauses, for it simply isn't plausible to suppose that if you've promised, then you've just jolly well got to do it, no matter what. However, I don't think that this does undo the project. The reason is this. Let us suppose that other things *are* equal, in a given case, in the sense that there are no "other things": Jones has no other obligations, there are no other moral considerations operating. To hold that in that case (5) really does follow from (4), and so on, is to agree that here, 'ought' follows from 'is'—and that is just what Searle wants to show. For what Jones does in (1) would have been shown, in that case, to affect Jones's normative situation. His promising makes a net difference to what he ought to do. But to say this is to say that we have an 'ought' that we didn't before, and if it came from (1), then surely we do have a case in which an 'ought' emerged from an 'is'. And so Searle's thesis would be confirmed.

But, is it? In one view (Anthony Flew's), the problem comes in at step (1) → (2): 'promise' is a normatively loaded notion.[43] To say that Jones promised Smith to do something may indeed be to say that Jones has an obligation to do what he promised to do; the only question, then, is, did he indeed promise, in the relevant sense? But to say he did is to commit us to the norms involved, and this cannot be extracted from any pure statements of fact.

The Case of Mad Harry

I want to agree with Flew that Searle's argument can't do quite what he claims for it, but I wish to launch a different and, I think, more straight-

---

[43] Anthony Flew, "On Not Deriving 'Ought' from 'Is'," *Analysis* 25, no. 2 (December 1964): 25–31. Reprinted in *The Is-Ought Question*, ed. W. D. Hudson (London: Macmillan Press, 1969), 135–43.

forward criticism. After all, it surely *seems* as though 'Jones said "I promise . . ."' is a matter of fact, and it's hard to see how one who says this cannot be said to be promising. However, consider steps (2) → (3) and (3) → (4), which purport to take us from 'Jones promised' to 'Jones is under an obligation.' Does it follow that she *is* under an obligation? Here we need to split a difference. Look at sentence (4), which says that Jones is under an obligation to pay Smith $5. Clearly step (4) à (5) is valid: sentence (4) surely does entail sentence (5), that Jones ought, at least prima facie, to pay the $5. But what about sentence (3), 'Jones placed himself under an obligation to pay Smith $5'? Does it entail that Jones is under such an obligation? No.

To see this, consider

(1′) Mad Harry says, "I vow to destroy Manhattan tomorrow!"
(2′) Mad Harry vowed to destroy Manhattan tomorrow.
(3′) Mad Harry undertook an obligation to destroy Manhattan tomorrow

Well, does this entail (4′)?

(4′) Mad Harry *is* under an obligation to destroy Manhattan tomorrow.

And therefore (5′)?

(5′) Mad Harry *ought* to destroy Manhattan tomorrow.

Our question about Searle's argument now turns on this: Does Mad Harry's having made a vow to destroy Manhattan tomorrow entail that Mad Harry ought to destroy Manhattan tomorrow? Not on your life! (Especially if you live in Manhattan![44]) But this isn't because vowing doesn't in some sense involve the "undertaking of an obligation." It does—that's what vowing is all about! Still, it does not follow that there really is an obligation resulting from that act of "undertaking" it. For however much the person who vows thereby *thinks* that he is under an obligation to do what he vows, the fact is, he could be (and in this case is) mistaken about that.

The problem is this. To promise is indeed to "undertake," or to "place oneself under" an obligation: one who promises, no doubt, thinks that he (or she) is "undertaking an obligation." And this is, indeed, a very impor-

---

[44] Note: this was originally written well before 9/11/01.

tant aspect of promising and many other acts in which we commit ourselves to various things. Our ability to do that is crucial to social life, in
fact. When we do those things, we certainly do them with a view to
becoming "bound," thus obligated, to do those things that we have put
in for. So from the fact that Jones said 'I promise,' it certainly follows that
if he was sincere, anyway, he would then come to think he is under an
obligation. But does it follow logically, without further normative
premises, that he *is* under one? No.

Semantic Subtleties

Expressions such as 'undertakes' and 'place oneself under' are ambiguous, in a crucial way. If I place myself under a bridge, then there has to
be a bridge that I am consequently under. But if I place myself under an
obligation, is there then an obligation that I have placed myself under?
Possibly not. It might be more like "placing myself under the protection
of the Queen": I cannot do that without the Queen's cooperation—uttering a sentence or two doesn't cut it. Or suppose I undertake to dig the
Panama Canal: does it follow that there is, eventually, a Panama Canal
that I have dug? No. Logicians have made a distinction between 'referentially transparent' and 'referentially opaque' contexts. A sentence appear-
ing to assert a relation between something that there is and something
else is transparent if we may infer from the truth of the sentence that the
second thing exists; if we may not make that inference, then it is
"opaque." The truth of 'Jones dreamed about a dragon' doesn't entail that
there is a dragon Jones dreamed about; but 'Jones went flailing about the
room' does entail that there is a room that Jones flailed about in.

What further conditions besides Jones's promising do we need, then?
Well, for one thing, we need Smith's cooperation. Suppose I say, "I
promise you I'll marry you!" Am I then under an obligation to marry you?
Not yet, I'm not. For you, after all, may be quite uninterested in marrying
me, and it does take two! If Smith refuses to accept Jones's promise, then
the deal is off, at least so far as Jones's effort at promising goes.

Even if Smith did accept it, it still wouldn't follow that there is an
obligation—not even a prima facie one. Suppose Jones promises Smith
that he, Jones, will help Smith fix up the bomb with which Mad Harry
will try to blow up Manhattan. Is he then morally obligated to do it? I
should hope not! (Nor should we say that this is because "other things
aren't equal." Why would the fact that the very thing I've promised to do
is a piece of criminal insanity count as an "other" thing?)

So this attempt to get from 'is' to 'ought' without further normative
premises falls through.

What are the further normative premises? For this, plausibly, we turn to Hume. The promising device is indispensable for many important arrangements on which we depend for various benefits. We should regard promises as acts that create obligations, in all those cases where our mutual interests really are served by their doing so. That's far from saying that "oughts" are simply created by the verbal acts of speakers.

Reviving Naturalism

Philippa Foot on Moral Beliefs

Philippa Foot's "Moral Beliefs" makes a different kind of case against the emotivist and intuitionist views. According to those views, there is a gap between evaluative conclusions and whatever facts one might have brought forward in support of those conclusions. Someone might say, for instance, "that a man was a good man because he clasped and unclasped his hands, and never turned NNE after turning SSW."[45] In short, what one person counts as evidence for a certain moral claim might not be regarded as even relevant by another, or as counting exactly the opposite way. Is this really possible, though? Foot claims not.

She agrees with some of the assumptions of the emotivists and prescriptivists: that moral words have to apply via general principles rather than purely to individual cases, and that they are connected with doing and choosing. But, she insists, this does not "go far enough."

Commendation and Its Objects

What she wants to know is whether we can really commend some action—just *any* old action—without reference to a "background" that makes sense of our commendation. Is commendation really independent of the object of commendation? Her thesis is that it is not, and that many mental attitudes are "internally related to their objects." For example, in order to be said to be proud of something, one must claim that that thing is somehow one's own accomplishment—that it is some sort of achievement or advantage. In order to be said to fear something, one must suppose that that something threatens one with some harm. Her main claim, in general, is that "it is quite impossible to call anything you like good or harm." Injuries to the eye, for example, must affect its sight; injury to x

---

[45] Foot, "Moral Beliefs," 366.

must adversely affect the function of x. Hence the notion of danger is restricted. So what about 'good'?

To call something good, according to Foot, is to relate it to a schedule of virtues we recognize. But is this parochial? Can we suppose that "it is logically possible that in a quite different moral code quite different virtues should be recognized"?[46] It is "just crazy to suppose that we can call anything the point of doing something without having to say what the point of that is."[47]

But there is the question of what answers that question. Suppose I say that I do such-and-such because I simply like it. Does this count? And if so, is there anything I can't, logically, like? Pain, perhaps? Moral judgments "commit the will," and here's where the fact-value gap looms: "for is it not one thing to say that a thing is so, and another to have a particular attitude towards its being so . . .? I shall argue that this view is mistaken."[48]

She offers the example of injury: can we be indifferent to what renders bodily parts unusable in their normal functioning? "The proper use of his limbs is something a man has reason to want if he wants anything."

Once the question whether a man is courageous is settled, for example, by showing that he will climb dangerous mountains, then is there any room left over for discussing the issue whether that is good? "I can speak of someone else as having the virtue of courage and recognize it as a virtue while knowing that I am a complete coward . . . I know that I should be better off if I were courageous, and so have a reason to cultivate courage, but I may also know that I will do nothing of the kind."[49]

Moral Weakness

This latter brings up an important question, which has been the subject of much philosophical thought since Plato: is it (or how is it) possible to know the good and yet not do it?

Plato's formulation raises two issues, one of which we can table here. Emotivists might be thought to be challenging the idea that we can "know" what is good, by denying that goodness is a matter of "knowledge." But even if we were to accept that, there is still an issue. We can rephrase it in a less tendentious way: is it possible to believe that x is good and yet not do it, or try to get it? We can believe that x is a good thing and not do it because x is impossible, or because y is even better

---

[46] Foot, "Moral Beliefs," 371.
[47] Foot, "Moral Beliefs," 371.
[48] Foot, "Moral Beliefs," 371.
[49] Foot, "Moral Beliefs," 374.

and we must choose between x and y. ("Vanilla is good; but chocolate is even better, and here I can have either one, but not both.") But can we agree that x is good, agree that under the circumstances there is no problem about doing it, and that nothing is under the circumstances still better—and *still* not do x? Or is this to use language idly, to engage in hypocrisy, or something equally unwanted?

Consider the drug addict who, we think, cannot resist the next dose even though he truly believes that being a drug addict is bad for him? Are we confused in describing him thus? Or is it the drug addict who is somehow confused? This, we should note, is closely related to what we now understand to be the "naturalistic fallacy" problem. Moore's theory, and some versions of naturalism, seems to make what is alleged to be goodness a matter of indifference. If we think that is a fundamental objection to any such theory, then how can we accept that the drug addict agrees that he would be better off not taking drugs, yet take them anyway? One proposed way out is to talk of "weakness of will" ("moral weakness"). The drug addict, we might say, is not indifferent to goodness: he really would prefer not to take the drugs. But he can't resist.

Philippa Foot's case above, though, may be somewhat different. She agrees that she would be better off being courageous, that she has reason to cultivate courage, but also she "knows that she will do nothing of the kind." But this may not be any sort of "weakness." It may, instead, be a rational judgment that even if it is not impossible for her to become more courageous, it is simply not worth the effort. I, for example, would dearly love to be able to speak and read French fluently. With a great deal of work, I suppose I could do so. But I simply judge that I can better spend all that time doing other things (such as writing philosophical papers in English). This may not be weakness of will, and it also doesn't involve any cutting of the link between goodness and preference. It simply recognizes that we sometimes must choose among goods, and that choosing one over another does not imply that the one not chosen is not good. ("Elaine is terrific, but Griselda is even better; therefore, I shall marry the latter"—makes perfect sense. But "Elaine is terrific, but Griselda is a complete wipeout; therefore I shall marry Griselda" is, shall we say, very puzzling.)

Are Criteria of Goodness Logically Open?

Do emotivism and prescriptivism imply that it is "possible to call anything you like good or harm"? Is the connection between what is virtuous and our various attitudes and interests "logical"? Foot's thesis is unclear here. She points to general facts about us and our environment which make it clear why and that we have certain general interests to which the virtues cater. What difference would it make whether these facts were "necessary" or not, so long as they are facts? Emotivists are indeed given to saying that there is no logical connection between properties of choosable objects and our choice of those objects. But suppose we are simply built in such a way that there is no real possibility of our not preferring them?

For example, consider happiness. Aristotle and Kant, and many other philosophers, have long supposed that we simply cannot be indifferent to it. They may or may not be right about this, but it is a plausible claim, on the face of it. Suppose it is true. Then the emotive theory could still agree that if someone thinks that x will make her happy, then that person will also say that x is good, since we know that she must favor x in that case. The conclusion might be that perhaps it doesn't matter whether there is a "logical gap" between descriptions and evaluations. Suppose the world changed in enormous ways so that courage ceased to be a virtue, and so on. *Now* it would be hard for Foot to maintain what she does. The emotivists, on the other hand, would see no great problem about handling the new attitudes that went with the new environmental/physiological regime.

Evaluating under Descriptions

One thing about evaluations that is now perfectly clear to everyone is that when we evaluate something, we evaluate it as a thing of some kind or other. And very often, the "kind" in question supplies a purpose or end that things of that kind are to be used for. What it is to be a good vacuum cleaner is a very different matter from what it is to be a good vacation spot or a good argument. And when someone fails to tell us in just what respect, under what sort of descriptions, he is evaluating something, we are rightly puzzled.

Consider two interesting examples: Here is my box of breakfast cereal, which alleges that it is the 'almost perfect food'. Does the description 'food' tell us enough so that we can know what it means for food to be "perfect" (and therefore, to be "almost" perfect)? No. The box continues by listing the nutrients in this food, showing that the food in question has almost all of those now considered to be essential to health, and has them in the proportions suitable for that purpose. But imagine someone who simply didn't like the taste of this food very much. Would she agree that it was "almost perfect"? It would be quite reasonable for her to dissent. She might say that the really perfect food would be absolutely delicious, as well as absolutely nutritious. Perhaps others discussing this with her might claim that taste is irrelevant. But that hardly seems reasonable. In any case, we could easily help matters out by saying, "Oh! You meant *nutritionally* almost perfect! Why, sure! But then, there is also the category of gastronomic aesthetics; and in that category, this stuff doesn't cut it!" Other purposes can also be imagined, though 'food' suggests mainly those two. ("This food is perfect for blocking drains" isn't on most of our agendas.) That maneuver is easy enough so that anyone can see it's relevant. Much more difficult would be to decide whether the perfectly rational person would discount gastronomic aesthetics in favor of nutritional virtue. That is discussable, and not so easy to resolve. We'll worry about them a bit later.

Another, much less trivial example: there has been a controversy in the past few decades concerning racial differences. Psychologists have come up with evidence, for example, that black people do, on the average, less well on I.Q. tests than whites, and that Asians do better than whites. Some have also come up with other statistical differences among the races. Now suppose that someone says, "Asian people are smarter than white people. Therefore the Asian race is superior to the white race." Does his conclusion follow from his premise? It wouldn't in any case, since his argument implies that the only thing that matters about a "race" is its average level of intelligence. But additionally, the trouble is that it isn't obvious that the expression 'good race' means anything at all. Good for what? Good how? Being a race doesn't suggest any particular aspect in which evaluation makes any sense. (Emotivists could point to the rhetoric of the Nazis as illustrating the flexibility of evaluative language, as emotivism has it. But Foot could reply, reasonably, that the Nazi rhetoric was arrant nonsense. Why couldn't both be right?) Until we are told more, we just don't know what is being claimed. Except for one thing: such a person is likely to be claiming that the Asian race is morally superior, with, perhaps, an implication about how Asian people should treat white people. We will discuss such claims later on, noting here only that it is obvious that no such conclusion follows from the sort of premises being used.

Means and Ends

In some of these cases, the relation between the item being evaluated and the appraisal we make of it is that of means to end. We know what we want to achieve, and the question is whether this will achieve it.

Even in the most obvious cases, this is an inadequate account, however. Suppose we are evaluating a certain car, the question being whether to purchase it as opposed to some other car. What is the "end"? Practically any car will get you from here to the grocery store before they give out.

No car will last the rest of your life, going all the places you might possibly want to go in it (unless you don't have long to live). Obviously there are matters of degree to be concerned with here. But there are also lots of other things that aren't just matters of getting from A to B. How fast will it go? How often will it need repairs? How much does it cost? How much fuel will it use? What will its exhaust fumes do to those who must inhale them? And—an important item with most people—how does it look? The obvious relevance of that question in this mundane context points to a major question about means-ends evaluation. For when we assess the look of our potential new car, what, we may in turn ask, is this "for"? Is there some "end," some purpose, in a car's *looking* a certain way? We return to such interesting questions below.

At least we have to say that when we evaluate item x as a means to end E, our evaluation of it qua means to E in particular is just one thing to take into account. There will be a set of other matters we will certainly agree to be relevant. These matters, in addition, will vary with the individual. No one car is best for all comers, regardless of what they want.

Which Ends?

Evaluation of something as, broadly, a means to selected ends is itself no simple affair, it turns out. But additionally, there is the question as to which ends to evaluate things in relation to?

The main options on this question have always been two:

(1) that the "nature of the thing" in question sets the ends for us, and
(2) that which ends we go for is up to us.

There is an understandable temptation to pair this distinction with that between the objective and the subjective. This matter needs to be explored a bit further, for it is not very clear how the notions of 'objective' and 'subjective' are to be applied in this context. The following discussion may help.

"Natures"

A long tradition has it that the good of a thing is a matter of its "realizing its nature." It is also widely repudiated by contemporary philosophers. This is partly on the ground that the notion of 'nature' is too unclear to be much use, and partly due to the influence of the naturalistic fallacy idea.

Well, what does "nature" have to do with it? Let's take three suitably diverse examples:

(1) a bowling ball
(2) a stone
(3) a person

In what sense does the "nature" of each of these determine the ends of the thing in question? One thing to note right away is that the word 'nature,' as it occurs in such expressions as "the nature of x,' does not refer to the "natural" by contrast with the "artificial." Bowling balls are not natural: they don't grow on trees, for instance. Yet bowling balls do have specific properties that distinguish them from other things. Those are what we mean by "the nature of" a bowling ball. (An old-fashioned term of similar intent is "essence.")

Artifacts

The bowling ball may seem an easy one. After all, it was made by somebody or other. Wouldn't the *manufacturer's* purposes for the thing be *its* purposes, then? However, the manufacturer made it for some people to use in a certain set of ways. Perhaps it is the interests of those who bowl that determine the "ends" of the bowling ball? These two sources of ends—the maker and the user—come together whenever the maker either is the user, or else makes the thing to order, or, say, for potential sale to, certain users.

Clearly, there is something right about this. One of the things that is right about it, moreover, may be seen when we ask what to say when we propose to use something for a purpose other than the one the maker had in mind for it, and/or other than the one that most typical users would use it for. For instance, I turn my bowling ball into a lamp base, or use it as a gigantic bearing in some Rube Goldberg machine I'm making. When I do this, am I doing something wicked? May others say, "naughty, naughty—that isn't what those things are for!"? Obviously not. There is nothing the least unintelligible about this, and anyone who thought it morally offensive would, at the very least, have a pretty rigid moral code—not to mention conceptual problems which we will go into later on.

On the other hand, there is plainly a role for "nature." Suppose you want to use your bowling ball as a pen. You're going to have real problems there! Perhaps you get a bathtub, fill it with ink, dip your bowling ball in it, and proceed to make awkward (and exhausting) swashingsabout on a huge piece of wrapping paper, managing in the end to get something intelligible on the paper. Does this show that bowling balls might be pens after all? Sure, if you like—very bad ones. And when you try this with, for instance, mountains or galaxies, you're going to run out of luck altogether. Clearly what the thing *is* tells us what can be done with it. Some things are naturally suitable for some ends rather than others, and artisans further improve the situation by reshaping, mixing, and performing various other operations on natural materials. The goal of this entire endeavor is to arrive at an object whose nature is such as to be conducive to the efficient performance of the end in question.

Natural Objects: The Case of Stones

When it comes to bowling balls, it seems clear that it is we who select the ends for which a thing is to be used. But what about things not made by people? Are the "purposes" of stones, say, fixed by nature? Reflection suggests that they are not. Actually, it suggests more: that the idea that there is such a thing as the "purpose" of a stone, as such, is off base. What is a stone for? Clearly there is no straightforward answer to this question. There are many things we might do with a stone. If it's a pebble and we are small boys, we might well want to see how far we can throw it, for instance. In a notable case, David used one as a weapon to vanquish his much heftier rival; and people do wonderful things with rock gardens; and so on. Yet, obviously, no one of these is *the* use for a stone. Probably there is no end of possible uses of stones, and we surely have little or no idea, at present, of most of them.

That's important, actually. That there are not fixed purposes in nature is not something to sneeze at as a finding; many early philosophers appear to have thought that there were, and that they mattered.

Natural Objects: People

What about the nature of a person? What's interesting about the example of humans is that it brings up the question which ends a person who *had a choice* about ends would choose, and why? A proponent of the classical view on these matters could now point out that presumably it is something about you, the way you are constructed, so to speak, that determines what you will choose. Being human, you will prefer water to arsenic when the quenching of thirst is what is in question. For that matter, it is the fact that you are a human rather than, say, a rock that makes you ever thirsty at all. The nature of a person evidently has much to do with this.

But what? Just as the bowling ball's characteristics limit what can plausibly be done with it at all, and also make it quite especially suitable for one activity in particular, namely bowling, so it may be that our characteristics limit what we can plausibly do with ourselves. It may even be that there is one activity that the human frame is quite specifically suitable for. To be sure, this latter seems highly dubious. For example, Aristotle's and Plato's proposal that this one activity that humans are suited for is *thinking* has its problems, especially in the case of people with no particular interest in mathematics and philosophy.

However, the case may stand with that, there would still seem to be the question of why, given the choice, we should choose to do what we are most suited for? Perhaps some would say that we don't really have the choice, that our natures simply close the question of what to choose.

But this can't be right. For if there were simply no possibility of choosing anything else, then we wouldn't have to choose at all. When I am standing at the top of the stairs and you give me a strong shove, I have no choice: down I go. But this isn't what the following of a way of life is like. Or rather, it isn't what any kind of system that purported to guide one in following a way of life could be like. You may have to decide whether to become, say, a banker rather than a schoolteacher. Information to the effect that you have the talent to succeed at the former and not at the latter would be very helpful, but supplying it wouldn't actually make the choice for you. Only you can do that.[50]

Functional versus Nonfunctional Terms

This is the place to remind ourselves of an influential discussion in the work of Aristotle. He argued that just as the flute player or the soldier, and so on, have a purpose, so a person has a purpose. But his argument appears to invoke an assumption that is clearly erroneous: namely, that the term 'person' is what I called a "functional term"—that is, a term with a functional definition, a word that is to be applied by virtue of the function of what it is applied to. We call a bowling ball a "bowling ball" in recognition of its intended and standard use. But we don't call mountains "mountains" for that reason, for there is no "intended and standard use" of a mountain. Mountains are so called because they are, roughly speaking, huge hills. There is no answer to the question what they are *for*. What they're for isn't the point of the term 'mountain'. (We could express

---

[50] An interesting relevant article here is David Falk's "Goading and Guiding," *Mind* 62 (April 1953): 145–71.

this somewhat more fancily by saying that utility isn't the point of being a mountain. Only that might suggest to some that there is a "point in being a mountain," but really it's a point other than "utility." Those who say that have missed the point also, I fear.)

Trying to think one's way through the subject of how to live by reflecting on the nature of human beings, or better yet, about the nature of one's self in particular, which is roughly the classical approach to ethics, is a large matter that we won't go into just at the moment. (We will return, briefly, to it much later on.) Suffice it to say that there is no obvious reason to suppose that nature can tell us what to do in any simple way; but also that on the other hand there are lots of obvious reasons why our nature severely limits our available range of options in life. Even there, the range of options is constantly expanding as technology and other inquiries proceed, so that really one should say that human nature limits our options at any given time, relative to the available technology.

In one obvious sense nature does limit us, in fact to just one option: the one we actually take, whatever it is, at each and every point in our lives. But we are not talking about that. What we are talking about is the number of options that are in some sense open. It is not hard to see how some quite intelligent person might confuse the one with the others.

Intrinsic Value(s)

This still leaves us with the subject of intrinsic value on our hands. Let's return to the subject, tabled some pages back, of buying a car in part because of the way it looks. Looking one way rather than another doesn't seem in any obvious way to be a "function" of a car, as such. Yet looks do matter to us. If we ask how they matter, we can give various answers. We might want to impress someone, for instance. Yet the most plausible answer is that they just *do*: that is, there isn't any further thing that the look of something might bring about that is why it matters. It matters for its own sake.

Ultimate Ends

What is worth having "for its own sake"? The car will get us from A to B, but why do we want to do that? Perhaps to visit a friend. Well, why do we want to do that? Because the friend is lonely, perhaps, or entertaining. But why is the fact that a friend is lonely, and you have some time available to visit her, a good reason to do so? What is it about visits with friends that makes that worth doing, as opposed to any number of other things one could do instead?

That's the kind of questions we expect from philosophers. It may be asked whether these questions are themselves reasonable. Must there be an answer to the question, "Why, ultimately, do you want to go to Elmira to visit a friend?" Some philosophers nowadays think there need not be such an answer. But these questions seem to be perfectly reasonable, so long as we are allowed to answer, somewhere along the line, "There is no further reason: I simply do want that."

Certainly we must agree that one needn't have the answer to this question firmly and specifically in mind as you make your preparations for the trip. Yet we can very often say that if it weren't that we expected to achieve some end E, we would not have done several of the specific things we did. In the case of friends, there is an obvious partial answer: we like our friends. That's a large part of what makes them "our friends"—of what is meant by the word 'friend'.

But now, we may also ask, "Well, why do we like our friends?" Again, some answers can be seen to be better than others or unacceptable. Suppose someone says, "I like him because he is so good at golf," when she doesn't, in turn, care the least bit about golf. Her answer in that case is, at least on the face of it, odd; more information, at the least, would be needed. On the other hand, that he has a warm heart, a ready smile, and a strong commitment to her welfare are very good reasons indeed. But let's admit that even such reasons won't ever be conclusive. There will be just something about him that you simply like, even though you may not be able to describe it.

Another kind of unacceptable answer, for a different reason, is this: "I like him because he is so good at fixing my car." An excellent reason for going to him with your car problems, indeed—but how is it a reason for *liking* him? Perhaps there's something about the way he does it, or perhaps he's very interesting to look at, so you just like to watch him as he fixes your car, and so on. But in the absence of some such answer, our reasons for having dealings with this individual aren't the kind that fit in with friendship, whereas "liking" someone does. There could also be a moral question here: suppose we appear to befriend someone, but our real reason is just to secure his services as a mechanic. We're exploiting, or using, that person. This is often (and plausibly) thought to be morally questionable. It isn't the kind of relation to a person that constitutes friendship, and to go on as if you do have that kind of relationship is to mislead, and to mislead about something important.

It does seem as though there are a subclass of experienced relations to other people that we seek out without any further motive. These are just experiences we like or enjoy having; though 'like' and 'enjoy' may seem too shallow to describe the sort of value a certain friend has. But now, does this take the matter to a still deeper level? When we just enjoy being in the company of a certain person, is our enjoyment of that person something we can abstract from the various aspects of our dealings with her that we do enjoy? Or is it, on the contrary, that the things about her that we enjoy, are things we enjoy because we think them *good?* "She has a fascinating personality," we say. Is that a personality that produces a certain effect—fascination—on us? An effect that we in turn value? A difficult question!

The Aesthetic

Turn to the cases where what you enjoy is not a personal quality or relation, but an inanimate thing or event: a splendid sunset, for instance, or a spectacular mountain. Or again, a work of art, which is produced by someone, the artist, but what she produced is detached from her and now hangs on a wall; or a symphonic performance recorded on a compact disc, which you now hear through your stereo system, its composer having been dead for centuries. What we like in the latter case is a sequence of sounds in a certain period of time; in the case of the picture, a set of visual shapes and colors with certain complicated relations to each other; in the first case, the sunset, perhaps the same sort of thing as in the picture, but also perhaps the sense of the immensity of nature, or whatever. In all these cases, there is a set of experiences that we value for their own sakes. We don't want these experiences because they lead to still other experiences, or, say, because they enable us to make money. On the contrary, we will spend money in order to have such experiences, and we will have other, less desirable experiences (such as that of driving our car through heat and heavy traffic) in order to have the first sort. Experiences such as these are indeed "at the end of the line": their value is in the having, right then and there. Because that is so, however, they also have a useful property that Bentham dubbed 'fecundity': a fine experience will also resound in the memory, and indeed, once one gets to know some such, the prospect of another, as well as the recollection of a previous one, may enliven an otherwise dull day.

Are Experiences the Only Ultimately Valuable Things?

One final question: is everything that we value for its own sake an "experience"? Is the point of life to have certain kinds of experiences? Could it be part of the point of life to bring about certain states of affairs having no connection with one's own or anyone's experience? It is hard to think of examples, but suppose you put a box of stones on the backside of Pluto. You are sure that neither you nor anyone else will ever see this or have any experience of it whatever. G. E. Moore has a famous discussion of an analogous case.[51] He asks us to imagine one exceedingly beautiful world, and another exceedingly ugly, neither of which would ever be seen by anyone, and asks whether we should not prefer the one to the other, and to do something to bring it into existence, if we could. We can update his example by supposing that one has but to push a button, and the beautiful world will come into existence; if we do nothing, then the other will. The question then is: is it rational to push the button?

One trouble with saying the latter is that there would be the experiences you have in the course of trying to bring about that state of affairs. Yet those who do such things might say that what makes those experiences valuable is only that they are the experiences involved in trying to bring about this independently desirable state of affairs. "That this box of stones should be on the backside of Pluto—what a great thing!" Does that make any sense at all? While I am inclined to doubt it, I am not entirely sure. On the other hand, I am entirely sure that I would think that anyone who went to an enormous amount of trouble and expense to do that would have to be at least slightly crazy. Whereas someone who takes hot showers simply because he enjoys the tingle of the droplets on his skin has a value that seems not only intelligible but reasonable, and it seems so even if I don't happen to get off on hot showers myself.

Another interesting question concerning the hypothesis that what ultimately matters are experiences is posed, fascinatingly, in Robert Nozick's imaginative experiment concerning the "experience machine."[52] You go into the machine and it supplies you with any experiences you can possibly desire: the experience of conquering the world, say, or of conducting the Philadelphia Orchestra. The only snag is that none of the things you experienced in the machine would actually be happening! Question: would you nonetheless board the machine in preference to continued contact with the real world, even though that contact would provide you with much less interesting experiences? Nozick's experiment is not totally fanciful. Perhaps the drug addict has faced precisely such a choice, and prefers the machine—cocaine or whatever.

Tentative conclusion: (1) We have "ultimate" preferences, preferences for which we can give no further reasons at all; and (2) it seems proba-

---

[51] Moore, *Principia Ethica,* ch. 3 (sec. 50).

[52] Robert Nozick, *Anarchy, State, and Utopia* (New York: Basic Books, 1974), 42–44.

ble, but not altogether certain, that what we have ultimate preferences for are always certain experiences. (*Note:* We must not attribute any kind of certainty or fixity to ultimate preferences. They could change, and, surely, do. We must also ask what significance, if any, attaches to the second tentative conclusion.)

Finnis on Self-Evident Values

I noted that G. E. Moore held that there are certain states of affairs having much higher value than anything else: love and aesthetic appreciation, roughly. Another philosopher, John Finnis,[53] shares Moore's view that there are some self-evident goods, but adds to the list. He proposes seven types (without claiming to be definitive): "Life," Knowledge, Play, Aesthetic Experience, Sociability (Friendship), Practical Reasonableness, and "religion" (by which he does not mean only formal religions, but also a serious concern with the sort of issues that the formal religions address. He might perhaps have said "philosophy" instead.)

Let's consider, as an example, his arguments about one of these— knowledge. Finnis says that this good is "self-evident, obvious. It cannot be demonstrated, but equally it needs no demonstration." He explicitly rejects the relevance of such considerations as that there might be psychological roots of the urge to seek truth, or even that all men by nature desire to know. For that matter, he wants to insist on the self-evidence of the good of knowledge even for those who don't actually care about it. The claim in question does not, he insists, rest on "any particular desire of my own or of my fellows." Nor, he says, is it relevant that "not everyone who might be asked would affirm that truth is a value worth pursuing." And he claims that "I may ignore it or reject it, but again and again it will come to mind, and be implicit in my deliberations and my discourse, catching me out in inconsistency."

One point to get out of the way concerns a possible confusion. The value of *truth*, namely, is quite a different subject in principle from the one he is mainly talking about. Valuing truth is a matter of preferring truth to falsehood, of not wanting to be deceived. But ignorance need involve no deceit whatever. It isn't that somebody is fibbing to us: it's that we simply don't know. Granted, we don't want to be in possession of false ones; but still, the question is, is it really valuable to be in possession of as many true propositions as possible?

---

[53] Finnis's view is expounded fully in his book: John Finnis, *Natural Law and Natural Rights* (Oxford: Clarendon Press, 1984).

His argument raises many questions. One is this: if the good of knowledge is literally self-evident, then why or how could anyone ever doubt it? And why all the supplementary arguments, to the effect that the goodness of knowledge is "implicit" in this or that activity? Another, and more important, question is that the view itself involves a puzzle: what is "knowledge," anyway? Knowledge isn't an experience, for example. Discovery is an experience, and one that fascinates and involves many people. But knowledge is more like a capacity to give the right answer when a question comes up, say. Until some occasion arises for attending to what one knows, the knowledge itself seems to lie in storage in the mind rather than in the forefront of consciousness.

Now, much knowledge is of undoubted practical use. Whenever we do anything that is predicated upon the world's being one way rather than another, then knowing which way it is forwards that action, and not knowing hinders it. Of itself, this would be enough to confirm that knowledge is in general a good. But here we hardly need to go in for "self-evidence." For if we raise the question whether knowledge, on this account, is of extrinsic or intrinsic value, the answer would seem to be: extrinsic. If we want to do something, then it would be well to know how to do it.

Now, Finnis's view is vague in a crucial respect. How much value should we attach to knowledge, and therefore to its pursuit? The answer, surely, is: no particular value, and certainly a degree of value that will vary wildly from person to person and for that matter from subject to subject. For any given person, it's easy to think of examples of knowledge not worth pursuing, given one's array of interests. Is Finnis arguing that we ought to be interested in its pursuit even if we are one of the latter? Is his idea that we can invade native societies and force them all to go to university?

The same would surely go for all of his other categories. How social should we be? How concerned with 'religion'? How much art? How much play? A person can live a good life devoted almost exclusively to any of these, neglecting all the others, except, perhaps, "practical reasonableness"—which presumably is the ultimate appraiser and decider of all these things and so cannot be overdone. On the other hand, you can certainly spend too much time thinking, as in "he who hesitates is lost."

Moreover, surely Finnis is not denying that there are bad things in each category. There is bad life, bad play, bad art, perhaps even bad knowledge (would humankind have been better off not knowing how to make nuclear weapons?) The general claim, as an allegedly self-evident proposition, that each of these kinds of things is good, becomes doubly puzzling, doubly unclear, when we reflect on this.

It is not clear whether Finnis thought of his theory as supporting some kind of intuitionist metaethics. Finnis has "the skeptic" (probably J. L. Mackie—they were at Oxford together many years) arguing, as does Mackie, that "our belief in the objectivity of values amounts to a belief in very queer 'things,' perceived by a very queer faculty of 'intuition'."[54] His reply is "But we should not be deflected. It is obvious that a man who is well informed, etc., simply is better off than a man who is muddled, deluded, and ignorant . . . whether I like it or not. Knowledge is better than ignorance."[55] But why should this be a question about 'objectivity' in any very interesting sense of that term—a sense, in particular, in which what is objective is what is so *irrespective of any facts about human minds?* Plainly that can't be what Finnis has in mind. And when he says that knowledge is good whether one likes it or not, one may wonder. Couldn't a person be driven crazy by the pursuit of knowledge, and come to wish that she had been a simple savage? When Finnis proclaims it to be self-evident that she is wrong in such a judgment, what is he doing? Is he claiming that knowledge is good even if it makes us miserable? Would that be a plausible claim?

In any case, we should see that views rather like Finnis's could be held by (1) an emotivist—obviously, as I hope is clear from my remarks about Blanshard above, but more surprisingly, perhaps, (2) also by a naturalist. Which brings us to another example of that kind of theory. After so much immersion in the intuitionist and emotivist theories with their background claims that naturalism is in principle unacceptable, we now turn to a very sophisticated later account in which the claims of naturalism will look very much better.

Sparshott: Getting It about Right

F. E. Sparshott offers this interesting analysis of goodness.[56] Happily, his analysis is easy to state, for he encapsulates it in a formula: "To say that x is good is to say that x is such as to satisfy the wants of the person or persons concerned."

This interesting formula locates several places at which there could be disagreement about goodness. He identifies them as follows: "that x (1)

---

[54] Finnis, 72.

[55] Finnis, 72.

[56] F. E. Sparshott, "Disputed Evaluations," in *American Philosophical Quarterly* 7, no. 2 (1970): 131–42. Sparshott is the author also of one of the most delightful, and unreasonably neglected books in the literature, *An Enquiry into Goodness* (Chicago: Univ. of Chicago Press, 1958).

is (2) such as to (3) satisfy (5) the (4) wants of the (7) person or persons (6) concerned." He offers an extensive commentary on each point, but we must be much briefer.

(1) Does the thing in fact *have* empirically ascertainable properties, which both parties agree would make it good if it had them? This would often be a straightforward factual matter.) Sometimes it would be a very difficult factual matter, to be sure—but still, factual.

(2) Even if it has them now, is it *such as* to have them—does it reliably, repeatedly have them, and have them by virtue of the nature of the thing in question rather than some incidental or extrinsic property?

(3) Does it "satisfy" only in the sense that one who wants such a thing as this gets what he asks for? Or does it satisfy in some further sense, say of actually allaying the craving that led to it? Does it produce the *sense* of satisfaction? This is very important; we all know the experience of disappointment, where we got what we asked for, but it turns out to be not to our liking. Question: should we say that if we don't like it, then it isn't what we "really" wanted? We often do.

(4) Is the "want" in question an outright need, or a mere whim, or a standing general interest, or what? In short, which of the total set of conditions that might be classified as 'wants' is the thing in question to cater to?

(5) Are the wants mentioned the *relevant* ones, the ones that are in question here? Do we have "the" wants, or merely "some" wants?

(6) Who is "concerned"? And which concerns are relevant concerns— which are to be attended to? (Some people, we think, are relevantly concerned, say affected or implicated, while others take a concern in what might be none of their business.) This kind of question is extremely important in ethics, for people frequently do take an interest in other people and their interests. When they do, there is the possibility that we would be satisfying busybodies rather than the people for whom they are supposedly concerned. This aspect will loom rather large in some discussions in normative ethics later on.

A further point about 'concerned': someone may fashion a concern about something—it's the thing to do, he's a busybody. But someone else is concerned in the sense that the thing really affects her, given her situation and person. Clearly, satisfying the first sort of concerns is not fundamentally important; it is the second kind that counts, and the first kind are subordinate to it. I take a concern, but if I do so rightly, it is because you are really concerned, and I merely take an outsider's interest in your case or situation.

(7) Who is a "person"? For example, are neonates, or cats to be considered such? Consider the abortion question. Are fetuses "persons concerned"? Arguably they are not. They have no developed consciousness,

no sense of their own or anyone else's interests. Of course there is the vital question of why we should be concerned about persons anyway, whether or not we count newborns or fetuses among them. Meanwhile, it is very clear that distinction (6) plays a major role in this controversy: persons take a concern for preborn humans, whether or not those organisms take a concern for themselves.

As Sparshott points out, some of these are pretty straightforward, but some are decidedly not. The question of how to settle disputes about whose wants count and who is a person might be quite intractable. Sparshott says that if disagreements turn out to be "matters of taste or attitude, then the formula turns out to be covertly emotivist."[57] But, after some analysis, Sparshott concludes that while many disagreements are not simply factual, yet they "involve an element of weighing up . . . the importance of factors whose relevance was not reasonably deniable."[58]

This brings up two crucial notions: importance and relevance. Neither, he agrees, is easy to explicate, yet neither can be "plausibly made out to be a matter of how anyone feels." Driving a car through rush-hour traffic, he points out, "involves ignoring some movements in one's vicinity, attending marginally to some others, concentrating on a few, taking into account some theoretically possible eventualities and not others, and making more or less allowance for those one does not take into account. None of these factors are calculable in practice, but the impossibility of calculating does not make any aspect of the process inexplicable, unjustifiable, or in any sense irrational."[59]

Sparshott's proposal has a great deal going for it. The question is, does it identify goodness with properties to which the naturalistic fallacy criticism really applies? The question is a tricky one. Consider in particular the case where the person concerned is oneself. How could I possibly be indifferent to what *I* am *concerned* about? In saying that I am concerned, after all, I am, obviously, saying that I am not indifferent. There is no problem, in this case, with the needed "magnetism." On the other hand, suppose that the only persons concerned are other persons, and suppose that they are not persons about whom I am particularly concerned. In that case, I could say, "well, this is good, but I don't care." This can be so when we are talking about the good of others, as we often are. It is not obviously irrational for me to be unconcerned about the good of others. Immoral, perhaps? Perhaps—we'll be getting to that issue soon. Here we should note only that not all goodness is moral, and that the

---

[57] Sparshott, "Disputed Evaluations," 135.
[58] Sparshott, "Disputed Evaluations," 140.
[59] Sparshott, "Disputed Evaluations," 141.

question is whether Sparshott's account transgresses any reasonable version of the naturalistic fallacy problem. The proposed "line" between facts and values, so far, seems to be due essentially to the problem of motivation, of "magnetism." When we explicitly talk about someone else's good, it is less than clear that there is necessarily any magnetism to account for. Only in the case of one's own good is that clear—and Sparshott's theory does account for it in that case.

While it is obvious that questions like the last one are of major concern in many ethical controversies, it is not obvious how one is to resolve them. But while it is not obvious, is it wide open? That depends on how we understand the formula—and whether it is the right formula. The central idea of the formula, certainly, is the wants of persons. The term 'wants' is used in a very broad way: ideals and compulsions, whims and long-standing basic interests, are all wants in the sense Sparshott intends. It will be a major job for the person having these wants to decide which ones take pride of place, which are more and which less important; if we can't do that, we can't make up our minds what to do, ever. But be that as it may, if the satisfaction of wants is the basic concept in ethics, then our focus is very much narrowed from views holding that various things can be good whether anybody takes *any* kind of interest in them or not.

Do suggestions of the latter kind make any sense? G. E. Moore supposed it made sense to say that a beautiful world unperceived by anyone at all nevertheless has some value—though not, he thought, very much.[60] But simply to think that something is "beautiful," surely, is ipso facto to evaluate it. Not only that, but whoever evaluates it thus shows that he has some interest in it—that he "wants" there to be such things, in Sparshott's appropriately wide sense of 'want'. It is plausible to think that Moore's "unseen world" example is incapable of refuting a view that value is essentially connected with *valuers*—with the wants, interests, desires, of persons doing the evaluating.

Sparshott's analysis has a great deal going for it. It succeeds where metaphysical intuitionism fails, in accounting for our interest and concern about what we say is good or evil. But it also succeeds where emotivism fails, to give a manageable sense of the rational relevance of some considerations rather than others. The idea that just anything might be good or bad is absurd, if by this is meant that they might be so whether we have any interest in them at all, or not. The Sparshott recipe enables us to make reasonable progress with many disagreements, while explaining too why some may be intractable.

---

[60] Moore, *Principia Ethica,* sec. 50.

Is Sparshott's formula naturalistic in a sense that violates the naturalistic fallacy? But there's something wrong with that "fallacy," when we think about it. The fallacy principle looks good when our analysis of goodness tries to invoke nothing but features of things external to ourselves. But it doesn't look so good when we start taking our own interests and wants into account. Does it in fact make any sense to say, "I want this very much, from the bottom of my soul, and moreover I am quite sure that it will satisfy that want, in a stable, enduring way—yet it is not good"? I take it not. It might not be good for someone else, of course. But in that case, as the Sparshott analysis implies, we need to examine the thing in the light of *the other person's* wants, not *mine*; motivation on my part is not automatic. To be sure, the question of why and how much the wants of others should matter to us remains open for the present. It is fairly obvious that they may not matter to us, in any given cases. Just what that does for *morals* is an important and interesting question; we will consider that question at length in the next part of this book.

Good Reasons in Ethical Theory

What is also clear, I think, is that Sparshott's proposal and his discussion of it bring up the need to be clear about another matter that has been, perhaps implicitly, hanging in the background so far: the matter of reasons in practical matters. What is it to act reasonably or rationally? How do values relate to reason? Sparshott's theory, as a theory proposing to account for all of the relevant variables in valuation, may well be regarded as precisely such a theory. To be a relevant variable is to be a variable that it is reasonable to take into account. We will focus now on analyses explicitly invoking the notion of reasons.

Concluding Thought on the Meaning of 'Good'

The term 'good' is applied in three contexts.

First: there is goodness or badness as means to ends. Something is good if it leads or contributes to the achievement of the end in question. Ends are of all sorts, some being evils and others good. But the evil man will intelligibly apply the notion of good to the means for achieving his ends, evil though they are. The terrorist regards some methods of carrying his explosives as better than others; the saint regards some ways of rendering assistance as better than others.

Second: there is goodness "of a kind" in the sense that something is said to be a good or bad example of the kind of thing it is. This is not the same as the first: there may be no sense that the thing in question is "for" anything: one galaxy may be a better example of a galaxy, and in that sense, a better galaxy than another. In terms of Sparshott's analysis, the superior example of an F is the one that satisfied better the wants of the F-fancier, the classifier for its own sake.

Third and finally: there is intrinsic good, good that makes no reference to anything further. This is reducible neither to the first nor the second. This good is about ends: not the goodness of means to them, but rather the goodness of the ends themselves. If we say that the opening movement of Mozart's Quintet in E♭ for Piano and Winds is "good," we are saying neither that it is conducive to something (though it might well be), nor that it is (merely) a good example of a classical sonata form movement (though it happens to be that); we are, however, saying that it is a very specific kind of thing that we who are interested in that sort of thing admire, like, enjoy, want, or favor, very much. Those who think that something might be intrinsically good without exemplifying any of those will have to be asked to explain themselves. There is no problem why those not interested do not have any of those attitudes, though for those of us who do see the point, it is difficult to see how someone of normal hearing and perception could fail to be interested in it—how they could fail to see the beauty of that music.

If we ask *why* we want things like that, it seems entirely reasonable to say that we don't know. Perhaps eventually something about our nervous systems will explain why we go for such things. And it is fairly obvious that we will often be quite sure that there are properties *in* the work in question which are what make it so good, despite the unfortunate fact that millions of people—most people, apparently—don't see this. Two things will be easy to say. One is that those who don't see this have missed the boat, or are missing something, are deficient in some way. Another, however, will be that despite this lamentable failure on their part to see what is plain to see, we are not justified in doing anything about it, short of reexposing or immersing them, if they're willing to listen, to the sort of stimuli in the object which does move us so much. And with that we turn to the important notion of *morality*.

Morals

Two Meanings of 'Moral'

This subject of what 'moral' means will preoccupy us for most of the rest of this book. Our first question is: *what is it?* And this, I think, quickly leads us to the need to make an important distinction. In Aristotle's

Ethics, the moral is identified with "control of the passions," the right principle of which, he famously claims, is to aim for the "mean." We will defer discussion of that principle until much later. Here the general point to be made is that Aristotle has indeed put his finger on part of the central idea of morals, which is that we can't go ahead and do just any old thing we like. We are instead to curb or restrain ourselves, to act in ways not necessarily responsive to what we just happen to want at the moment.

That said, however, there is another distinction that is not the same, though related. Here the question is: *who is involved?* Are we exercising these controls because we think that we *ourselves* will be better people or live better lives as a result? Is it essentially a matter of what is good for myself, leaving others to one side? Robinson Crusoe could think himself to be doing either well or badly in this respect, exemplifying a subject that, with some danger of being misleading, we could call 'prudence.' It's misleading because it is not a given that the *prudent* life is the *better* life, even for oneself. But no matter. The point is that there certainly is a subject there, and an important one—but it is a different one from the sense of morals in which it is *essentially* social.

Consider famous maxims such as the "golden rule": 'do not do to others what you wouldn't want them to do to you.' Or consider the anthropologist's sense of the term, so that he might catalogue, say, the moral rules of the Zuni or the Dobu. Or look at the Ten Commandments of Judeo-Christian fame. Apart from the union-rule specs about confining your religious sympathies to this particular version of the deity, all of the substantive ones are about how we are to treat and regard our neighbor—not ourselves.

One of the major questions has always been *which* neighbors? Is it just fellow members of the tribe, or is it more than that? There is strong conceptual pressure in the direction of the "neighbors" being *everybody*. Most importantly, on any version the tribe is, as it were, the minimal unit. How to treat fellow members of one's family, say, is important, as is how to treat fellow employees and associates in any number of groups engaged in enterprises you share in. But morals especially applies to our dealing with miscellaneous others—people we don't know at all, or scarcely at all.

A moral theory should address these questions seriously. What is the point of morals? Why are we into this neurotic-seeming engagement, in which we are called upon to set aside or at least severely inhibit our pursuit of our various "passions" and indeed, our own theory of the good life?

First we will inquire, then, into the meaning of 'right' and 'wrong' in their distinctively moral application. Second, we will consider the role of moral *rules*, or *principles*, or at any rate *generalizations* in all this. And third, we should ask whether some distinctively different vocabulary, notably the vocabulary of *virtue*, should be regarded as more fundamental than that of *rules*.

Having asked all that, we then will proceed to substantive theory. Our ultimate question is a decent answer to the question, what *are* the basic principles of morals? But to put it that way is to presuppose that there is "an" answer rather than, say, a host of answers, perhaps one for each individual, or one for each culture, or at least a great many as advocated by assorted moral theorists down through the millennia. Should we think that some one relatively specific view could possibly be thought to be the one right one? Or is it a mistake to think that any such thing is possible? Readers who can't stand the suspense may or may not be gratified to hear that I will indeed be proposing, in a sense, just "one" theory, though along with it will come an explanation of why many different theories can be plausible, at certain levels, and why we can hardly expect easy answers at those levels.

Defining 'Moral'

In the preceding, I emphasize a rather sharp distinction between personal ethics—the subject of *how to live*—and *morals*, in the distinctively social sense. In this latter sense, the subject of morals is, putting it very generally, *rules for the group*. Groups are composed of individual people, and nothing of the normative kind proposed for any sort of group, large or small, can make sense if it does not make sense to individual agents who are the only entities capable of addressing the question, "What shall *I* do?" The question, "what shall *we* do?" can only be the question, "what should I try to tell everyone in the group in question, or their leaders, to do?" Groups as such can't address any questions, and cannot do anything. When they are said to do anything, it will be because many or all of the members do something. And so the question of morals can be distinctively and securely put in the following terms: what should you or I or anyone do, *as a member of society*—as one who interacts with an indefinite array of other individual people?

What makes this an important question, one to be separated rather strongly from the other general sort of question? After all, the *most* general question is, simply, "what should *I* do?"—the category of morals is a subset of that more general subject, and moral principles must be a subset of all of the general principles, or rules, or whatever we call the cognitively accessible inputs to decision-making, that there are.

There is a definitive answer to this question of the distinctiveness of morals, though, like so many other profound matters, deceptively easy to state. This answer is *the separateness of persons* (to use an expression similar to that of John Rawls.[61]) Each person is a distinct individual, with a mind of his or her own. Only individuals, strictly speaking, *have* any ideas, any problems, any interests, any principles. But some people may and frequently do have *different* ideas and principles from other people. And that's why there is a problem about morals.

More generally we can say this. All people have, at any given time,

(1) a set of what economists have come to call *utilities*, comprising the things people are interested in, the things that matter to them, the things they care about or that concern them. This can equally be called their set of *values*.

(2) a set of *powers*, which individuals can utilize in action. There will be bodily capabilities, such as the use of arms and legs and lips; and there will be skills, acquired either from teaching or exercise and experience; and there will be intellectual, artistic, and emotional resources that can be brought to bear, when individuals decide what to do.

Rawls rightly complained that a theory like utilitarianism seems to put all of us, as it were, into one basket, making out society to be one big individual instead of the many particular, "little" ones whom you and I encounter in our lives. That has been one of the classic ideas in moral theory, conspicuously utilized in the utilitarian view, though not confined to it. But if it literally requires any such thing, it must surely be wrong. People almost always "identify" in varying ways and in varying degrees of attachment, with some or many groups. But for Jones to identify with the Welsh, say, is not literally for Jones to be part of a big mind that is the Welsh mind. It is, rather, for Jones to sympathize with and to tend to act in various ways like other Welshmen—both of which he could also fail to do, if he so elected, and indeed which, without having decided to, almost all of the other six billions in our world do not do. Identification is something individuals do, though in doing so they relate in certain ways to groups. Obviously it is possible to raise the question whether one *should* do this, and even if one claims that one cannot possibly avoid it, there will be options in action that can be addressed and rejected despite such membership and identification. Individuals make up *their* minds, and consult *their* interests when they act. And because this is so, it is futile for *me* to tell *them* that *they* should do this or that on the ground that it will promote such-and-such an end—an end that, it turns out, they simply do not have. An individual's rational actions are a function of *his* inputs, not anyone else's as such. And that, in brief, is why morals are

---

[61] John Rawls, *A Theory of Justice* (Cambridge, MA: Harvard Univ. Press, 1971). Rawls uses the expression 'the distinction between persons' and famously argues that utilitarianism does not take it seriously. See p. 27 and more generally the following section (sec. 6, pp. 27–33).

distinctive. In that part of ethics, *moral* theory, we seek principles, rules, sets of virtues that can credibly, plausibly, be applied to the behavior of *people in general*, and not just to some one or some few.

Moral Relativism

Down through the centuries, a recurring thought has been that morality is in some basic and essential way "relative." By this is meant, not that morality depends on how we are, for it does. It is meant, rather, that some *variable* group, or even individuals as such, determines what is right or wrong in a way that makes it true that people in one of the relevantly varying groupings ought to do certain things, yet people in one of the others ought to do certain quite different things, and that the variation is due simply to their membership in these different groups—that there is no *further* reason, no basis for action that can transcend such membership.

To get anywhere with this idea, it is crucial to distinguish three different kinds of theories that may be so called. Relativism could be proposed,

(a) as an *explanatory* theory, describing differences among various people in respect of group membership, or possibly even among individuals. *Anthropological* relativism is the thesis that there is quite a lot of variation in the actual mores (that's what anthropologists call the moral rules and customs of particular societies) of (at least many) different societies.

(b) as a theory about the very *meaning* of moral expressions such as 'right.' This we may call *metaethical* relativism; or finally,

(c) as a substantive, normative theory about what people ought to do. It is this especially that is usually called *moral relativism* without qualification.

Moral relativism is popular because of the plausibility of claims of the first type. It is thought that experience shows that what is right in one tribe is wrong in another. From this it is sometimes inferred that these people can't even talk to each other in a clear way (theory [b]), or that what is right for people really is a function of their group membership (theory [c]); or sometimes both. In all of these cases, the question is whether relativists have succumbed to confusion.

So let us first get clear about their logical relations. On the face of it, the trouble with the move from (a) to either of the others is the "is-ought" gap we have been concerned with. But we do not need to get into the underlying meta-considerations of that "gap" in order to see what the fallacy is here. For in general, from the fact that Jones *believes* that p, it does not follow that p. Jones could be wrong. If morality is something it is even possible to be right or wrong about, then there is no fundamental reason why some very large group of people could not be wrong about it as well. We were all told in fourth grade that there was a time when everyone believed that the world was flat. The claim was probably inaccurate, but it is obviously the kind of claim that *could* be true. Very large numbers of people in our contemporary world almost certainly believe that there is a phenomenon called "global warming" that threatens to eventuate in various calamities for humankind at some time in the foreseeable future. The belief is certainly vague, and in any sense in which it can be made clear, is almost certainly false. But there is no problem about the possibility that they really do believe it. That does not settle the issue of whether those things really are happening and going to happen.

So unless morals are a "matter of opinion" in some sense that really rules out even the possibility of error, then the basic reason usually proposed for moral relativism is simply fallacious. The moral relativist would have to do better than that. What, then, might he do? He may be tempted to move to theory (b), which has a sophisticated ring to it—metaethics, after all, is a relatively recent and rather intricate theoretical subject. But theory (b) has a basic problem from which it is extremely difficult for any theory to emerge into the light of day. If, when a member of culture X engages in any sort of discussion with a member of culture Y, what X is saying when *she* says that what the Ys are doing is "wrong" while what Y means when *he* says the same thing about X is *different*, then they cannot be disagreeing with each other. This observation is enlightening to beginning students of ethics everywhere. I can't deny what you're saying if I don't understand it. Yet the perception of *disagreement* is among the major sources of moral relativism—it is thought that the Xs really do differ from the Ys in a way that invited description as disagreement: the Xs, for example, regard polygamy as okay while the Ys think it is terribly wrong. It would be disappointing if it turned out that all the Xs mean is that polygamy is in accord with a certain set of rules accepted by the Xs, and all the Ys meant is that it is not in accord with the set of rules *they* accept. Where is the disagreement, then? After all, if they are reasonably intelligent, they can easily enough find out, from the anthropologist or from their own observations, or just by chatting with each other a bit, that indeed the Xs *do* have such a rule and the Ys do indeed have the other rule. So what?—we must ask.

Now moral relativism in the third and usual sense of the term can be brought into the picture. The relativist may now say, "And, guess what? They're both right! Xs really *should* practice polygamy and Ys really shouldn't! In general, people ought to do what their tribal rules tell them to."

Up to some point, the moral relativist's advice is plausible and easy to accept. Do these people put their forks on the left, or on the right? In polite company consisting of Xs, you too should put yours on the left; or Ys, on the right. No problem. But suppose that Xs are of the view that anybody—including Ys—who fails to put his or her fork on the right should be hanged at daybreak. What now? It will not be quite so obvious that this is a sensible piece of advice for the Y's to go along with. We may want to insist that where you put your fork really isn't a subject calling for the death penalty for nonconformers, and that any culture claiming that is in serious error on that point—custom or no custom. Would that advice be misguided? I don't think so!

In general, the trouble with moral relativism is that it is a theory that doesn't have any "teeth" unless people do in some quite serious way differ in a sense that implies *disagreement*—and yet what it seems to have to say about this is that *both* parties are right. A disagreement in which both parties can be right, however, is not a disagreement at all—it is merely a misunderstanding. But to describe such contemporary concerns as terrorism, proper responses to environmental issues, women's rights, and no end of others as "mere misunderstandings" is to have missed the boat. These are real issues, people really do disagree, and we need, in a serious way, to try to figure out who is right. The right view could very well call for much accommodation by many to practices they previously disliked; but that it doesn't actually involve any disagreement at all, and all parties' views can simply be accepted as they stand, is not sophisticated—it's just sophomoric.

There is a lesson to be learned from contemplating moral relativism, however. The lesson is this: it is the *point* of morals to apply *interpersonally*. A moral claim, a moral "principle" or rule, purports to tell us who may proceed and who must give way in various possible interactions among people. It purports, indeed, to impose a *uniformity* on people. It purports to overrule those who want to do otherwise. All of this is described in terms of "purporting," on purpose. The job of moral philosophy *is* to try to find rules that can credibly perform that function. If there are no such, then morality is impossible—a will-o'-the-wisp, an illusion. Cloaking that in the language of "subjectivism" or relativism is a pointless evasion.

The reader may have noticed, by the way, that moral relativism of type (c), the standard understanding of relativism, is incompatible with relativism of type (a). For moral relativism *does* purport to tell *everyone* what to do: namely, to adhere to the mores of his or her tribe, or whatever the group selected as the relevant variable for moral purposes may be. The relativist does disagree with someone else, namely the "absolutist" who thinks that there are some moral rules *other than* those calling for adherence to tribal customs that we should instead be following, even when they do collide with local practices. Both are advocating morals in the same sense: a general rule for all, the same for everyone. The contents of certain of the rules they propose are very different. But relativists cannot defend their choice on grounds of the unintelligibility of the rival view. And once this is seen, relativism will also very soon be seen to be a dramatically implausible view. Indeed, epithets such as "lunatic" come soon to mind, when we find ourselves called upon to approve of various outrageous, inhuman, murderous, or bizarre practices merely because they have been and are in fact practiced by certain groups.

The Notion of Social Rules

Just what is a "social rule," anyway? And are moral rules, indeed, social rules? They are; but to say that moral rules are social rules is misleading. Normally, the expression 'social rules' is used in social-science contexts, as describing phenomena in various societies—as a synonym for 'mores'. But we want to be able to claim that a given society's social rules might be wrong in some way, in need of improvement. Moral rules—the real McCoy as we might put it—would be the rules that *ought to be* social rules. And secondly, the term is misleading in that it seems to imply that these rules exist "outside" of us, like the legal rules of the land, which emanate from the legislative building a thousand miles away. But we want moral rules to be *internalized*. A moral rule, if there are any, is something that any and all individuals *should* have "in their heads."

In what sense, then, should we say that moral rules are "social"? The answer is that moral rules tell us what to do taking into account the fact of our fellow persons existing in the same social world as ourselves. What we ought to do is affected by the presence of others, each with their own unique sets of desires and of powers to affect us, for better or worse, and a good deal of what we do does or might affect them. An individual whose personal behavior was completely unaffected by that fact, if conceivable at all, would be, for one thing, probably very dangerous, and for another, not very long for this world. On the other hand, an individual who fails to take due account of the claims of her neighbors, on some occasions, is perfectly normal. This last goes far to explain why we need morality. What you do matters to me; what I do matters to you; and we both are sufficiently intelligent to appreciate the fact in general. We are also both sufficiently imperfect in one way or another that we could easily overlook it every now and then, with more or less unfortunate consequences.

John Stuart Mill, in his discussion of the idea of justice, proposed that "the sentiment of injustice came to be attached, not to all violations of law, but only to violations of such laws as ought to exist, including such as ought to exist, but do not; and to laws themselves, if supposed to be contrary to what ought to be law."[62] With a modest amount of restating, Mill's idea is that a moral rule is something that ought to be recognized as a social rule, and ought to be somehow impressed in the minds, the practical operating systems, of all individuals. This, I think, zeros in on the idea of morality quite well. But it contains two variables that need to be accounted for if our analysis is to be both reasonably complete and also noncircular. Obviously, we need to know what this word 'ought' is doing there. If it is in effect a reiteration that morality is what morally ought to be done, we have not got very far. And secondly, we need to know more about this "recognition": what's involved? Here are a couple of suggested answers.

First: To say that these "ought to be" social rules is to say that there are good reasons why anyone should so recognize them. The moral 'ought' is accounted for in terms of the more fundamental, but not essentially moral, 'ought' of general practical reasoning.

Second: We "participate" in morality in two ways. One way is by doing what it asks us to do, by living up to it—by *being* moral. But there is a second way and it is essential to understanding morals. This second way may be described as participating in "moral administration." Each of us can and often does *respond* to the behavior of our fellows, and prominent (often) among the ways we do so is that we tend to express approval or disapproval. And why do we do that? Primarily, in an effort to induce those other people to do the things we express ourselves about. To praise someone, say, is to provide a psychological input of a kind that would normally stimulate that individual to continue to behave in the way for which we praise him. We may call this, broadly, by a term used often in psychology: "reinforcement." We *positively* reinforce behavior when we praise it; we *negatively* reinforce behavior when we blame people for it. Those are mainly verbal methods, but we can do more: we can reward and punish. Positive reinforcement in the intended sense is behavior on our part that is aimed at increasing the likelihood of compliance; negative reinforcement is behavior on our part that is aimed at reducing the likelihood of noncompliance.

There is a close analogy, at least, between morals and law on this view. Law is enforced, but by a specially designated set of persons, the police (and associated auxiliary personnel). Morality is also enforced, but

---

[62] Mill, *Utilitarianism,* ch. 5. Published in numerous editions.

not by the police: rather it is enforced by *everybody*. More precisely, it is *to be* enforced by everyone, though of course this too is a job at which we can do better or worse, more or less.

If we press the analogy further, we note that law is *legislated*. But what about morality? In what sense if any is it legislated? The short answer is that it is certainly not legislated by a legislature, or any particular, designated set of persons, the "moral government." For there simply is no such thing as a *moral government*, in any normal sense of the word; rather, the "governing" is done by *everybody*. And that too is the answer to our question. Morality grows, "like Topsy": it doesn't originate in some specific party laying down the law. It does originate, though, we may be sure. As time went on, long, long ago, people began to cuss each other out for doing or not doing certain things; they began to do so in imitation of others doing likewise; and they began to notice what sort of behavior on the part of others would be more welcome to themselves, what less welcome, and to note what makes the others aware of your noticing of this, and so on. Morality, in short, is a network of interaction among people in society. But it is not just any old interaction. Rather, it is interaction of a general type, with formal properties applicable to all.

Morality, in short, is the society-wide set of rules that ought to exist and which it is to be everybody's business both to observe and to *reinforce among their fellows*.

Morals and the "Common Good"

My general analysis here is much influenced by a famous idea of St. Thomas Aquinas, who tells us that law is "a directive of reason for the common good, promulgated and enforced by those who have the care of the community."[63] St. Thomas was especially focusing on law in the legal sense, but he thought that it also applied to morals. Insofar as it does, we need to recognize that those who have "care of the community" are *everybody*, and that promulgation is not by some designated committee but, again, by everyone, so that the "natural law"—as he referred to it—becomes obvious and second nature to all. Those are the features I have been emphasizing in the preceding paragraphs. But now we want to consider the insertion of the phrase "the common good" into the picture. In what sense, if any, can we say that morality is for the common good?

At this point we need to remember that our analysis is notional: no particular society's actual morals are necessarily, or even probably, per-

---

[63] Thomas Aquinas, *Summa Theologia, Treatise on Law*, Q 90.

fect—especially not in every detail. In saying this, though, what standard are we implicitly invoking? St. Thomas's suggestion, which I think is essentially right, is that it is the standard of the *common good*.

In so saying, we bring up a notion that many have regarded as intolerably murky; we need to "un-murk" the idea. Its potential for being clarified is much greater than such critics seem to appreciate. I think there is a trackable cause for any confusion: it comes from overlooking, first, the point that these are *rules* intended to guide or direct the behavior of *everyone*; and second, that each person is an individual, different from each other in assorted ways.

Our model for the direction of the behavior of people in general can't be one that can easily be associated with emotivism. For although humans are quite capable of "emoting" at each other, we really have to ask, as we saw in the preceding discussions—what's the point? If the point is to attempt to induce the other person to act in certain ways, different from what they might otherwise do, then we shall have to adapt our emotive expression to our purpose. We don't just shout at people; we don't just wave our hands. Rather, we attempt to *persuade* them to do better. And if we are to do this, we must hook the proposed sort of behavior somehow into *their* practical frameworks, even though a bit of emotive expression might actually help to do that. A rational actor assesses *his own* utilities and powers, and acts so as to do his best in relation to those. So a rational influencer must provide for, or discern in, his audience, premises that they can see to be relevant to their behavior. Sympathy is one possible source—but it is highly variable, and we seek rules for all. Self-interest is far more promising, though people's interests differ, and so we need to appeal to what we can be pretty sure is there—in fact, to the *common good*. Common, because we are concerned about people generally; and good, because to act is to attempt to promote something the agent agrees to be or sees as good.

Why would, or how could, anything like "morality" work? The answer is that it will and can only if there are principles, or a principle, such that everyone can see that he or she could, given the general social situation, *benefit* from operation under the proposed rule. The benefit has to be something agreed by the persons in question to be beneficial. And it has to be realizable, at least if everyone does act as the rules call for.

But that brings up a very thorny problem. Is the common good in question realizable not only *if* everyone so acts, but also *only* if they so act? The difference is enormous. People could agree that if we all did this, we'd all be better off—but point out that many will not. And if the good will not happen *unless* all do act, then there is little point in any particular person so acting, for unless 'all' is a pretty tiny group, there isn't the slightest chance that all *will* so act.

On the other hand, if a lot of the desired good will in fact come about even if not everyone acts—albeit, the more the better—then there may still be incentive for individuals to act. And too, if the cost of urging people to act, praising them for acting and blaming for not acting, is not high, but a return is at least decently likely, then we may rationally participate in this aspect of morality.

There is another thing, of considerable importance. Once we start urging others to act, we put pressure on ourselves to act as well. For hypocrisy is morally objectionable. The person who makes a large point of advocating a course of action that he then fails to engage in himself, if caught out at it, will be something of a laughing stock. He will also have, so to say, "let the moral side down."

Let's get back to the idea of the "common good." There are two sets of distinctions to invoke here, by way of narrowing down feasible concepts. First, there is the sense of 'common.' And second, there is the question of what the relevant criterion or criteria of goodness might be.

1. 'COMMON . . .'

Common good can be understood in roughly three ways.

One way can be dismissed fairly quickly: 'common' can be understood in the sense of an *aggregate*: we add up this person's good, that person's good, and so on, and come up with a total, by addition. This view has two problems. The lesser one is that there isn't much "common" about it: if Jones has a piece of this thing, and Smith a very different piece of a very different thing, where is the sense of 'common'? Consider a basket of apples. Now chop them all up so that there are no individual apples discernible, though the mass is the same as before. But now we don't have anything "in common" among distinct apples. Similarly, we may have nothing in common among people, on this reckoning.

The much more serious problem in terms of the theory being developed here is that no individual need have an *interest* in the aggregate good. What matters to Jones is, pleonastically, what matters *to him*; and this may not include much, or any, of what matters to someone else. Not only is the sense of commonness undone, but the allegiance of particular people to the cause, so to say, of promoting this good is dubious to nonexistent. And that is essentially fatal, if morality is to be a rational institution. Thus what is needed is common good in the sense of something that is genuinely *in common* among all people—something shared by and the same for each, so that each has a stake in it, as it were.

So far, so good. But, that said, another problem looms before us: *how good* is the good that is in common between me and you, as compared with the good I recognize that is *not* in common? Suppose we would all enjoy going down to the village square and participating in some festivity. But I would also enjoy staying home and playing music on my stereo system, or . . . whatever. Clearly I might easily prefer the latter to the former. The commonness of the common good assures that each has *some* interest in it, but does not assure that each has *enough* interest to induce him to prefer its pursuit to something else not a part of it.

Clearly, it would be nifty if we could come up with a good such that it would be positively irrational to prefer anything else to it. But that is a very tall order. Socrates supposes that the good person will be happy on the rack. But Aristotle thinks that is silly. The good person should be ready to endure some costs, indeed—but not beyond some reasonable point, beyond which he would simply be sacrificing himself to no avail. Aristotle is plainly right on one level, and it is the most relevant level: we cannot *expect* all to sacrifice themselves, at least not frequently and wholesale. When we can expect people to endure some costs is an important question, to be sure. Meanwhile, however, we shall have to settle for a morality such that people can see the point in having it, the point in supporting it, and some point in enduring at least considerable costs on its behalf.

2. '. . . GOOD'

In fact, we have almost covered our second question as well. Consider the thesis that the common good is, say, what St. Thomas himself supposed: the good according to Roman Catholicism. The trouble with that assumption, however, is that a great many people (most) do not share it; and some would roundly repudiate it, or worse. When I say that this is "the trouble" I am not saying that I think St. Thomas to be in the wrong about the intrinsic merits of his belief (though I do think that). What I am saying, instead, is that it is not a good candidate for the special job that the *moral* notion of good needs to serve. What's wrong is not only that a great many people do not accept it, but also that there is, so to speak, no way to "sell" this good to someone not already disposed to "buy" it. Attempting to argue people into accepting a particular religion is a notoriously futile task. The safest assumption is that it can't be done—and the best course of action is to point out to those who think it can that they are in for a long and frustrating job of it. But we can now look at another candidate, less controversial in one sense, but burdened with the same problem: the good is being immersed in classical music. I am ready to wax fairly eloquent on behalf of this particular good, to which I am personally very attached. But I too am doomed to failure if my idea is that we should all share it: for many will not see it, no matter what I do to try to persuade them. Now what?

Well, "what" is quite easy to see, in both cases. When we move up to the moral level from that of personal values, the solution is to allow both of us to pursue our interests, so long as we don't thereby significantly infringe on the pursuit by the others of *their* interests. In the case of religion, this is religious tolerance. In the case of music, it goes under the general heading of freedom of "lifestyle." The basic idea is reasonably clear, and the reasoning behind it is extremely strong. Common good has to be *common* as well as good. In the present case, and at least a great many others, that common good is, simply, freedom. What's "common" about it is that all of us have pursuits which we want to be able to pursue without impediments from other persons who don't share our particular interests; and that with regard to the good we are contemplating here, that of freedom, *only* other people *can* provide it. The only people who can provide me with the sort of freedom that is in question here, namely social freedom, freedom from the depredations and interferences of our fellows, are all the rest of you out there, who could make life miserable for me but happily, for the most part, do not. Similarly, I could, in many cases, do something to make your lives miserable or short, and, fortunately for you, I don't.

Later we'll be addressing this kind of solution to this kind of problem in the light of "social contract" theory, or somewhat more technically, of game-theoretic reasoning. Here the point is just to illustrate the enormous difference it makes whether we are just asking (1) how good—how interesting, how enjoyable, how nice, how profitable, and so on—a given pursuit is, or (2) when we are asking, What is the rule for us *all* to be guided by? The solutions to these two questions are so different that, indeed, the second one hardly even makes sense in terms of the first one. My choosing to be "free" has no content, ordinarily. I can't just "choose" to be free from *you*, for your actions and dispositions are involved in that; but my "choosing" to be free from *me* is either just nonsensical, or is a way of getting at certain possible personal problems—hangups, as we might say—that I might have but which are immensely variable from one person to another insofar as they are any sort of factor at all in our various lives. In any case, they are not as such the subjects of morals.

We can helpfully generalize yet more. Consider theories to the effect that some value or other is "intuited." Well—we say—fine and dandy. But why should we be impressed? Are the intuitionists claiming that we *all* have this experience? But, alas, apparently some of us do not. Now, what? The intuitionists may well bill their proposed principle or judgment as "rational." But how is it rational for the person who doesn't see it? Why should it be rational for *me* to act on *your* intuitions? And why should *I* be disposed to applaud when *you* propose to act *in relation to me* the way *your* intuition tells you to? Of course, I may, if I'm lucky, be quite happy with the content of your intuition. But suppose I'm happy with it for some quite other reason, such as that I just like the idea of acting that way? Presumably you won't think that will give it the *imprimatur* of morals. But that's my question about your intuition: why should I think that something's being intuited by you gives it that imprimatur?—Or even, it being intuited by myself, come to that? If I were to intuit something, no doubt I would think it is true. What one intuits, presumably, seems obviously true—that's what we mean by calling it an intuition. But does it even *seem* to be true *because* I intuit it? Or is it, rather, that somehow it looks as though there are reasons, in the nature of the case, that make this thing plausible?

Take for example, murder. If you look at murder from the point of view of the victim, it's not hard to see a serious objection to it—hey, I end up *dead*! Do I really need an intuition to think that *that's* a bad idea? I can't see that there's much of a problem about why I would object to a procedure aimed at, and likely to succeed at, converting me into a corpse. And now, if somebody says, "well, it's not only that, but there's the fact that murder has this intuited property of *wrongness* (which, by the way, I can't otherwise explain!)"—I don't really see why we should be any more impressed.

The reason for wanting to make objection to murder into a *social rule*, though, is very clear. We can't improve on the reasoning of people like Hume and Hobbes about this, which I will summarize in my own words here. We can easily see how murder might look pretty good from the point of view of the *murderer*—he might be gaining a lot of money, or he might simply hate his victim something awful. And indeed, we can all easily see how somebody out there might get an idea that killing us would improve things for him. This puts us in a proper fright, considering. Now, there are a lot of us, and we don't differ all that much in respect of what it takes to kill somebody. As Hobbes so trenchantly puts it, "as to strength of body, the weakest hath enough to kill the strongest." Or near enough—perhaps only 98 percent of my fellows have "enough," but I reckon that will do, thanks! So we have a problem. And what are we going to do about this? We have to consider what our potential assailants might gain, and what we might lose, and then take whatever measures may be needed to reduce the probability that the assailants will assail us. One of these measures is the one called *morality*: we implant a sense that this is not to be done. If it succeeds, and none of us get murdered, then we will all be a lot better off than if instead we were quite likely to be murdered by one of those who do have something to gain from it.

And if it doesn't, we'll have to resort to warfare: organized police, say.

But prospects of the first being successful are pretty good, so long as people believe that their own deaths would be a very bad thing, and that we are better off being prevented from murdering others if the return is that we are not murdered ourselves. And as to the second, the police—well, that is the subject for another book, for one thing. But at this point, there is a simple observation to make: we only have police because we have the sort of problem that is indicated when we declare murder to be wrong. And there is simply no way that any number of police can substitute for the dispositions of the many people they undertake to police.

The resulting arrangement, morality, is fairly fragile. First, there will be people who are ready to cheat—to enjoy the benefits of others' acquiescence in the rule against killing—yet to enjoy for themselves the benefits, as they suppose they are, of murder. And second, some few people will adopt schemes of personal values in which they somehow come to believe that their own lives are worth almost nothing, or even that they will do better being dead here on earth, because to be so means being alive somewhere else (in Martyr's Valhalla, or whatever). The rest of us have a problem with both of these kinds of people, and part of our solution is that we will be *very* hard on the murderers we manage to catch, as well as very disposed to catch them. Moreover, in the nature of the case, we will need *collective* security here. Everyone is to be disposed to disapprove, and help to apprehend, the murderers of *anyone*, not just themselves.

Will we also, though, need to disabuse the deluded fanatics, as we think them, who fall into that second class? That depends on what you mean by 'need.' We need to disabuse them of those notions if we are to be safe from those people, yes. But that may be impossible, for the same reason that it is impossible to talk you into adopting my religion, or out of adopting yours. If so, however, one thing will be perfectly clear: those people make themselves deadly enemies of the rest of us, and we accordingly would be perfectly justified, so far as it goes, in making sure that the fanatics do not get to the point where they actually murder us. If that means taking such drastic action as blowing up their meeting houses, so be it. How would they be able to *complain* about this? That is: to complain in such a way as to make the rest of us think they have a point?

The example of murder is a useful one here. Values are involved, obviously, and facts: the value of life, and facts about vulnerability and aggressive capability. The latter give rise to a very strong case for, as I called it, collective security. The hypothesis here is that that is what morality is: the points or planks in a platform aimed at making life better *for all*, except those members of society whose values or proclivities make it impossible to accommodate them on the part of the rest of us—the bullies, sadists, dominators, and the like. Do those exceptions worry us? Of course—in practice. But do they worry us at the level of moral theory? Does their existence show that morality is pointless or arbitrary? They do not. On the contrary: they make it clear why life is difficult, but that very difficulty adds to the urgency of the moral program, the moral "point of view," as some call it.

Intuition and Suffering

Many writers hold that we have a duty to refrain from inflicting pain on others because pain, or suffering, is intrinsically bad. The view affords a classic arena for assessing the methodology of intuitionism. There are two questions to ask. The first is whether, indeed, pain is intrinsically bad. But the second is whether that fact, insofar as it is a fact, supports a moral rule (or "plank" in my preceding account's terminology) against inflicting it on others.

We are, I take it, naturally averse to pain. Or is it only *almost all of us* who are? Is it conceivable that one should not be averse to it? Some people, certainly, are able and willing to put up with a lot more of it than others. People intent on accomplishing various things, such as climbing Mt. Everest or making it to California in a covered ox-drawn wagon, have been ready to endure a great deal of pain in the process. That doesn't show that they don't dislike pain, of course, or that they don't regard it as bad. It does show that the precise scope of the claim that pain is intrinsically bad is rather unclear. We can, for example, distinguish between pain, discomfort, annoyance, irritation, general unhappiness, and some other conditions not easy to relate to these things, such as boredom. (Is boredom bad because it's painful? Or only bad when it becomes painful? Or is it quite distinct from pain, but nevertheless something we don't like?) Questions such as this would occupy many pages in a treatment aiming to do justice to the subject.

Not having the space, let alone the patience, to attempt this, I content myself with the observation that the notions of pain and pleasure both seem readily susceptible to broader and narrower uses. In the broad sense, we might use the notion of 'pain' simply to refer to all experiential states to which we are as such averse. In the narrowest sense, however, pain would be one among many of those states, to be distinguished specifically from the other things mentioned—discomfort, and so on. Presumably the claim that pain is intrinsically bad is to be affirmed mainly in the *broad* sense. And at that level, the claim that it is bad comes very close to being a tautology: to be painful is to be an experienced state to which one is as such averse. If we confine the notion of pain to its narrowest uses—in which a toothache is indeed painful, but the feel of cotton under your tongue is merely unpleasant, and being accused of some terrible vice is extremely unwelcome but causes no pain—then the thesis that pain is "the bad" and pleasure "the good" is clearly false.

The problem for those who wish to convert the *evaluative* thesis—that pain is bad—into a *moral* thesis is that the aversion is to a *felt* or *experienced* state, and only the person who experiences that state can be its subject. To say that x is bad, as Sparshott affirms—I think rightly—is to say that x is such as to dissatisfy the wants of the persons concerned; but the person immediately concerned is the person feeling the pain. It does not follow that A is averse to B's being in pain. Again: most of us are fairly sympathetic. If we see on television a man in a distant land writhing in agony, we will be sorry for him—perhaps. But then, avowed enemies of some group of which that victim is a member may rejoice in his pain. It is in B's interest that A take a sympathetic interest in B's pain, yes—but not the reverse; and this holds for almost any pair A and B. Few doubt that the pain experienced by B *is* bad *for B*. But many who agree with that do not care much about the fact, or even take it, perversely, as a point in its favor. The common good does not appear to include the pleasures of others, as such. That is to say: a notion of the common good that does not *impose* any values on people who do not already have them, will not include the sort of item that would be there if everybody were significantly averse to the pains of all and sundry others. It will, we may agree, include the pleasures and lack of pains of each person for his or her own part.

Suppose that intuition is called in to bridge this particular gap. The claim will be made, say, that all pain is bad *as such*, no matter whose (or what's—the pains of animals will presumably get included). But is this a useful claim? It is so only if intuitionism is a useful approach to strictly moral philosophy. But I have argued that it is not and cannot be. Intuitionism, as so often in philosophy, answers questions by begging them. It avoids the need for honest labor: why, indeed, *should* we people, all of us, adopt as a standing attitude that we avoid inflicting pain on others?

The plank will need much refining. The dentist inflicts pain on others, who pay him well for what he does. We shall have to say that we are not to inflict *net* pain on others, or more accurately, not inflict pain that is, all things taken together, and so far as that particular subject is concerned, *unwelcome* to him or her. That means we are back to our more general nonharm condition, the avoidance of pain-infliction being included only as a part of that more general program.

Once we have all that, will an intuition add anything? It will, I think, provide a *name* for what we now have: a moral injunction to us all to have a fundamental aversion to doing what worsens, on net, the situations of others—insofar as it is possible for us to avoid this without entailing even greater worsening for ourselves. But intuition will not provide an *explanation* of anything.

Moral Realism

A popular view of moral theory in recent years has gone by the name 'moral realism.' Here's a good sample definition: "Moral realism is the view in philosophy that there are objective moral values. Moral realists argue that moral judgments 'describe moral facts.' This combines a cognitivist view about moral judgments (they are belief-like mental states that describe the state of the world), a view about the existence of moral facts (they do in fact exist), and a view about the nature of moral facts (they are objective: independent of our cognizing them, or our stance towards them, etc.). It contrasts with expressivist or noncognitivist theories of moral judgment . . ., error theories of moral judgments . . ., fictionalist theories of moral judgment . . . and constructivist or relativist theories of the nature of moral facts."[64]

But just what does the view come to, really? If Agnes wants to say to Bob that something is good or bad, right or wrong, and so on, presumably she won't find it either necessary or interesting to add that what she has just said is *true*—what else, after all? A favorite comic line goes, "I'm not making this up!" If Agnes adds this affirmation to her statement and Bob accepts it, would it make any difference to Bob's behavior? As was observed back near the start, it will always make a difference to his verbal behavior, and presumably also to, as we might call it, his cognitive behavior. But what about his behavior regarding the very subjects of those predicates? If Bob agrees that x is wrong, yet makes no effort whatever to refrain from doing x himself, he is hypocritical. His judgment is not *sincere*. Do moral realists mean to say that such hypocrisy is perfectly all right? Is it their view that those who make moral judgments, however earnestly, need do nothing in consequence? Often the judgment will be about matters regarding which one is not in a position to do anything, of course. In that case, the issue is moot. Even there, however, one can show enthusiasm, for example, or dismay, at the doings of others. Is the moral realist claiming that such responses are *irrelevant* to morals?

The emotivist position, as it is called, centers around this very point. To accept that the universe contains some fact about matters outside ourselves, independent of our minds, is to imply nothing about what, if

---

[64] Wikipedia entry on Moral Realism by Geoffrey Sayre-McCord [http://en.wikipedia.org/wiki/Moral_realism]

anything, one will be disposed to do about it. To accept any evaluative claim is to imply that one will oneself, or that the "persons concerned" will, if they accept the claim, do something about it. The behavior of the evaluator is relevant to the fact of his holding the view in question at all.

But ethical claims are about something, and this requires that there be descriptions of the something that they are about. If realism is the thesis that there has to be a basis in fact for our evaluations, then realism is beyond controversy. Why do I like this cheese? Because it tastes *like this*. Is its specific flavor relevant to that evaluation? How could it not be? Are flavors facts? On that point, we get into semantics. Flavors are sensed by those who taste the things that have or produce those flavors. Those experiences really happen. If what makes them really happen are neural and other physical events, fine. If not, fine: whichever, they are occurrences, and if we are to say that they are not "real" because they take place in minds, then the question is: don't they *really* take place in those minds?

Presumably moral realism is not just a program of metaphysics, a contribution to the mind-body problem. Its claim is that there are "specifically moral" facts, which apparently is supposed to mean that over and above all of the facts, in the usual sense of that term, which we would cite in support or in critique of some moral claim, there are *other* "facts" which *constitute* their moral character. But this claim borders on the unintelligible. Here is my friend Jones, the very soul of kindness. He wouldn't hurt a fly (fact); he would go way out of his way to help anyone in distress (fact); and more things of that kind, including, if need be, facts about his mental states attending these doings. Having said all that, the thesis that Jones is "kind" is well supported. Do we need, now, an additional thing, the kindness of all those kind acts? Could this additional thing be present even if Jones's behavior had been entirely the opposite? Presumably not.

Well, why not? Do moral realists suppose that once someone is aware of all the "facts" in which the wrongness of something consists, then that person will be moved to act accordingly? We who accept some moral judgment do think, surely, that anyone confronted with the same facts would indeed also accept the moral verdict in question, and we hope he would also be moved to do whatever was appropriate in that case to do about it. We hope that, yes. But facts alone don't guarantee it. And *calling* the judgment a "fact" will do nothing to ensure that fellow investigators into the situation will indeed come up with the same judgment that I do.

All this, however, is on the assumption that we are excluding facts *about ourselves* from the admissible set of what is being called "fact." Once we allow that, however, things are different. For if we include the fact that I have this or that attitude toward something among the "facts" relevant to the issue of rightness or wrongness, then it will indeed follow from the facts that I will have the disposition to do this or that regarding the matter at hand.

The conclusion seems to be that moral realism does not offer any new insight into morals. It adds, if anything, some misleading terminology, and another opportunity for question-begging arguments in moral theory.

Error Theories

Some recent philosophers argue that the very vocabulary of morals contains an "error": we suppose that wrongness, say, is a real quality, and can hardly help doing so, and yet we are wrong—there is no such quality. That view has become known as the "error theory." It has the oddity that it builds the error into the very fabric of value: to have values at all is to make this mistake.

But is it a mistake? Whenever we evaluate anything, as we have seen, we require a description of what is valued, and in particular, a description such that *it* is what really *has* the value, as distinct from various other aspects of the item in question that are not what give it value. Benevolence is a value, and what has it is the objective property in benevolent people of doing nice things for others. There need be no mistake about that, and when there is, it is sometimes detected and then reverses the value-attribution in the case of that individual. But it doesn't reverse it as regards the value of benevolence *as such*. And if we ask what *that* value consists in, we will be able to point to the satisfactions, in the objects of benevolence, which give it its point. Are satisfactions subjective or objective? The trouble is that the answer is obviously *both*. Satisfaction would not exist apart from a "subject"—notably, us. But for all that, we often really do feel satisfied. (Recalling the distinction made in the discussion of Sparshott's analysis, we can alternatively point to the fact that the person in question really did get what he wanted, even if he doesn't *feel* satisfied. Both that condition and the feelings, in the cases where they too happen, are objective in the sense that they really exist. And what other sense do we need?)

Values are obviously objective in the sense that people do actually have them. They are also objective in the sense that anyone claiming that something, X, is valuable thereby claims that there is something about X that makes it so. And the various subjective reactions he has as a response to those facts do also exist. No doubt the question is this: will this objective basis of a reaction inspire a similar reaction in *others* who contemplate the same facts? Alas, that cannot be guaranteed, people being what they are. The wonderful urgency in the opening of the finale to Haydn's "Rider" Quartet (op. 74, no. 3) somehow fails to stimulate some people to the enthusiasm that is surely its due. What is there to do about that? We lamely resort to the same thing recommended by the intuitionist: urge our subject to look again. But failing that, then what? He is apparently not the person to take to the concert hall next time around.

Does this last require us to withdraw our attribution? I don't think so. We who are in the know about such matters know what we're talking about. But when it comes to ultimate values, we know also that people differ in their capacity to perceive and appreciate. Values are certainly not objective if that means that they have nothing to do with subjects—with perceivers and feelers able to respond with a discerning appreciation or criticism of what is perceived.

Those who argued for error theory were, however, most concerned with morals, not with aesthetics. And in morals, as will be seen, there is an entirely different kind of reason for maintaining that "values" are not highly variable or subjective, in the most relevant sense of that term.

Evolutionary Theory

There is the important possibility that we can find decent evolutionary biological explanations for humans entertaining various dysfunctional stories. "Natural selection made the human brain big," Gould wrote, "but most of our mental properties and potentials may be spandrels—that is, nonadaptive side consequences of building a device with such structural complexity."[65] But notice that nonadaptivity involves a value assessment. Are either aesthetics, or many other evaluations, or, most pertinently, morals, nonadaptive? No way! Morality, as I shall argue now—and if it isn't already obvious—is highly useful, and can be made even more so by pruning its maladaptive features. That story comes next—starting with the theories that have, I shall argue, the counterproductive features that can reasonably be called "errors" of one kind or another.

Meanwhile, we'll conclude this survey and account with a note about "evolutionary ethics." The original idea was that something's being right is a matter of its being conducive to survival. Of what? The obvious answer would be, the species, the human race. But in the first place, evolutionary theorists are divided between a big majority who think the essential mechanism is not the species but the individual, and a minority

---

[65] Quoted by author Robin Marantz Heig in "Darwin's God," *New York Times*, March 4, 2007.

who think it's the species and not the individual. And in the second place, and far more important: survival, as such, surely underdetermines ethics by a very, very long shot. Yes, not killing other people is arguably number one on the moral agenda. But what about keeping our promises? Is there a big evolutionary payoff here?

A prevailing problem with evolutionary ethics is that it can look pointless. Aristotle remarked that if everything was for the sake of something else, then all action is "empty and vain." Why do we reproduce? So that our offspring will reproduce. And why do *they* reproduce? . . . So that *their* offspring can reproduce. Hmmm . . . The whole thing sounds almost comically empty. Human life is full of interesting things: the singing of birds, the changing of the seasons, the sound of the horns in Mahler's Seventh Symphony, the argument of Hume's *Inquiry*—what on earth does all this have to do with the perpetual reproduction of species? Yes, we have to be born first, and people are a good thing, for sure—the presence of lots of other people makes *my* life immensely better. But that just sheer existence is the point is a kind of cosmic put-down, not a sensible moral philosophy.

Evolutionary theory can explain a bit. But not very much. Even sex, for example. Evolutionary theory maybe makes it unsurprising that people are interested in sex. But have a look at the fashions in the *New Yorker* or on TV; read a decent novel with a romantic interest; for that matter, just have a modest look at any of the opposite sex (or same, if that's your interest) and ask whether your particular interest in the particular ones you find interesting isn't enormously understated by observing that, yes, it would be possible to have children by them (unless it's the same sex, of course . . .). The interest of individual people, even on the level of sexual attraction, is far too great to be written off as a footnote in a great big biological program of species-perpetuation.

—Isn't it?

* * *

In this part, we have delved into *metaethics*, the subject of what ethics is about—what its basic ideas mean and how they relate to each other and to anything else. Our review divides the subject into values generally—"goodness"—and moral values in particular. This isn't the same as the distinction of value and *rightness*, or of value and *obligation*, but certainly right/wrong and obligation are the most typical and distinctive moral notions. We began with the problems of *naturalism*, the claim that ethical notions can be exhaustively defined in *descriptive* terms, making goodness and rightness to be further properties of various actions and other things. The thesis that there is a "naturalistic fallacy" is the claim that naturalism is impossible, and we considered the interesting very general argument for it called the "open question test." The originator of the challenge, G. E. Moore, concluded that goodness is a unique, unanalyzable property, a view we found strong reason to reject. A major twentieth-century response to Moore was *emotivism* which held that ethical claims are essentially just expressive, and not descriptive as such at all. While the charge of fallacy is challenging, we ultimately concluded that an analysis of goodness in naturalistic terms could solve the problem, and do so in a way that both utilizes some insights of emotivists and yet provides an understanding of how discussions about goodness can be rational. We then turned to morality, in a "narrow" sense in which it is distinctively social. A morality is a set of rules—"marching orders" for people in general, evolved from social interaction and "administered" by everyone. Philosophically, we want to know whether such a set of rules can be reasonable, and argued that it can, if general observance of such rules could plausibly work out for everyone's good, understood in their own terms. This provides a transition to our second part.

PART 2

Normative Morals:
A Review of
Popular Theories

Introduction

The most general distinction within ethical theory is that between metaethics and normative ethics. The object of metaethics is to understand what ethical concepts are, or more narrowly with the meanings of words such as 'good,' 'ought,' and 'right' in their ethical uses. The object of normative ethics, by contrast, is to understand what are the basic principles or rules, or more generally the right general account of what actually is good, right, just, or such that it ought to be done. In brief, normative ethics is what most people think of as "ethics, period": what they want to know is *what they ought to do*, and not what it means to say that they ought to do it.

As was said at the outset, this distinction must not be taken to imply that the two have nothing to do with each other. The point of metaethics is to tell us what normative ethics is about, and how it might work. The point of normative ethics is to tell us, hopefully, what's right and wrong. But the way in which philosophers can "tell us" such things is still, generally speaking, by logical analysis of ideas, plus, in this case, a good deal (I hope) of common sense plus acquaintance with general science insofar as we have that.

When people ask for ethical guidance or insight, what are they asking? To begin, let's reinvoke the distinction between ethics, in the broad sense, and morals, in the narrow sense identified in the last many pages. We previously distinguished two importantly distinguishable subjects. One subject is the one in which the inquirer wants to know whether we have any *duties*, any *moral requirements*, any matters with regard to which there may be some kind of principled insistence that we not do just whatever we like, or perhaps even whatever seems to be good for us, but instead must toe some kind of moral line. That is the area we are concerned with here in part 2. The other possibility is that he is concerned with a different kind of question—the general question of what to do in life—perhaps, even, what is the meaning of life? That subject is the topic of our last and rather briefer part 4.

There are many ideas about morality, and a notorious amount of disagreement. Some think that the extent of disagreement is incurably great, and that to seek the true general principles of morals is to chase after a will-o'-the-wisp. At the opposite extreme, some philosophers suppose that there is just one very general abstract principle that is basic to all of morality. There is also some disagreement about what that one principle is, even among those who think there is such a thing. In between, we have views that maintain that there are several, but not a great number, of basic ethical principles—the "ten commandments" of Judeo-Christian fame exemplify this. Then there is the view that really each and every actual case has its own specific relevant values, and they simply can't be captured under a small or even a sizable number of headings at all. It is, even, occasionally held that each and every act is a distinct and unique case, no generalization being possible or desirable. And, it is sometimes held that morality is "relative"—that different people or groups of people just do have their own morals, irreducibly, and that there is no general or universal answer to the questions of ethics. Finally, there are some who think we should not be talking about rules and principles at all, but only of virtues and vices. Clearly there is a great deal of work to do in this area.

Moreover, we should note a still further distinction: between "theoretical" ethics and "applied" ethics. The idea of the latter is to look at quite concrete and fairly specific problem-areas and try to work out good solutions to the main, or at least to typical, problems in those areas. We do not, in the present treatment, get into applied ethics except in a quite incidental way, or to illustrate some more general approach. But a great question of theory is whether we can actually have general theories that are genuinely relevant, in a helpful way, to specific practical issues. And again, even among the many philosophers who do think that we have a reasonable knowledge of the general principles of morals, no one supposes that you can go straight from there to the details of practice with no further investigation.

Meanwhile we will begin this part of the book with a review of a number of influential moral theories—most of them, I think, wrong, but all of them interesting and instructive, because at least moderately plausible in one way or another. We will then move on to a more constructive treatment.

Moral Relativism, Again

Moral relativism is, in general, the view that what we ought to do varies systematically as a function of whose "code" or set of rules we are operating with—those of the group we are associated with, in some way. We have already opened discussion on this topic in part 2. Here we will consider only the third of the three versions of moral relativism distinguished there: moral relativism as a substantive, normative thesis. As such, it is a "one-principle" view: that *one ought to do whatever one's society rules that one ought to do*, or that we *are morally permitted to do only what it allows*. Since presumably those sets of rules will vary a lot, moral relativism could alternatively be said to be a many-principle view, with the principles in question limited in their application to just the members of the relevant group. That is the temptation. But it won't work, as we will shortly see. Meanwhile, the reason for accepting the particular set of rules in question is *always the same*: namely, that they are the rules of one's society. (What that means is not so obvious either, a point we'll table for the moment.)

That brings up the subject, which group *is* meant by 'one's society'? Or for that matter, why groups at all? Why not just individuals? *Individual* relativism would hold that what is right for you differs from what is right for me, just because you are you and I am I. But at that point, we might as well be talking about egoism, an important topic that we will address next. *Group* relativism is the standard kind of relativism, however, and more specifically, cultural relativism.

Defining 'culture' for this purpose, and explaining where one culture leaves off and the next begins for purposes of analysis, will be no easy job, and raises major problems for the theory, as we will see shortly. Note that there are indefinitely many possible groups that conceivably could figure in some version of ethical relativism, and the aspiring relativist needs to explain why we should use the one he chooses rather than some other—something of a theoretical millstone around the would-be relativist's neck, but not something we'll worry about further here.

The choice of 'culture' is made plausible by three things. In the first place, on any construal, culture affects us in major ways. We are brought up in a culture, and its influence is extremely extensive. In the second place, cultures can be, often are, and more especially have historically been quite separate from each other. That is important, as we will shortly see—things have changed. And third, the morality of a group is generally taken to be a part of its culture. That is where social science comes into the picture. The emergence of cultural anthropology as a serious subject of study probably is the main single cause of moral relativism's being taken so seriously.

Whether the group to which morals is taken to be "relative" is culture or not, in fact, doesn't actually matter very much, as we will now see. Relativism has abstract problems just as such. So while, for purposes of convenient discourse, we will take it to be the moral view that one ought to be guided by the moral rules of one's society, whatever they are, in the end the whole idea will be found to be misguided, in a most funda-mental way.

An Ambiguity

There is a major source of ambiguity, or worse, to be on the lookout for here: what do we mean by 'one's society'? For starters, this can either be:

(1) the society in which one was brought up—the society from which one *came*, or

(2) the society that one is in fact among at a given time—say, as a tourist, or an international businessperson, a visiting anthropologist, a lost mariner, or an immigrant.

But these two are enough to generate conflict. The general theory says that I am to do what "my culture" says to do. Well, suppose I come from Arcania and I am currently in Zania, and suppose that the Arcanians tell me to do x, while the Zanians tell me to avoid it. Now what? Does our theory tell me to do as the Arcanians say or as the Zanians say? The problem is that I can't do both—they disagree. (In fact, that they do was a major stimulus to the whole idea.)

Note that it is now no use saying, "What the Arcanians teach is right for the Arcanians, what the Zanians teach is right for the Zanians." For our problem here is that we have an Arcanian in Zania-land, and the respective teachings seem to conflict. Which do I do? Saying that both are right, leaves us puzzled—it gives no guidance.

It is clear that the aspiring relativist is going to have to take a choice here, and not obvious which he should take. For after all, "cultures" are the sort of things that people are born into and raised in, and the idea that cultures are the basic source of our morals surely stems from that sort of fact. On the other hand, normative ethical relativism is "liberal"— its idea is that every culture is right, in some very fundamental sense. So when anthropologist Professor Fred visits culture C2, his professional shtick, as it were, bids him fall in with the local rules, however different they may be from those of Chicago, where he came from. Reflection on that leads to more basic questions. It is obvious that moral relativism has a crisis at the point described—which, after all, is going to be extremely frequent, when you think of it. And it's hard to see how the problem can be solved in any other way than by trying to decide which of the two conflicting cultures has *the better of it*. But moral relativism's idea is that a culture's mores are right *for that culture* just because it *is* that culture.

Why should we think that? Why suppose that the mores of a culture are right for that culture, anyway? If there's a useful answer to that question, the possibility then arises that in some cases, perhaps it has got it wrong—perhaps the rules it actually has could be improved for the purpose in question. Perhaps someone else has a better answer.

If we say that the rules of morals, ideally, are the *best* rules for a given cultural situation—including those situations in which people turn out to be involved in two or more cultures at once—then we will have departed fundamentally from the germinal idea of the theory. And that would be a useful thing to have seen.

The Basic Question

We are interested in moral relativism as a proposed answer to the philosophical question, What is it that makes an act fundamentally right? The proposed answer is: the fact that it is in accord with the moral rules of one's [some?] society. The question we now need to ask is: Why would this be the right place to turn? What's the point?

Metaethical relativism, in effect, argues that this is the "place to turn" because there *isn't any other place*. But since, as we see, there are many "places" and not just one, and these places can give different directions, that answer turns out to be useless. People have sometimes rebelled against their societies, thinking that some other view is better. They can't have thought that what their society says is right is in conflict with what is "really" right if 'right' means 'what my society says is right'! On this view, Jesus Christ's proposal, in the Sermon on the Mount, that instead of hitting back at those who hit us we should turn the other cheek, would be shown to be simple nonsense as soon as it is noted that the hit-back view is the prevailing one in that part of the world. I don't think Christ would have been impressed by that argument, and rightly so!

Note that metaethical relativism seems to be incompatible with normative ethical relativism. For this theory says that what anybody, anywhere, at any time, ought to do is whatever the local moral rules say to do. But that is, on the face of it, a universal theory, and therefore requires a nonvarying sense of such terms as 'ought' or 'right'.

Question: is the normative ethical relativist telling us that the local moral rules must be right? Why? Are the tribal elders infallible? That is not a very credible view, to put it mildly. But further reflection on it leads to a basic concern about relativism.

The Fatal Flaw in Moral Relativism

Can we imagine our society being wrong about something? If we can—if it is possible to raise the question whether one's own society has it right—whether what it tells us to do really is what one ought to do—then it would appear that we must be able to go deeper. The mere fact that our society disapproves of something is not, in itself, sufficient to show that it's wrong. But if some underlying consideration is what makes the society's rules the right rules—or, as might happen, the wrong rules—then relativism is evidently wrong as an account of what's fundamental in morals.

What would be the relativist's reason for thinking that we should always obey the local moral rules, no matter what they are? One possible idea would be that the village elders always know best. Not a plausible view! Or should we say that society has absolute authority in matters of morals? But why? Where would it have got it? We have dismissed the suggestion that it's a matter of superior knowledge on the part of society. What then?

We may also dismiss the suggestion that society *by definition* has this "authority." To say that x is right is not simply to say that x is in accordance with the local mores. What we need is an answer to a reasonable question: why should we take those mores to be authoritative? Why, that is, should the fact that society tells you not to do x be a sufficient reason why you shouldn't do it, as relativism seems to have it?

We are, in short, looking for a rational morality—a morality that does actually provide us with requirements which we have good reasons to accept.

Force and Reason

As in political and legal philosophy, we must distinguish between two interpretations of the view that society's word gives you reason to do something: (a) because they'll hit you if you don't, and (b) because society's word is a *good* word, somehow.

"Reasons" of type (a) are in their way good—compelling, anyway—but they don't count for this purpose. It's not just that might does not make right, though in a clear sense that is true. But rather, it's that such reasons are purely prudential reasons, not moral reasons: that is, they do give you some sort of reason in terms of your own interest for doing x, but they don't show that x is right. Now this reason wouldn't exist in a given case if the people with the muscle weren't threatening you. And our question is: *should* they be threatening you for this? We are supposing that there might be a good answer to this. If there's no good answer, then society is just bullying you, rather than answering you. A fight decides who wins: but, obviously, it doesn't decide who's right. And who's right is just what we want to know.

So we are left with a serious question: what is the underlying reason that makes society's rules right—if they are? Which social rules *deserve* to be enforced? The qualification 'if they are' turns out to be essential, for it now seems clear that society could be wrong. Not only could it conceivably be wrong, but it must be true, in a great range of situations where the individual is subject to conflict from rival social mores, that some society *is* wrong about something quite important for the individual caught in the dilemma.

Moral relativism, as a fully general theory of the most fundamental kind about morality, must be wrong. That is very far from saying that there is nothing to it at all. There is room for a principle of going along with one's society on various matters, as we will later see. What there is not room for is relativism as an answer to the question, What, at bottom, makes something right?

Egoism

Our question here concerns the foundations of morality. We will investigate this, first by looking at some instructive failures. By far the most important of these is egoism. As a first approximation, let's say that egoism is, roughly speaking, the view that, for each individual person, it is *that person* who is the basic source of whatever truths there are about ethics. I said "roughly speaking" on purpose: refining and being more precise about the idea are utterly essential if we are to have any luck dealing with it. For indeed, the idea as I have just stated it can reasonably be taken to be not only true, but necessarily true. But the view we are especially concerned with here is another matter. That is the view that the individual's interests are to be taken, just by themselves, as a sufficient criterion of moral rightness. To investigate egoism further, we will need to begin by making some important distinctions. The first is the distinction between *psychological* and *ethical* egoism. On the face of it, these look very different.

Psychological versus Ethical Egoism

Psychological Egoism is the theory that an individual always does whatever maximizes the satisfaction of that individual's self-interest, no matter what happens to others; that is, that one's actions are determined by self-interest alone. The *ethical* version of egoism, by at least apparent contrast, says that we *ought* to act in the way that the psychological version says that we *do* act: that each person *should* act so as to maximize his self-interest, paying no fundamental attention to anyone else. We must start with the psychological version. For those who accept any ethical version often do so because they think that they have no choice: this is just the way people are, and therefore the only theory about what they should do that makes any sense.

Let us see.

Butler's Distinction: Formal versus Substantive Egoism

The eighteeth-century British philosopher Joseph Butler made a crucial distinction concerning egoism: between the theory that we ought always to act on interests *in* ourselves, and the theory that we ought always to act on interests *of* ourselves.[1] It's interesting how much can hang on one tiny, two-letter word! The second view, he saw, was obviously necessary. Whenever we act, we must act on our own reasons. These have to be things in *our* heads, as it were. I can't act on your motives; you can't act on mine. By contrast, the first is "real" psychological egoism: it holds that although it is logically possible for people to act in a non-self-interested way, it is psychologically impossible for them to do so. We are "wired" to act exclusively in a self-interested manner.

Assessing Substantive Egoism

Is "real" psychological egoism true? Clearly it doesn't seem to be. All of us know people who do a great deal for others without thought of reward, who make great sacrifices for them, and so on. Surely these people are not acting out of pure "self-interest"?

Careful reflection on such phenomena shows us the need to make a still further distinction: "deep" or "ultimate" egoism versus "shallow" or "everyday" psychological egoism—what we may also call "phenomenal" egoism—the sort of egoism that can be tested by ordinary observation. And as such, it is wildly implausible. The world is full of people who act for the sake of others, who even sacrifice their lives for them. Perfectly ordinary people exemplify this daily: mothers, for instance, not only frequently but almost continually act so as to promote what they see to be the well-being of their children, always at considerable cost and sometimes at very great cost to themselves. Surely it is odd, perhaps even crazy or meaningless, to call these people 'self-interested'?

Perhaps it is. But such phenomena do not refute the "deep" version of this theory. According to the deep version, there is some state of ourselves that we aim to maximize when we act. However, this is such a "deep" one that we can't find it in ourselves just by looking. Perhaps there is a "pleasure center" in the brain, say, that controls all that we do. How would *we* know? As a wag used to say, "we just work here!"—'Here'

---

[1] Joseph Butler, *Sermons in the Rolls Chapel,* esp. Sermon xi. I cite the edition published by the London Tract Society, 1858. A more familiar source is *British Moralists,* ed. L. A. Selby-Bigge (Indianapolis: Bobbs-Merrill, 1964), 356–59.

being, in the lived, phenomenal world where things appear to be happening that we can take in from our limited, here-and-now situations.

The "Deep" Theory: Too Deep

But is the deep theory of any interest? For moral purposes, I think, no. For it is, like the purely formal theory identified by Butler, compatible with any overt behavior whatever. No matter how charitable, kind, or selfless someone may be so far as day-to-day observation goes, it may still turn out that somehow, deep down inside, he's acting "selfishly."— Well, so what? Since the deep theory doesn't predict that we will act in any observable way in particular, it doesn't matter whether it's true or not. It does matter that people are nasty or nice. If there is some level at which both are acting the same, that cancels out. It is the differences that count. It matters to us what people do—whether their actions tend toward our benefit or our harm, especially. It does not matter whether in some ultimate way all of them act from the same fundamental motive, beyond the perception of the rest of us. (Or at least, it does not matter unless the scientists who figure out what this ultimate thing is also find ways to turn it to good use for us all.)

Self-Interest and Rationality

Still another version of what started out as "egoism" is the theory that the only *rational* thing to do is to fulfill self-interest. Is this theory right?

First, we should notice that someone proposing this might be proposing a theory about how to live, what to do—a sort of evaluative theory, rather than an explanatory one. But a theory of rationality isn't that. It is, instead, a theory about practical reasoning. What it says is that we should "maximize our utility." But what does that mean? The answer is provided by the "formal" theory identified by Butler. That theory says that when we act, our action is rational if it is intended to bring about the maximum of what we want—whatever that is.

Decision theorists in recent years have operated with a notion of *utility*—that which is "useful" for the individual. The classical utilitarians supposed that there is some psychological "quantity" that we aim to maximize when we act. In Bentham's view it was pleasure. But we don't need to suppose that. All we need to suppose is that I, as a person, have some interests or desires, whatever they may be, and that when I act, I am trying to promote these as well as I can. Rational action demands that I have ends that can be identified, and that I organize my actions so as to promote them coherently—but that's all. It does not follow and is often not true that those ends exclusively concern certain states of myself that are identifiable independently of anyone else.

Take playing tennis for example. Someone might be happy bouncing tennis balls off brick walls, say; but for every one of those, there are hundreds who enjoy playing tennis, that is to say, hitting those balls across a net on the other side of which is another person hitting them back, and what's more, trying to hit them back in such a way that the opponent can't return them, within the identified limits of the court. And for every one who would try to gain points by cheating there are dozens who would not, insisting instead on playing by the rules. Rationality simply is not adequately characterizable in terms of self-interest in any but the vacuous sense identified by Butler.

Selfishness Is Bad for You

No version of this theory need recommend selfishness or reclusiveness. Most of us are very social beings: we like to do things with our friends and loved ones, we read the newspaper out of interest and sympathy at the lot of strangers around the world, and so on. And consider how you deal with your friends. What kind of a friend would be always trying to pull the wool over his "friend's" eyes, making as much money as possible from him, and in general treating him strictly as a sort of chump? How absurd!

One who has such attitudes suffers from a vice, the vice of selfishness. (There's a book by Ayn Rand entitled *The Virtue of Selfishness*. The title sounds odd, but we soon find that she's not really talking about what is normally called selfishness at all.[2]) This isn't a matter of moral rules, though moral rules will also come down against selfish actions. But here we speak of self-interest, a different thing. And the point is that it is in your interest, in all likelihood, not to be selfish. On the contrary, it is in your interest to be generous, helpful, kindly, cheerful, and supportive, especially to certain selected people, such as your friends, lovers, children, or associates. That's just the way we—or most of us, anyway—are. Given that, selfishness is indeed a vice. Taken very far, it can also lead to immoral actions.

Consider Bentham's view, that maximum net pleasure is the aim of all our action.[3] But if pleasure is thought to be the aim of all our actions,

---

[2] Ayn Rand, *The Virtue of Selfishness* (New York: Signet Books, 1964). See for example pp. 23–24.

[3] Jeremy Bentham, *Pinciples of Morals and Legislation*, ch. 4, "Of the Value of a Lot of Pleasure or Pain, How Measured," in any of the many editions.

what is "pleasure"? Contemporary philosophers have generally agreed that if we take the term at all strictly, the theory is much too narrow. To see why, consider its opposite, pain. When the dentist hits your tooth's nerve with his drill, or if someone jabs you with an ice pick, and you've had no painkiller, what you feel is pain, for sure. But what about when the dentist stuffs a pencil-shaped wad of dry cotton behind your teeth. Is that sensation *pain?* Or is it something else? It surely is *uncomfortable.* But it's not at all the same thing as pain in the narrow sense just noted. Similarly with pleasure. You can get a fairly definite sensation of pleasure, perhaps, from a nice drink when you're quite thirsty, or when your lover rubs you the right way. But you don't get any such things when you read a good book, have an interesting conversation or, likely, when you are out for a pleasant walk. None of this proves that there isn't something in one's mind which one is always aiming at whenever one does anything. But it does prove that it's no easy matter saying what this is. Maybe Moore was right after all—maybe "satisfaction" or "utility" is an irreducible, indefinable mysterious entity in the mind. Or, better, maybe it's something we all recognize and find obvious. A recent author suggests the term 'enjoyment' for this purpose.[4] I think we should accept that.

Moral *Egoism*

Now turn, for a moment, to moral egoism, the view that what we ought to do, what is one's moral duty to do, is to promote one's own maximum interest no matter what happens to others. *A morality,* we recall, is *a set of rules that everyone is to live by, and everyone is to encourage everyone to live by.* Moral egoism (of the "substantive," or "real" type) means that what we will bring up our children to do, what we will praise and encourage in each other, what we will condemn people for not doing, is the promotion, *by any means whatever,* of the agent's self-interest, no matter what that may be. So suppose it is in A's interest to kill B. And suppose that A and B both live in a community governed by moral egoism. What is B supposed to tell A to do? What is he to approve of A's doing? Evidently B is supposed to approve of A's murdering B, since, after all, that is the action of A's that is maximally in A's interest. If so, then what is B likely to think of the "morality" in question? If rationality is anything like egoism as a theory of rationality, then the obvious answer is: not much! Indeed, moral egoism would be irrational for B in this case.[5]

---

[4] Roger Crisp, *Reasons and The Good* (New York: Oxford Univ. Press, 2006), 103–11.

[5] A classic paper about egoism is the one by Brian Medlin, "Ultimate Principles and

On the other hand, perhaps moral egoism says that B should disapprove of A's proposed action. For after all, that action is not in the best interests of B. And so the action of approving of A's action would also seem not to be in the best interest of B. At least, if B's approval or disapproval had any influence, then B obviously ought to utilize it in the way most conducive to B's interests, not A's. Perhaps that's what egoism says—"Approve only of what is in your best interest to approve." Yet the action—killing B—is, we suppose, in A's best interest. And there's the problem. When interests conflict, it is not possible for each party to come out best; and yet egoism says to approve, of the actions which make "the" agent come out best. But this is impossible, if 'the agent' is any agent, in other words, both agents, and their interests are in conflict. Somehow, a procedure is needed that can tell us which is right. Egoism as it stands can't do that. In short, moral egoism seems to be an absurd theory if it's to be taken as a theory of morality.

As with relativism, this is by no means to say that there's something altogether wrong with self-interest—an idea that has been very much too popular, though understandably so, in the history of this subject. It is to say, rather, that we have work cut out for us, to try to find the right general idea for the needed scheme of interpersonal rules. Self-interest will play a major role in that scheme, yes. But not the only one.

Before continuing in the direction of what I take to be the right moral theory, for the sake of completeness, let's look, at a few others.

Virtue

One way to do morals is to figure out what is the *right way to live*, and then get the resources of society behind the goal of getting everybody to live that way. Philosophers taking this option expound it, generally, in terms of virtues. A virtue, as they analyze it, is a quality that enables a thing to perform its function well. The moral and various other sorts of virtues are what make us function well. And in the case of *moral* virtue in particular, that's what enables us to *act* well, action being generally the province of moral theory. The general idea, then, is that we are all to be as virtuous as possible.

There is no real need to think of virtue theory as an "option," the alternative being to embrace what looks more like moral rules. We can

Ethical Egoism, " in *Australasian Journal of Philosophy* 35 (1957): 111–18. Reprinted in *20th Century Ethical Theory*, ed. Steven M. Cahn and Joram G. Haber (Englewood Cliffs, NJ: Prentice-Hall, 1995), 316–21.

and do have both sets of terminology in use, and both have their uses. But virtue theorists tend to claim that virtue is the more basic of these notions. Is that possible? Virtue, as we have just seen, is a state of character, for one thing. And for another, a virtue is a disposition to act in certain ways. It is not clear that this is "another thing," really: perhaps virtues are nothing more nor less than dispositions to act. If they are something else, then there is a general problem with virtue theory so far as morals is concerned: namely, that it looks very much as though I simply don't have any business going on about the inner nature of your soul. On the other hand, I do have a very real and obvious interest in how you act, for that is what affects me.

Moreover, if virtues are indeed essentially dispositions to act, then it is hard to see how virtues can be evaluated independently of the actions to which they give rise. My actions of taking walks and eating right, and so on are virtuous because they make me feel and perform better. It's not the other way around: that I should feel better in order to be virtuous. And turning to the moral virtues: how could honesty be a virtue if living up to one's agreements weren't independently virtuous?

Virtue theory as characterized here looks "paternalistic": the idea is that society and/or perhaps the state knows what its "children" should do and the job is simply to get them to do it—no back talk, please! Is this objectionable? Yes—especially for anyone whose view of how to live differs from the official version. If we aren't enamored of that version, we may object to having people make us conform to it. How objectionable it is will be a function of how much it collides with our preferred view.

The famous view of the ancient Greek philosophers Plato and Aristotle goes roughly as follows: humans are composed of three "parts" (rational faculty, emotions or "passions," and appetites). The main subject of moral virtue was the second part, the passions, and the proposed principle is to get us into such a condition that we tend to control our emotions to the right degree.

And what is that right degree? There is claimed to be a sort of midpoint or "mean" that we should strive to observe, and Aristotle had a lot of fairly specific-sounding advice about where it lies. The point to emphasize is that this "mean" was supposed to be *objectively* determinable. It wasn't a matter of what you happened to like or want. But what does this mean? And how would you demonstrate that the mean is here rather than there? For that matter, how would you show somebody that going for one of the "extremes" wasn't the best thing after all?

And that's where the theory runs out of gas. On the one hand, Aristotle tends to define the mean as "neither too little nor too much." Since 'too much' and 'too little' are themselves normative terms presupposing that the right amount has already been, at least approximately, identified, this specification of the mean is simply useless for theoretical purposes. On the other hand, Aristotle was clear that an "arithmetical" mean—supposing we could even make sense of the idea that we can feel, say, 50 percent of our total possible supply of anger—was crazy, as it obviously is. Indeed, he also noted that the right amount had to do with circumstances, persons, situations, and other variables. So his account doesn't get us very far, other than to say, what is after all both true and important, that the concepts of too much and too little are almost always applicable in practical matters. However, Aristotle does not explain what makes them so. One way to explain it would be to propose that too little is when more would make you happier, too much when less would do so. But that brings in happiness as an independent variable, rather than as simply the condition in which one is acting maximally virtuously. Virtue theory was supposed to explain happiness rather than presuppose it.[6]

In any case, we now re-remind ourselves that we're looking here for an *interpersonal* rule, one that applies to everyone, not just Selma Smith or Jack Brown. We may be sure that the relevant "means" for those two will lie in different places. But morality is supposed to tell them both the same thing, somehow. Telling them to seek that mean has two short-comings, in addition to the one just cited.

To see what these are, remember that our basic question here is, What is the *social* status of theories of that sort—theories about how to have a "good soul"? Here are two ideas about that:

(1) One idea is that a reasonable person will see that these matters are important and will thus be motivated to develop appropriate behavioral responses to her or his emotional needs and so on, by herself. It's up to the individual, even though it's up to that individual's "faculty of reason," rather than just being totally without controls. Still, it's individual, it's bound to be variable, and that creates a serious problem for those who would impose social guidelines.

(2) The other is that it is the business of society in general to *impose* norms along these lines. Consider, as an analogue, how much you should weigh. This is a matter of considerable concern to lots of people nowadays. There are health aspects to it—you can be so thin, or so fat, that you get sick. Then there are aesthetic aspects: many people want to look good and have ideals of beauty to which they would like to conform. But do we think that our society may get together and force us to lose or gain

---

[6] Virtue theory has had a recrudescence of popularity in recent decades. See especially Philippa Foot, *Virtues and Vices* (Berkely: Univ. of California Press, 1978) and her later work, *Natural Goodness* (Oxford: Oxford Univ. Press, 2003). Another interesting contribution is Rosalind Hursthouse, *On Virtue Ethics* (Oxford: Oxford Univ. Press, 1999).

weight for any of these reasons? No—even though some people act as though they do.

So, which is it to be? Well, if the question of how irascible or how generous we should be is like the question about weight, surely it too should not be thought to be proper material for the publicly promoted rules of morals. And on Aristotle's view, it is hard to see how they could be anything but that. Yet surely we don't think that whether murder is to be permitted is on the same plane as whether we should wear our hair long or short, or wear green shoes. Virtue theory either doesn't account for, or misleadingly and circularly "accounts for" the crucial dimension of interpersonal validity. It either comes on as high-handedly paternalistic, or it leaves us with the uncomfortable possibility that some very evil but extremely virtuous persons might be what we should all be emulating.

Many people are still under the impression that religion and morality are closely connected—so close as to be really just about the same thing. This now qualifies, in most contemporary philosophers' judgments, as one of the exploded views about our subject, but it is still useful to consider it, both because it is still influential and because several other moral theories, as we will see, share its errors.

Religious Ethics

The sort of religious ethics we will look at here is *theological* ethics, that is, the view that ethics has some fundamental connection with the idea of God (or gods? For reasons brilliantly explained by Plato,[7] we won't bother with polytheism here. Also, we also won't consider nontheistic religion, if such there be.) The theory we are considering—call it the "God Theory" may be expressed thus:

Act x is right = x is *commanded by God*

(Two notes. First, remember that we are not here directly concerned with nontheistic religions. And second, the word 'command' needn't be taken very strictly. All we need is that some act or attitude of the deity's is what determines the rightness of actions on our part.)

---

[7] Plato, *Euthyphro*. There are countless editions of this classic dialogue, and it is available on the web as well. The main problem with the religious theory, which we are about to identify, has indeed come to be called "the Euthyphro problem." Plato's brilliant little piece is one of the history of philosophy's definitive demolitions of an influential idea.

The question now is: why should we accept such a thing? Suppose an ordinary person claims that being right is a matter of being in accordance with *his* commands: "Act x is right if and only if act x is commanded by Elwood P. Jones." Call this the "Jones Theory" (JT, for short). Mr. Jones, we will suppose, resides at 237 Slippery Rock Road, Muddsdale, Ontario. Phone him up, he'll tell you what's right and wrong! We all find this obviously ridiculous, including, very likely, Mr. Jones himself. After all, Jones is nobody special, we think (and he agrees.) What's he got that *you* haven't got? What possible reason could there be for always obeying Jones?

In the case of God, however, the situation is supposed to be different. There are two central features associated with the idea of God that might be (and invariably are) thought to figure importantly in morality. They are (1) supreme power, and (2) supreme goodness. Let's consider each carefully.

(1) Supreme power, taken by itself, doesn't look too promising. After all, there can be very powerful people who are very evil. Indeed, many religions conceive of a devil figure, "Satan," who is extremely powerful yet perfectly evil instead of good. And just consider what an extremely powerful person could do. Suppose he says that murder is just fine, contrary to what you may have been told; or that the most important of all moral duties is to paint your third left fingernail blue; or that you must lick the boots of all persons of Abyssinian descent; or . . . Surely it is silly to think that such things become *right* just because a very powerful person tells you to do them? We'll talk about obeying the law below—a special case of this same general idea. Meanwhile, it seems clear that power by itself isn't the right thing for this job.

One might try a variant of the "power" idea, though. A supremely powerful being would also have to be supremely intelligent and to know everything (if you don't know everything, there will be things you can't do because you don't have the needed information; so you won't be able to be omnipotent. Thus, omnipotence entails omniscience.) The following, which we may call the Omniscience Theory (OT)might be thought obvious:

OT = If someone who knows *everything* tells you to do x, then x is right.

Why would this be so? First, let's divide all knowledge into two sorts: (a) knowledge of right and wrong, and (b) knowledge of everything else. Suppose our Omniscient Person (OP) only fulfills (b). But then he might be a mad scientist or some other sort of crazy, all ready to use his incredible knowledge for horrible or bizarre ends.

Even if our OP fulfills (a) and not just (b), is it plausible to suppose that OT is true? Not quite: for after all, Satan knows what's right and wrong—only he's against what's right, and in favor of what's wrong—oops! So—just *knowing* what's right and wrong may not be enough.[8] (Our discussion of metaethics included the plausibility of the view that it doesn't really make sense to claim to "know" what is right and yet be *against* it. Yet we all recognize that there is some sense in which we can somehow do that. We'll leave further discussion about that to later sections, where it will become acutely important.)

(2) But there is a still more fundamental difficulty, as we will now see when we look at the other version of the God Theory. Consider, then, the other major property of God: perfect goodness. This needs to be *moral* goodness. We can't depend on the commands of, for example, a perfect basket-maker or—worse yet—a perfect assassin to tell us what's right and wrong. Only a perfectly moral person could do that reliably. If the morally perfect individual is also omniscient (is an 'OPP'—Omnipotent and Perfect Person[9]), as God is supposed to be, then indeed we could be quite certain that whatever *he* says is right *is* right:

x is right if and only if an OPP *says* that x is right.

(Or, x is right if and only if an OPP says to do x—pretty close, anyway, since certainly such a person could never tell you to do what you oughtn't to do. . . . Could he?)

Now a crucial problem arises. For if we have to know what constitutes moral perfection *before* we can know what God is like, then we have to be able to know what's right and wrong independently of the existence of God. What's right and wrong, therefore, does *not* depend for its *truth* on the existence of God. That is a lethal result for religious ethics, *if* it is proposed as an account of the *fundamental* idea of morals. But that is exactly what we are here concerned with. That many people derive, as they suppose, moral instruction, solace, and the like from their religions is not here in question.

One thing definitely is in question, though. Many people think that God is needed to *enforce* morality. That remains a logically possible option, in a sense. But it raises plenty of problems for the religious person, for if an omnipotent person is supposed to be enforcing the rules, then one would think that everybody would always be obeying them. If

---

[8] The ancient Greek philosopher Socrates seems to have thought it was, but we can't go into that here.

[9] Any resemblance to a certain corps of law enforcers in my home province of Ontario is purely coincidental.

they aren't, it suggests that the OPP hasn't done a very good job of enforcement, and that seems puzzling in the case of a supposedly omnipotent as well as omniscient being—unlike, say, the case of the other OPP, the Ontario Provincial Police, who, due to limited budget, limited information, and limited authority (among other things) don't always do it right. Nor can it be true, surely, that what makes something wrong is that someone *will* hit you if you don't do it. There is a general sense that moralities like that are primitive and barbaric. We have that sense because they *are* primitive and barbaric.

The long and short of this is that evidently moral knowledge cannot in any interestingly fundamental sense come from God. God could cause us all to be the way we are, but still, it is evidently something like the way we are that we have to appeal to in order to find out what's right and wrong, rather than what, if anything, *caused* us to be that way.[10]

Authority Theories in General

The God theory has something in common with several other theories. These theories may be called "authoritarian": they claim that morality consists in obeying the commands, or conforming to the will, or what is called for by the plans, of some allegedly supreme authority. Nontheological versions of the authority theory might make, for example, the dictator or the government this supreme authority. What's wrong with all of these views is the same: we would need some independent guarantee that the authority is telling us what is indeed the right thing to do. The sheer fact that he *says* it isn't good enough. We need to be sure that his credentials, so to speak, are right: that given what we know about what is right and wrong, we can expect this person or committee or whatever to give us reliable directions. Which means that we must already know what is right and wrong before we could turn to the authority for an answer.

Among such views, clearly the theological one is, in one important respect, the strongest: God, after all, is supposed to be an all-powerful and perfect being. No earthly dictator or committee can match up to that specification. On the other hand, earthly dictators may obviously really exist, whereas the existence of God, either in general or of any particular sort, is bound to be highly, and insolubly, debatable.

---

[10] This was a large advantage of the view of St. Thomas Aquinas, who has God creating the world, but then has the nature of the world being responsible for morality—"Natural Law" theory. His instincts were sound on this matter.

A contender for the strongest secular version of such a theory would be the theory that what society tells us to do is right. For this purpose "society" would have to be derelativized, else the theory will succumb to the problems we saw in moral relativism. Even if this is done, we would next have to distinguish between what society says and the *reason* it says it. This reason might, for instance, be that the practice in question was for (an appropriate version of) the Common Good. Then the point can be clarified. The sense of 'what society *says*' is something like, when individual people condemn, or punish, or reward or praise something, and do so reacting as members of society. But anybody could get such a thing wrong. Maybe the practice in question would *not*, after all, be for the common good of society in the long run?

Insofar as an "authority" is someone or some agency or group able to "lay down the law," its credentials lie in its being somehow in close relation or access to the underlying consideration, whatever it is, that makes what is right right. When that is so, the question is whether the presumed authority is doing its job properly. Thus, Professor Jones, the authority on snails, is an authority because he knows a lot about snails. But obviously Jones doesn't *create* or *lay down* the facts about snails: rather, she goes out and finds out what's what with those creatures. The facts are prior to Professor Jones. Similarly, any moral authority is so only because, for some reason that the theory has to explain, the authority in question is peculiarly well situated to know what's right and wrong. But its rightness and wrongess is logically prior to and independent of the existence of that authority. With the theological version, that in principle is supposed to be no problem. The fact that there are thousands of different, irreconcilable, and uncomfirmable views about the supposed deity in question, not to mention that many of us are pretty sure there is no such thing anyway, present further unvaultable hurdles to the view. Meanwhile, the point is that we are looking for *the* foundations of morals, and our conclusion about all authority theories, from top to bottom, is that they are in vain for that purpose.

Theological Ethics—A Major Practical Problem

No theological view can be publicly proven in the sense that knowledge about chemistry can. Many may claim that it can, but they do not expect the same result as in the case of a real problem about chemistry. Obviously there is an enormous variety in people's religious views, and there is no way that A can expect B to accept A's view as to which if any of the different faiths is right. If morality *depended* on religion, then, it would necessarily mean that every different religion is going to have a different morality; and since religious differences cannot be resolved by rational methods, it would follow that their moral differences can't either. That's going to lead to real problems—and has. Conflicts such as the Thirty Years' War, which devastated northern Europe, and all the many, many other religious wars there have been, as well as ongoing strife in today's Middle East, illustrate the point well enough. And that is an intolerable situation for a set of principles that is supposed to apply to *everyone,* and to *publicly direct* their behavior. If a set of principles is going to do that, it's going to have to apply to people *regardless* of their religion *or lack of one.*

Thus the idea of having this rule depend on things that vary from person to person or group to group is ruled out from the start. A morality for everyone—as may be pretty obvious already—is going to have to opt for a right of religious freedom. Obviously that is not an idea that presupposes the truth of some one religion among the many; or of atheism either.

Authority theories, then, including the most extreme one—the religious theory—simply won't do. The foundations of morals must lie elsewhere.

Conscience

The Conscience Theory is the view that people ought to do what their consciences tell them to do. It says that it is right for A to do x *if and only if* A's conscience tells A to do x.[11] This theory will clearly have difficulties analogous to those of the God Theory. Will conscience be understood just as a sort of "black box," about whose operations and principles we have no idea? If so, absolutely anything could conceivably be recommended by conscience. Yet can just anything *be* right? And should there not be reasons why something is right, when it is? If so, the "black box" conception of conscience would render it in principle incapable of supplying them. Conscience Theory, on that understanding of it, would be akin to idol worship.

On the other hand, if we take 'conscience' to be simply a name for *one's moral sense,* then it will be quite unsurprising that any given person will think that he should do what his conscience tells him. For on this understanding of what conscience is—and it's a lot more plausible than the "black box" view—a person's conscience will simply be *what she*

---

[11] A historically main source among philosophers of the Conscience Theory is Joseph Butler. See Sermon iii, of *Sermons in the Rolls Chapel,* cited above in n. 74.

thinks is right. But then, it will also be obvious that a person might be wrong in thinking that something is right. The sheer fact that we sometimes change our minds is evidence for this: how can I change my mind about something that I can't possibly be wrong about? And the fact that others sometimes disagree is further evidence: obviously, if we really disagree, then we can't both be right. To disagree is to attach opposite truth values to some sentence: it is for one party to affirm that something the other says isn't so. There's no problem in two people having mutually incompatible views in this sense, but there is definitely a problem in supposing that they are both *right*.

Like the God Theory, and authority theories generally, if we were to accept that people may do whatever their consciences tell them, then we are going to be in a pickle whenever their respective consciences give contrary results. If A's conscience says that abortion is wrong, and B's says it is right, then how is C going to go about fulfilling the ethical requirement to let people do whatever their consciences tell them? For Alice, in thinking that abortion is wrong, is thereby thinking that nobody should be allowed to have one, whereas Bertha, in thinking it right, is thereby thinking that everybody should be allowed to have one. If Constance is thinking of having an abortion, do we now say that she *may* have one, in view of Bertha's conscience? Or that she may not have one, in view of Alice's conscience? And again, if Mr. Heydrich's conscience tells him to go forth and slay all Jews, do we then allow him to proceed? Or do we instead forbid him on the ground that Mr. Goldschmidt, among other Jews, thinks otherwise? In short, the idea that morality can be helpfully explained in terms of conscience is a losing proposition.

There is room for misunderstanding here. In a spirit of ethical liberalism, for example, we might propose that a person, whoever he or she is, should be permitted to do whatever *that person's* conscience tells that person to do. Note that if we say this, it can hardly be that the reason why we should permit this is that *our* conscience tells us to. And secondly, that kind of liberalism, in the case of the abortion controversy, actually endorses precisely the view that the "liberal" side supports—that people should be allowed to have an abortion or not, as they choose. Obviously the "conservative" side which denies precisely that isn't going to be very happy with this "compromise"! And finally, as usual, we come up against the dedicated conscientious Nazi. Do we seriously want to say he should be allowed to do whatever he wants—incincerate Jews, say— just because *his* conscience tells him to?

Again, I remind the reader, to dismiss the idea for this purpose is very far from dismissing either the phenomenon in general, or its real utility. Beyond doubt, a very significant aspect of morality is conscientious behavior: behavior by people who are trying to do the right thing, even if they can't quite explain why it is right. We don't want to "knock" that. But we very definitely do want to knock the idea that conscience is the bottom line in ethical theory. It very clearly cannot be.

Convention

In effect, any very thoroughgoing espousal of relativism is probably based on conventionalism: the view that what is right is determined by conventions. It is the essence of a convention that it organizes lots of people's behavior by a subtle process of social reinforcement. Every society has a large variety of rules and conventions, explicit or (more often) implicit: what one wears, what one eats, where one goes when, and any number of other things are strongly influenced by the "way things are done here." It could hardly be otherwise, and even if it could we mostly wouldn't want it otherwise. The efficiency of life is much promoted by conventions.

The question before us, however, is whether conventions are the definitive, final word on what to do. Does it follow from the fact that there is a convention in my society that when in circumstances C, one is to do x, that if I am in C, then the *right* thing for me to do is x? Certainly not. The "unconventional" person may not be immoral.

What if it is a *moral* convention, though? On the account of morality I have given at the beginning, it is not so very easy to pick out a precise subset of all the conventions there are as being the moral conventions. A principal criterion here is that of just what kind and degree of reinforcement is applied. Do people stare in horror when you do x? Do they reach for their spears? Or do they just smile amusedly or wink, or giggle? All of these reinforce to some degree, but to different degrees and in different ways. We are especially interested, for reasons that will emerge very clearly as we go on, in those reinforcement activities which consist in making it very difficult or impossible for you to do what you wanted to do: execution and imprisonment are among them, but just imposing a stiff fine will be plenty off-putting. So will everyone's brushing you off on the street; but we won't try here to refine the matter farther. What we do need to ask, though, is whether we can have good reasons for objecting to the reinforcement of some kinds of activities: whether, then, conventions can possibly be improved or not—subjected to some sort of reasonable criticism. Part of the hope of philosophers down through the centuries has been to show that it can—that we needn't simply accept conventions as they are, but can sometimes find good reason for rejecting them, or altering them, or in many other cases no doubt, for sustaining them as they are.

Let us formulate a view about conventions that makes the appropriate contrast. The philosopher of the type I have in mind here holds, in effect, this: that we should obey a given convention, C, when C is a *reasonable* convention. And we can then issue a challenge to the Conventionalist: does he wish to state that conventions *cannot* be unreasonable? Or does he wish to hold that if there is a convention requiring that we do x, then that, in and of itself, is sufficient reason for doing x, no matter what x may be? If not, then it will be difficult to reject the proposal that the reasonableness of conventions is a real subject. Just how to nail down the idea of a reasonable convention is another matter. We will be working on that later.

The reason we should take convention quite seriously can be stated in what are now called "game-theoretic" terms. The paradigm of convention for game theory is the situation in which there is a sort of activity such that

(a) everyone will benefit from everyone's doing it the same way, and
(b) there are alternative ways of doing it any of which would produce that benefit; but
(c) there is really nothing to choose between one of these ways and any other.

This gives rise to what is called a "coordination dilemma." There is, due to (c) no reason for anyone to do it one way rather than one of the other possible ways, yet, by (a) there is much reason for all doing it in one of those ways. We then have a problem: which among the different ways of doing it, all of which would be equally desirable if we all do it that way, will we actually choose? How do we solve the problem?

One way, indeed, is to have a leader who just tells us which way to go. The traffic officer at the corner provides a pretty good example. It doesn't matter so much which people he tells to go which way: what matters is that we all follow directions so that we avoid bumping into each other and get where we want to go efficiently. Then there is the classic example of the rule of the road: if we all keep left, that's fine; if we all keep right, that's fine too. But if some go left and others right on two-lane roads with traffic going both ways, that sets us up for disaster. Having an authority tell us which side to take is one way to solve the problem. However, another very good way is simply to follow the established pattern, whatever it is, and regardless of why in particular people began doing it that way. Another way, however, applies in lots of real-world cases. In these cases, the problem has somehow been solved in the indefinite past when people simply fell into a particular pattern. Now along comes you, a newcomer—a tourist, perhaps—and what are you to do? The plausible answer is: do the done thing. There is, by (c) no point in doing anything else anyway, but by (a) a great deal to be lost by not doing it.

Convention should prevail whenever the situation really is a coordination situation. But many are not. Sometimes one way is better; but sometimes it is not true that we all do better if we all do it the same way—quite the reverse may easily be the case. (Composers and authors should write *new* works, not just rewrite the same old ones, for instance.) And so on. Much more will emerge along this line later. Meanwhile, the nature and limitations of "conventionalism" are reasonably clear from these considerations.

Legalism: Law and Morals

Still another theory of the authoritarian type is legalism, the view that x is right if and only if x is legal. Is this a plausible view? Given what I have already said, it will be obvious that a negative answer is in the offing. Let's see why.

We must first clarify the notion of law—and again, note the potential for confusion here. I will do this by contrasting law and morality. Every society has a set of moral standards—a "morality." And almost every society has laws. Both direct us to do certain things and avoid others. What's the difference? There are several. Laws are

(1) written down, definitely (in principle). When there are disputes about just what the law is, we have

(2) an official judiciary whose business it is to settle these disputes. Judges are to settle the disputes definitely. The rejected views are ruled out, the accepted views become part of the law itself.

(3) There is an officially appointed, state-sponsored enforcement procedure: the police, and so on.

(4) Perhaps most important, laws can be made, and unmade, by legislatures (or absolute dictators, or whatever the government has available for the purpose). The legislative body goes through a certain procedure, and out comes law. The question whether what comes out of the procedure, providing it has been properly gone through, really is law does not arise: for purposes of this theory, the procedure *defines* the law for that jurisdiction.

Morality, however, has none of those features.

(1) People can try to write textbooks on ethics, or draw up lists of "The Ten Commandments," but it would always be open to question whether these lists are the *right* ones. Someone else might have a different view. There is no document you can point to to settle these ques-

tions: any such document would simply raise those same questions. What are needed here are good analyses and arguments, not lists.

(2) There can't be a "moral judiciary." We can go to people we respect for their advice and opinions, but there is nobody whose opinion is official and definitive—nobody who is such that, if he (or she) says that x is the right thing to do, then x jolly well *is* the right thing to do. Invoking supposed transcendental authorities, such as gods, is of no use whatever, as we have seen.

(3) There is no special agency whose special business it is to "enforce the moral law." But practically everybody expresses approval or disapproval of other people's (and their own) actions from time to time. Some of them are even accepted, perhaps by quite a few people, as their moral mentors and as having the authority to do this. But others, equally human, equally mature and rational, would deny this. (Think of the Pope, for instance. Or the Chairman of the Supreme Soviet. Or the Queen; or a columnist in the newspaper. Or a role model—Angelina Jolie, perhaps?)

(4) Nobody can lay down the moral law—go through a procedure (writing the proposed "law" in stone, for instance, and having somebody carry it down a mountainside for dramatic effect) such that what comes out of it is, by definition, necessarily and unquestionably the Moral Law.

Morality just isn't like that. Morality is an informal institution. It has no particular origin—like Topsy, it "just grows." And it is indefinite, constantly open to criticism and revision, from any and all quarters.

Morality just isn't like legislated law. It is much more like the common law, and more accurately still, like the set of customs to which tort law appeals. That kind of law, like morality, has no particular origin—like Topsy, it "just grows," though the civil law grows from an accumulation of decisions, whereas a society's morality grows generally from social life. And it is indefinite, constantly open to criticism and revision, from any and all quarters. Some students of law hold that the proper model for law is the customary-based law that antedates what is now called the common law, and is thus not only more like, but really of a piece and continuous with, morality as I have just described it. Most of us, as one such student, Professor John Hasnas, points out—all of us in British Commonwealth/American-derived countries—"live under an extremely sophisticated and subtle scheme of rules, very few of which were created by government. Since almost none of the rules that bring peace and order to our existence were created by government, little argument should be required to establish that government is not necessary to create such rules."[12] Since my point is that legislated law needs

---

[12] John Hasnas, "The Obviousness of Anarchy," in *Anarchism/Minarchism*, ed.

to be founded on an antecedent set of moral principles, I take Professor Hasnas's trenchant arguments to be consistent with the general view being advanced here.

Is what is legal in the sense in which the legal is what is legislated necessarily what is moral? Clearly not. In the first place, a society could be at odds with its government in certain respects. When the Bolsheviks took over in Russia, they imposed many newfangled ideas on a public that had long been accustomed to doing things the "old way." Doubtless many people considered many of these laws immoral. They could have been right. It is very clear that laws can be wise or unwise, good or bad, just or unjust, realistic or unrealistic. In South Africa for some decades there were many laws that many regarded as downright paradigms of injustice (as did many people in South Africa). There is no inherent reason why we (or they) might not be perfectly correct in this. Laws, as such, have no monopoly on justice.

There are two different ways in which laws can be unjust. On the one hand, they can require people to do what is unjust. For example, the Nazis required people to turn their Jewish neighbors over to the Gestapo for suitable torture and murder. On the other hand, and more interestingly for our purposes, the law might require somebody to do something that it has no business requiring her to do. A law requiring every woman to wear pink lipstick—no further reasons given—would be an example. We commonly suppose that there are lots of things that the law should keep out of. So, interestingly enough, does the law, in many places. Canada has a Charter of Rights and Freedoms. It is possible for existing laws to infringe this charter—an interesting example being the former Canadian law on abortion, which was struck down by the Supreme Court of Canada. But the Charter doesn't define what is just and unjust. It instead identifies what the people of Canada, perhaps, think is so, or at least what the framers of the constitution thought about it. But any or all of these people could conceivably be wrong.

There are different levels of legalism. Here are three different views about our moral relation to the law:

(1) It is always right to obey the law, no matter what it requires, always wrong to disobey it.
(2) One should obey the law unless it requires what is positively immoral.

Roderick T. Long and Tibor R. Machan (Aldershot, U.K.: Ashgate Publishing, 2008), 111–31. The quotation is on p. 113.

(3) One should obey the law only when the law is *reasonable*—only when there is some good reason either for doing the action that the law requires even if it didn't require it, or good reason for requiring it.

Version (1) is legalism proper. Let us call this "strong" legalism, to distinguish it from (2), which may be called "weak" legalism. Weak legalism obviously recognizes that there is a difference between what is right and what the law requires, and recognizes that there could be conflict. However, it calls upon us to obey the law except in those hopefully rare cases in which the law requires immoral conduct. This would save it from the absurd implications that we ought to obey the law even if those who make it are Nazis making it in order to promote their awful programs— which type (1) would require.

Should we even accept weak legalism? Suppose your business, or you as a professional of some kind, are required by the law to do something onerous and costly and, in your judgment, completely pointless, though not actually immoral, so far as it goes. Do you really have a moral obligation to obey this law, supposing you could get away with ignoring it? Some think so, but it's hardly obvious. Many thousands of motorists who drive over the speed limit on Canada's Highway 401 every day evidently don't think so.[13]

The "Natural" Law

One fascinating idea as a sort of antidote to the problems of "legalism" is to move from the obviously unsatisfactory idea of making human law into moral law to the idea of a law that wasn't legislated by any humans, or gods, but instead, so to speak, by nature itself: We should do x because "that's what nature tells us to do."

Natural law theory has been extremely influential down through the years (it goes all the way back to the ancient Greeks, at least). Influential theories probably have something to them, somehow. The question is, though, just what is it, in the present case? The trouble is that there isn't any clear literal sense to the idea of "natural law" in which natural laws can be what they need to be here, namely moral laws—unless we simply *define* 'natural law' as 'moral law,' in which case we get no explanatory value at all from the idea.

---

[13] The median speed on his highway is said to be about 17 kph higher than the posted speed limit.

Consider the idea of a "law of nature," as in the sort of thing that scientists are looking for: the Law of Gravity, Snell's Law, the Law of Conservation of Energy, and so on. These laws have two characteristics. First, they *describe* nature: they tell us what is going on in the world. But they don't *prescribe* anything. The law of gravity says everything does attract everything else at a certain rate, and so on, but that's it—there's no "should" about it. And second, there is no sense to the idea of a natural law's being "obeyed" or "disobeyed." You do not "disobey" the law of gravity. If you jump out a window, you fall—no choice in the matter. Anything we can do is compatible with the laws of nature, and if anything is incompatible with them, then we don't do it, because we can't. Period. But morality has to be about what we can choose: we can do right or wrong. How, then, can moral laws be "natural"? Obviously they can't simply be laws of science.

What we need, then, is an idea that some proposed laws in the sense in which laws can be obeyed or disobeyed can, nevertheless, have some kind of solid "backing" or "support" in the laws of nature, properly so called. Examples come fairly readily to mind. We shouldn't roll around in poison ivy; we shouldn't sit in the fire; we shouldn't try to stay under water too long. Why not? Because we want to live, want to keep our skin intact, want to avoid death, and so on. If we are to talk of natural law as having any evaluative or prescriptive force, evidently it must be because it tells us how we can get what we want, what we see to be good for ourselves. Can it also tell us what is good for us—good *in itself*? Well, not exactly. But maybe it can tell us that we like some things better than others. Except—wouldn't we already know this? We'd know it by *being* ourselves, not by *studying* ourselves. In any case, things like that don't seem to address moral questions yet, either.

But here is a suggestion: moral laws are the best rules we can come up with for the governance of our general behavior in society, given the facts about ourselves and our relations to each other and to the world around us. This formula can hardly be denied. But it is very thin: what are those "best rules"? What makes them so? And, how do we find out? What is said later in this book is, really, an attempt to answer that question, at least in part. But it is not an answer that just leaps off the pages of the Book of Nature at us. We have to work at it.

Elitisms

Some cultures have sometimes had theories that look rather like what I will now call elitism. By this I mean, roughly, the theory that what is right is what is in the interests of, or alternatively what is proposed to the rest of us by, some selected, smallish subset of the population. A close and certainly more typical variant has it that what is right is to obey the orders of that smallish subset. The temptation to be elitist is obvious, especially if you think yourself to be one of the "elite." It is rife in academia, which is full of very bright people, know-it-alls who take enormous interest in the affairs of other people and frequently think they know better than those people themselves what is good or bad for them. So the view that they, the academics, should be in a position to tell the rest what to do is very tempting to us academics. But it should be resisted.

Marx (and, about twenty-two centuries earlier, the character Thrasymachus, in Plato's *Republic*) held that these theories really come down to the same thing: give somebody the power to tell people what to do, and what he will tell them to do will be what's in his own interests, when you get right down to it. It needn't be so, however. An occasional theocracy, for instance, may quite genuinely have been aiming to tell the people to do what they supposed was for the good of those people, not just for the monks or priests who gave the orders. However, lots of other elites have lived up much more straightforwardly to the Marxian model.

Can any version of elitism be true? Here it is very important to distinguish between *fundamental* elitism and *derivative* elitism. An elitism is fundamental if the ultimate factor held to be what makes x right is simply that x is in the elite's interests, or in accordance with its directions. It is derivative if it is held that we should obey the elite, not just because they are the elite but because obeying them is going to get us all farther in the long run, or be best for society at large, or some other such reason. In derivative elitism, there is believed to be some fact that connects the elite with some other theory, such as one of those discussed here. But we are only interested in the fundamental variety at the moment.

So what's wrong with elitism?—the same thing that's wrong with Jonesism, in the end. If you are a member of the elite, that's one thing. But what if you aren't? Then the question of why you should lick the boots of those particular people will arise. Maybe they are very strong and will beat you up if you don't. But that's hardly the sort of thing to make it right—it merely makes it prudent. If the elite are going to rule by naked force, let's at least not legitimize it by claiming that whatever they want is therefore somehow morally terrific. A morality that turns out to be just a device for promoting the interests of some particular group is a sham, and an insult while it's at it.

Imaginary case study: Some group—the Nazis of mid-twentieth-century infamy come to mind—decides that it is the "Master Race and therefore entitled to go around the countryside beating up on the previous inhabitants, such as the Poles. The Nazi leaders seemed to think that since the Poles were just "Slavs," they didn't count, as compared with the culturally sophisticated Nazis who proposed to move in instead. Now, suppose that they had something of a point, in that the Germanic people were indeed—at least quite a few of them–more sophisticated and brilliant than the people farther east who were there for centuries before: they are, after all, suppliers of a large proportion of the world's Nobel prizewinners, violin virtuosos, chess wizards, and so on. But would it follow that the Nazis have the right to move in and shove the Poles over, killing a large number, dispossessing most, and making second-class citizens of the remainder? Those who think so are espousing, it seems, some version of elitism.

It shouldn't surprise us much that the Poles weren't being all that accommodating. They didn't see why they should put up with this. Do sophisticated people really have more rights than less "advanced" people, just because they are more sophisticated? Should the brilliant inherit the earth? Should the meek, for that matter? There's something wrong with both views. Morality has to be for everybody, not just some subset of the people, some group or other. No particular group, however selected, gets to "inherit the earth."

The correct moral theory must provide a nonarbitrary answer to problems like that. Such a nonarbitrary answer is, for example, part of the genius of the business system, or the free market, as we will be calling it. We'll return to such things later on.

Innate Moral Reason

Egoism, far from being acceptable as a moral theory, looks to be just the reverse of moral. After all, don't we regard selfishness, egotism as a vice? So some have held that the business of morals is precisely to tame the ego: to clamp down on our mere individual desires and whip us into line with some universal sort of good. One such thinker was the great German philosopher Immanuel Kant (1724–1804). We will shortly say a little about the complexities of Kant's moral theory, but one feature of it is worth looking at here. Kant thought that all of us come equipped with two different sets of fundamental motivations. On the one hand, there are all of the usual desires, appetites, emotions, and so forth. These he called "inclinations." On the other hand, he thought, we also have this interesting device known as reason. In the case of ethics, in particular, the device in question is known as "pure practical reason." The idea is that morality is universal and objective, whereas "mere" inclinations are particular and subjective. Pure practical reason issues universal commands of morality, whereas Inclination tells us to do what we like and devil take the rest. Pure practical reason has the function of overruling our desires and inclinations.

Kant's theory, in that regard, has a big problem. He held that our "inclinations" were in the empirical realm, whereas reason is in the transcendental department. The empirical realm, he thought, was subject to the laws of nature. And the laws of nature, being laws, are *necessary*: there's no going against one of those things! But that leaves a problem: if inclinations are governed by natural necessity, then how is anything "else"—the transcendental department, as I called it—going to overrule them—as he clearly thought it ought to?

One can abandon Kantian metaphysics and make inclination overrulable, but that will only help if you can find a plausible theory of practical reasoning that will show us that it is *possible* to so overrule them, and that there is some good prospect of its being done from time to time. And here's where a similar problem will reemerge. Suppose somebody claims that there is a special kind of what he claims is reason that should overrule what you happen to want on a particular occasion. And suppose you hadn't noticed one of those things around: where is this alleged reason, you ask? How is this going to be answered, if the new sort of reason is indeed *wholly distinct* from what you *want*?

What you want, after all, is pretty important to you. In fact, it's difficult to see how there could be anything else at all from your point of view. Somebody holds out what he claims is a carrot, but you, stubborn old mule that you are, simply aren't interested. How is that carrot going to get you into action? How is any morality going to motivate you if it claims to be wholly unrelated to your desires, your interests, your goals—in short, your "wants"?

The plot thickens.

Kant's "Categorical Imperative"

Kant's most famous contribution to moral theory is his proposed fundamental principle of morality, the "categorical imperative," more precisely, the "supreme" categorical imperative. Kant contrasts "categorical" imperatives with what he calls "hypothetical" imperatives. Imperatives generally are "commands of reason"—they are what our practical rationality tells us to do. The hypothetical variety tell us to do what is needed to attain our various ends. There are specific ends, which he takes to be highly variable. Some want to play tennis, some don't, for instance. But if you do, then there are things you'll need to do in order to do that—invest in a carbon fiber racquet, for instance. But since we want to do them, we'll likely want to do those things anyway. Motivation isn't likely to be a problem (energy is!). To the extent that it is, reason of this type is there to countermand it: yes, practicing up on your tennis every morning at 6:00 A.M. is an imposition, but if you want to be a champion, that's what you have to do. But if we don't care about being champions, then we're free to do whatever else we want. This sounds right. Score one for Kant.

He also supposes we have a very general end—happiness, or perhaps overall satisfaction. There again, motivation isn't a problem—but finding the right way to achieve it is another matter. A considerable part of life consists in doing what we suppose will achieve it. Or perhaps *all* of life? Well—that's where the plot thickens, a lot. Kant is appropriately doubtful that we can work up a tight doctrine on such matters. Score another point for Kant.

Enter now the categorical type of imperative. These are supposed to be commands, as it were, of pure reason, and such that we ought to do what they say whether we like it or not, whether it'll benefit us or not. So motivation *is* a problem. Where would such things come from, and why would we think we should pay any attention to them? The supposed answer to this latter question gets Kant into big trouble, as we saw in the previous section. On the other hand, the general form of these categorical imperatives is very interesting indeed. The formula goes like this (in my words, not Kant's):

Act only on maxims that you can universalize.

This interesting but almost universally misunderstood formula needs some explaining.

First: a "maxim" is a "subjective principle of volition"—in effect, a rule issued to yourself, for getting something you want, because you want it. This is an excellent starting point, for it recognizes that we all have interests that we want to act on. If morality can be built out of that, it is on firm ground. The "hypothetical" imperatives noted above conform well to the idea of a maxim.

Second, *universalization* consists in addressing this rule not just to yourself but to everybody—exactly what a moral rule is supposed to do, remember—so Kant's principle is on solid ground in this respect as well. Another point for Kant.

Now we come to the heart of the idea. The "supreme rule" tells us to act only if our action is compatible with rules that are "universalizable." What does that mean? Here things are not quite so easy. There have been numerous interpretations in the literature, which we can't go into here. But a few pointers are in order. One of them is that it is better to ask what it is for a rule *not* to be such, since Kant's idea is only that we are prohibited from acting on the ones that *cannot* be universalized; it does not and could not say that we are to act on all the ones that *can*. (Interestingly, there is good reason to think that we could not universalize that, either: namely, many of them are incompatible with many others.)

Another is that we should explain this in a way that makes it intelligible, rather than in ways that invoke arcane notions that may sound good but which we don't understand, on the face of it. The main idea is this: if it would be *impossible for all the people to whom the rule is issued to act successfully on it*, then the rule is no good—it is "practically inconsistent." 'Ought'—as philosophers have put it—implies 'can.'

One way for a rule to fail this would be if the generalized rule is logically inconsistent. For instance, "Everybody, play at competitive sports only if you win!" Since winning in such a game implies that someone else loses, it is impossible for both to conform to such a rule. Of course, the losers could just refuse to play at all, but then they wouldn't be playing. But the poor sport *wants* to play. An analogous problem is illustrated by Kant's own example of the man who proposes to get a loan that he secretly intends not to repay.

Another way is that the rule could be "materially" inconsistent: "Everybody, get onto that bridge!"—but in fact, the bridge can't hold everybody. If what we ask everyone to do is such that the way things are out there makes it impossible for some to do it if others people are doing it, then we've issued a rule that turns out to be impossible for all to operate on. Kant's idea here is that that won't do. The solution in this case is the more complex rule, "get on the bridge only if there aren't already N people there" (where N is the maximum it can safely hold).[14]

More controversially: suppose that a rule is not inconsistent in any of the foregoing ways, but it's a rule that from most people's point of view would be self-defeating—like one-person egoism, for instance. Did Kant want to count this as "practical inconsistency"? I think he did. In any case, he certainly should have. And his use of maxims as his starting point requires this, for maxims are indeed what we address to ourselves as practically operative beings—as people.

So far, so good: a moral rule is a rule for all. But if what we claim to be a moral rule is one that simply couldn't be acted upon by everyone, then it's a bad rule; something has then gone wrong. Now his idea is that we reject any such rules as rules. Among the remaining ones, which everyone could consistently act on, however, we get to choose—as we

---

[14] A modern pioneer of this kind of theory is Marcus George Singer, whose *Generalization in Ethics* (New York: Alfred Knopf, 1961) is an interesting read, even if he doesn't quite get everything right. . . .

should, since they are, simply, our own principles of volition that we started with.

Kant's idea is that moral rules are addressed to us all as rational beings. Such beings run, as it were, on their own steam. If the idea is that a moral rule has to be one that everybody to whom it is addressed has adequate reason, from his or her own point of view, to follow, *provided* everybody else does so too, then we have a very powerful idea indeed. It is, in fact, the one we will be developing in this book. So understood, in fact, what makes the categorical imperative plausible is that it is essentially a defining condition for a rationally acceptable universal rule. If morality is to be rational, it *must* meet the standard he lays down in that principle. It is, then, reasonable to think of the principle as being a priori, just as Kant says. Score another point for Kant.

So far, so good. But if you think, as Kant seems to have, that somehow morality calls upon us to act against the empirical laws of nature, then morality is going to be impossible. Not so good! Fortunately, however, that idea is a confusion. People are in no way limited to something like maximizing their own pleasure, as we saw in our discussion of egoism. Can people curb their impulses? Of course—we do it every day. What's required is common sense and some analysis.

Some of that will be forthcoming shortly.

Bureaucratic Ethics: Rigorism

A different feature that is often associated with Kantian ethics concerns the operation of what we might call "low-level" moral rules. Kant supposed that if some sort of maxim turns out to be nonuniversalizable, we are then commanded to refrain from doing what such universalized maxims tells us to do. We can't all successfully lie to each other: lying involves taking somebody else in, and that person doesn't want to be taken in. Everyone's lying to everyone would be self-defeating. But Kant jumps from there to the opposite rule: *never* lie! He supposes that to do that is always wrong. Rules of that kind, if there are any, are what I call "rigorous"—for obvious reasons. And the moral theory that moral rules are always, or even mostly, like that we may call "rigorism."

Rigorism runs into problems, for example, in the case of lying, as a friend of Kant's pointed out. A murderer, M, comes to the door, seeking his victim, V, who as you know is at this very moment right there in the kitchen. You think fast. If you tell M the truth—that V is in the kitchen—that'll be the end of V, and moreover, you will have been uncomfortably close to being an accessory to the murder. If you say nothing, or shift from one foot to the other, M will barge in, suspecting the truth, and—

same story. But if you quickly and firmly point out that V just went down to the post office, that-a-way (right next to the police station, as it happens), there's a good chance that M can be caught and V spared. This third alternative involves lying. So there's our problem: do we tell a lie, or don't we? Kant seems to think we must not under any circumstances take this third alternative, even though it looks to most of us, I'm sure, to be obviously the best one by far. His reason? Well, moral rules are rational and rationality is universal, and a rule isn't universal if it has any exceptions, right?

Wrong, actually. People who insist on sticking to relatively simple rules, and damn the torpedoes!—"rigorists," as I'm calling them—are making a mistake. We can have rules that nevertheless don't have this kind of awful consequences. For example, the rule, "Don't lie!," can be understood as having more nearly the force of this: Don't lie, other (moral) things being equal. In cases where the other things are *not* equal, you will properly do something else, without having violated the rule. So V gets her life spared.

Rules that are properly overridable in the light of other considerations besides the one mentioned in the rule have come to be called *prima facie* rules, following the useful terminology adopted by W. D. Ross.[15] The duties they lay upon us are called prima facie duties; we can also talk about prima facie rights. Such a rule is one that holds so long as there are no materially relevant factors present counteracting the effect of the original rule, that might take precedence over the factors taken account of in the rule in question. These other factors must themselves be *morally* relevant. The fact that we don't like people who part their hair on the left doesn't entitle us to make an exception to the rule against killing them. And specifying which rules are to be taken as having moral weight is a job that would, logically, urgently need doing.

Rigorism is what I call "bureaucratic." The bureaucrat sticks to procedures and forms, regardless of their real utility in the case at hand. A cartoon from my college days showed a student, knife protruding from his back, dragging himself up to the admissions desk at the hospital where the receptionist, ever prepared, responds with, "I.D. card, please!" That, and countless billions of other examples, well illustrates the category. A theory of morality must give us a decent account of rules, telling us how to distinguish good ones from bad ones. While it's at it, though, it can and should tell us when rules should be ignored, overruled, stretched,

---

[15] W. D. Ross, *The Right and The Good* (Oxford: Oxford Univ. Press, 1930), ch. 2: "What Makes Right Acts Right?" Reprinted in *20th Century Ethical Theory*, ed. Steven M. Cahn and Joram G. Haber (Englewood Cliffs, NJ: Prentice-Hall, 1995), 87–105.

bent, or thrown out. The fact that "a rule is a rule" is not in general a very good reason for doing what it says to do. In fact, it is really *never* a sufficient reason, in itself. The reason for obeying a rule is to achieve the good purpose lying behind the rule, whatever it may be. Sometimes that end will be better achieved by violating the rule. Jaywalking when there is virtually no traffic, for example, gets pedestrians about their business more efficiently and just as safely as taking the long way, via the traffic-light-governed intersection.

Now, however, we are saddled with a big job. 'Other things being equal' is not a very clear qualifying expression. What are the "other things" that need to be "equal" and sometimes aren't? How "unequal" do they have to be? Saving people's lives is more important than telling the truth. We can turn the tables on Kant's rigorism by suggesting that the rule "Don't lie, even if telling the truth would kill someone!" is *nonuniversalizable*. All acting on that could get some of us killed, and that is hardly something that rational people are willing to accept. But Kant talked, often, as though the rules of morals were somehow purely abstract and a priori. Weighing the value of truth-telling against the value of saving lives doesn't sound like the sort of thing Kant thought he was into. But he has to have been wrong. Sir W. D. Ross left this weighing and balancing to intuition. We should hope to do better.

Where, then, do we go from here?

Particularism, Again

Some recent writers have called for junking the whole category of moral principles or rules—on grounds very much like those that led Ross to adopt his terminology of 'prima facie.' Prominent among them is Jonathan Dancy, who says, "morality has no need for principles at all. Moral thought, moral judgment, and the possibility of moral distinctions—none of these depends in any way on the provision of a suitable supply of moral principles."[16] His position depends in turn on a theory about reasons, which he calls *holism*. According to it, "a reason in one case may be no reason at all, or an opposite reason, in another."[17] Significantly, Dancy is also of the view that he need offer "no account of the distinction between the moral and the non-moral."[18] This should worry us. A theorist who sees no difference between evaluations of his

---

[16] Jonathan Dancy, *Ethics without Principles* (Oxford: Clarendon Press, 2004), 5.

[17] Dancy, *Ethics without Principles*, 5.

[18] Dancy, *Ethics without Principles*, 3.

own situation and those involving others has possibly missed the point of principles, which as here understood are distinctively moral, in that they impose requirements against our doing whatever we please, but also requirements that are intelligible and predictable. If there are no principles, how do we achieve either?

Dancy's strongest argument for this unusual view is that a given factor might count for a certain action in one context, yet that same factor count against it in another. Consider his example of causing pain. Is causing pain always, so far as it goes, wrong? He claims not: "if the pain is a statutory punishment for a recognized offense, you are not doing something wrong."[19] Now, the appropriate generalization operating here is that pain, insofar forth, is a bad thing: pain, that is, taken apart from effects, is viewed negatively by the person experiencing it. (Or is it always? What about masochists?) So, is causing pain wrong? It is if the individual on whom it is inflicted doesn't deserve to have it inflicted; but he might, in which case it, or rather, an appropriate amount of it, would not be. Is there a single invariant principle standing behind all this? That remains to be seen, but it is not obvious that there is not.

Does gravity cause things to fall? Not if they are immersed in a fluid of higher density than they; in that case, gravity will cause them to rise. Dancy should infer from this that there are no laws of nature either. Still, there is a general law of nature about gravity holding in both cases. Something like that could, for all Dancy says, be true in morals. This background law is not inordinately complex, as are the packets that Dancy attributes to Thomas Scanlon.[20] It is a law that relates all material objects to all others. Even its effects, however, can be counteracted by other forces. In physics, scientists still seek a unified field principle that will enable all of the different forces to be systematically related to each other. Might there be one such in morals? Yes. Might there be one such in ethics? That's much less likely. If one sees no distinction of the kind I've emphasized, between morals and ethics, then the possible role of principles in morals that do not function in ethics is likely to be lost sight of.

If there is such a general principle, it will be both *general* and a *principle*. It will be the former in two senses: first, it will cover an indefinitely large number of instances; and second, it will call for self-restraint on the part of those subject to it. They will be required to behave differently from what they might otherwise do, to do what they might not want at the time of action. And they would explain the anomalies so ingeniously brought out by Dancy.

---

[19] Dancy *Ethics without Principles*, 8.
[20] Dancy, *Ethics without Principles*, 135–37.

We should also agree with him that if we look at familiar fairly general and fairly abstract moral rules, such as to keep promises and to avoid inflicting pain, they will certainly not stand up as universal rules in the sense of having no exceptions or counterexamples. A medium-length list of moral rules is not going to do the job of telling us, invariably, what we morally ought to do.

This interacts, then, with the issue of foundationism discussed at the outset of this book. If morality has a set of "foundations" we would be able to say what it is in general about. This may in turn lead us to look in the right places for its fundamental principle. So we will table Dancy's challenge at this point.

Sentiment

Hume proposed that we all have at least a bit of sentimental attachment to other people—"some particle of the dove, kneaded into our frame, along with the elements of the wolf and serpent"—and that this provides the foundation of morals. He admitted that this might in some cases be very little indeed: "let them be insufficient to move even a hand or finger of our body; they must still direct the determinations of our mind."[21] This contrast between moving "the body" and moving "the mind" is evidently very important, for it is hard to see how morals is going to get much support from the former. After all, morals may often call upon us to do quite a bit with our bodies—certainly to refrain from doing many things with them. If the sentiment supposedly supporting morals is so diminutive that it will do almost nothing in the way of action, why should the "mind" be so different? And indeed, are there not villains without the slightest bit of pity? Are their actions wrong *because* they have a vanishingly small sentiment against them?

Or for that matter are they wrong because *other* people have these sentiments against them? We may be sure that the victims of his depredations, or their near and dear ones, are going to have ample sentiment about them. But again, what makes their sentiments correct, and his comparative lack of them not?

It's quite true that we have "sentiments" about moral matters, most of us. We are, most of us, very interested in what our fellows are up to, we don't hesitate to evaluate the deeds of individuals and public figures in moral terms, and we can get upset or elated at either our own or others'

---

[21] Hume, *Enquiry Concerning the Principles of Morals*, sec. viii.

actions, and do so in recognizably moral vein. But is the rationale behind these sentiments nothing but the sentiments themselves?

On one misguided but understandable misinterpretation of emotivism, that would morality might appear to look like: people simply sounding off at each other, with no real basis for doing so. If morality came to that, that would be bad news. The cynics would have won the day. We have to do better.

Utilitarianism

Utilitarianism is a monistic moral theory: it is the moral theory that the one and only fundamental moral principle is the *principle of utility*: which says that actions are right if and because they promote more utility all around—counting everyone's utility equally with everyone else's—than alternatives. All other moral considerations are supposed to be derivative from this one. Is murder wrong? If so, that is because murder doesn't promote utility. In general, if there is a moral rule to the effect that we ought to do x or refrain from y, then this has to be supported, in the end, by an argument to the effect that x maximizes utility and y does not.

Here we need to note that some writers have put forward this principle as explaining actual (de facto) morality: they have held that this is what underlies our actual moral beliefs and practices. Others have supposed that the principle of utility is, or at least was meant to be, an improvement on ordinary morals—to be, quite possibly, a revolutionary theory that might overturn many of our ordinary beliefs. I shall suppose that the latter is what was basically intended, but the difference won't matter too much here.

The Principle of Utility

There is much disagreement about many aspects of the theory. However, we may take the essence of it to be this: that an act's moral properties are due to its bearing on the level of utility. The principle of utility, whatever else it says, says this: "Maximize utility!"

But what does this mean? The two components each bring up a host of questions. Actually, there are three components: (1) Maximization, (2) Utility, and (3) the exclamation point. Let's consider them, in that order:

MAXIMIZING

The hard part of utilitarianism is getting a handle on the sort of calculations and measurements it contemplates. But once you can do so, maximizing is easy enough to understand, in principle: the agent, A, is to determine for each available option open to her the amount of net utility that act would produce. She then compares them in that respect. The one that produces the most utility is the one that "maximizes" utility.

What if there were two or more options with equal maximum utility? That brings up a question. If we are supposed to choose the one that maximizes, and if there is more than one act neither of which produces more utility, but both of which produce more than any other acts, then what should we do? Two suggested alternatives here are: (1) do as you like; and (2) choose at random, that is, allot equal probability to each one. This might give very different results in various cases. You might dearly love one alternative and find the other quite distasteful, for yourself, but due to their different effects on others, they come out equal. If you adopt rule (2) for such cases, you'll find yourself half the time doing what you very much dislike; if you adopt rule (1), you'll always choose the one that pleases you more.

The issue about moral dilemmas comes up here. We don't often feel that the way we can make our choices in very tough cases, where two acts seem equally strongly morally recommended, is by flipping a coin, nor by doing whichever we happen to "like" more. But is this an important problem? Some have thought so. I am inclined to think not, as a point of theory. In personal cases of decision, however, deciding between what seem just about equal alternatives can be perplexing, distressing, and downright painful.

CARDINALITY

The way in which an individual's utility needs to be measurable on the utilitarian theory is, in the first place, in cardinal terms. Those are expressible in numbers of "units" of utility. We must be able to say not only that A prefers x to y, but also by how much. To be able to say only whether she prefers it or not—"ordinal" measures—and no more would not give us what we need to talk about "maximization." This is especially because of the next requirement.

INTERPERSONAL COMPARABILITY

The utilitarian wants us to maximize "overall" utility, not just our own. That is its distinctive contribution to moral theory: we override individual interests on the basis of attaching equal moral value to equal amounts of utility, no matter whose. It is in a very important sense a highly egalitarian theory, interpreting a common and plausible idea that no one is any "better" than anyone else by holding that what counts to anyone, after all, is that person's utility, and then upholding the impartiality of morality by holding that equal amounts of it count equally, no matter who enjoys the amounts in question.

Can we make sense of the supposition that your values and mine can be quantitatively compared, in cardinalizable units? This is at least highly problematic. It's problematic enough to contemplate the measurement of any one person's values, intrapersonally, let alone measurement in such a way as to enable us to say that Jones is now enjoying five more units of value than Smith.

We don't talk that way in ordinary life, but that doesn't prove anything: we didn't talk that way about temperature either, until we had thermometers. We must distinguish between the questions whether utility is unmeasurable only in practice, or whether it is also unmeasurable in principle. Everyone agrees about the former, except perhaps in some exceedingly rough and general ways. The latter, however, is extremely difficult to establish. How does one go about knowing in principle that something can't be done?

One way would be to prove it. It has been demonstrated mathematically, for example, that you cannot square the circle (a problem on which people worked for years and years). Can such a thing be proven in moral philosophy or psychology? I rather doubt it.

UTILITY

What is utility? This is a funny question to ask, because utility is not an ordinary notion, like good or pleasure, that we can analyze. But we do have to ask what the utilitarians were trying to do with a concept such as this. The answer, I think, is that utility is supposed to sum up an individual's good. But 'individual's good' is a crucially ambiguous term. Does it mean

(1) what is *good for* individual A?

Or does it mean

(2) what individual A *thinks to be good* [for individual A]?

Clearly these can diverge, as any parent dealing with a recalcitrant child is aware. Or at least, our view of what's good for A can diverge from A's! Classical utilitarianism, I think, supposes that these two run together: that for any individual A, A is the ultimate "authority" on what is good for A. We have to go along with A because A is in the preferred position for knowing this sort of thing. That is definitely contestable, however.

And what is meant by 'good' in (1) and (2)? Also, why be talking about it at all?

I would think that it is because A's view of what's good for A plays a crucial role in A's practical reasoning. It's what makes A tick, so to speak. If that's right, then a moral theory that latches onto utility in the right way is onto something meaningful and important. The question is whether it does so in the right way. (I will argue later that utilitarianism does not.)

Utilitarianism presumes in principle that all of an individual's values can be integrated, and thus that they must be commensurable. For any two things whatever, the individual, it is supposed, either prefers one to the other or knows that they are of the same value. If none of these is true, it's not clear where that leaves us (or him!)[22]

The Modality of the Principle

Supposing we have some idea what it is to maximize utility, does the principle of utility tell us that it is our *duty* to do this? Many theorists have put it thus:

PU(1): For all acts, x, and for all agents, A, and for all circumstances, C, it is A's duty to do x in C if and only if A's doing x in C maximizes utility.

This seems to make it our duty to eat peach instead of strawberry if we like peach just slightly better and all other things are equal. That sounds awfully odd! On our rendering of what morality is, duty can be identified with what an individual may be *required* to do. There would be general negative reinforcement of x if x is regarded as a duty. Does the utilitarian want those who take strawberry when they might have got more pleasure out of peach to be excoriated by their community? Surely not. So it would perhaps be better to say this:

PU(2): For all acts, x and y, and for all agents, A, for all circumstances, C, x is *morally better* than y for A if and only if A's doing x produces more net utility in C than would A's doing y.[23]

---

[22] See Joseph Raz, *The Morality of Freedom* (New York: Oxford Univ. Press, 1986), ch. 13, 321–69.

[23] Those interested in pursuing the idea of utilitarianism a good deal further might look at the author's earlier book, *Morality and Utility* (Baltimore: Johns Hopkins Press, 1967) Among other things, the proposed switch from duty to preference is explained there, among other results suggested in the brief discussion here. I came, however, to reject utilitarianism, including my earlier book's argument for it, for reasons briefly indicated here.

This brings up the question how we would get from a principle for rating acts to a principle for requiring them. The question is whether we would require the best available act.

A proposal that we not require this was argued for in my earlier book, morality and utility. There I pointed out that threatening (and carrying out) negative reinforcement for an act is costly. Is it worth it to do this in the case of peach versus strawberry, we may ask? No!

If not, what things would be duties? Only those which a cost-benefit analysis in terms of net community utility would show a profit for negatively reinforcing. And which are those? Clearly this would require much thought and "calculation" on any account. But one plausible suggestion, due to J. S. Mill himself, is this: that we should use negative reinforcement only for acts whose net utility is negative: that is, which leave people worse off than they would have been had the act not been performed. Merely leaving them less well off than they would have been if the act is *not* performed is not sufficient for invoking this kind of reinforcement. (It is sufficient for invoking positive reinforcement, such as praise and reward. In effect, the proposal would be that our duty is to refrain from harming the community, but that it is morally meritorious to benefit the community.)

Is this suggestion wholly consistent with the utilitarian idea? That is hard to say, but probably not. The reason lies in the nature of maximization, as we have already seen.

Assessing Utilitarianism (I): Intuitive Discussions

The most familiar objections to utilitarianism consist in "showing" that it has implications that are unintuitive. But what does this mean, and why would it matter?

We have already discussed this considerably. The first point is to distinguish between arguments holding that the theory has implications that are unacceptable from the points of view of (1) general common sense, scientific theory, or logic, on the one hand, and (2) morality. Clearly, all theorists will accept these as reqirements that a decent theory must meet. A theory must consist with what we know, and logic, science, and in some general but indeterminate way common sense (but not common-sense *morality*) as well are what we know if we know anything. But to claim that it conflicts with morality is, obviously, to assume that one already knows something—when the theory might claim to have superior reason for rejecting it. The general issue, then, is whether we are entitled to our moral opinions if we don't have any theoretical basis for them. While it's hard to say that we are not—few if any would have acceptable moral views if that is so—nevertheless, the opposite point of view, that morals doesn't need reasons, seems to me more than equally unacceptable. Still, it is surely plausible to suggest that a theory maintaining that murder, say, is perfectly all right, but that flexing your ring finger is a mortal sin is one we need hardly take seriously, unless there is some quite terrific story we don't know about underlying it.

Does utilitarianism have unacceptable implications? The main problem here is that we cannot suppose it does until we know that it *has* some implications. And that isn't entirely clear. For unless we can "measure" utility in a reasonably precise and objective way, the question whether utilitarianism implies p will always be highly problematic, whatever we may think of p itself.

Thus consider the Raskolnikov case. This character in the famous novel *Crime and Punishment* by Dostoevsky murders a miserable and despised old pawnbroker in order to continue his studies at the university, necessary .in order to develop his known brilliance, with which he will eventually, he supposes, rise to a high position and do immense amounts of good for the Russian people. Raskolnikov reasons that the loss of utility suffered by the little old pawnbroker lady would be vastly more than offset by the amount of good her money would enable him to do in later life. So, does utilitarianism imply that Raskolnikov should kill the old lady? Many things would have to be decided before one could say that it does. It could hardly be denied in principle that it might: conceivably, there just might be more utility in the killing. But if we have no idea in real-world terms just how that would work, the point seems not of much importance. Worse yet: what if the act really *could* be justified, even to ordinary moral views?

A MAJOR QUESTION ABOUT UTILITARIAN ARGUMENTS

Is there any restriction, in principle, on the sources of "utility" to which the utilitarian can appeal in defending a theory? The interesting view of G. E. Moore (who was an "ideal" utilitarian, that is, he held that we should maximize intrinsic good and not just pleasure or satisfaction . . .) offers an instructive case.[24] Moore held that we should always adhere to the local moral rules, on the ground that if we break them, we know that we shall cause much disutility, namely, in the enormous numbers of people who would take offense at this; while on the contrary, he thought, we can never be sure apart from that that our revisionary view really would produce more utility in the long run anyway. But can the theory

---

[24] Moore, *Principia Ethica*, ch. 6, "The Ideal."

permit us to count as a relevant utility the fact that a given result *offends somebody's morals?* I would have thought this very questionable. For then one could defend any moral view just by pointing out that lots of people do actually accept it. Surely the fact that p is widely believed cannot be used, all by itself, to prove that p? Similarly, how can the fact that a certain proposed action would provoke widespread moral indignation be used as itself a relevant reason for thinking it actually wrong?

Suppose, for instance, that action x is widely held to be just, and that's why people would be very unhappy if one didn't do x. But isn't utilitarianism supposed to tell us what is just and unjust, apart from what people think? And it does seem very clear that unless utilities of that dubious kind are appealed to, it's going to be very hard to make a strong case against the Raskolnikov-type examples. For instance: if we allowed Raskolnikov murders for his reasons, it is alleged, people would be terrified that they might at any time be the victim of a similar atrocity. But if the murderer can make out his case, why should they be terrified? Why shouldn't they take the view that they ought to be willing to sacrifice themselves for so obviously worthy a cause?

RULE VERSUS ACT UTILITARIANISM

A large amount of scholarly energy has been expended in recent years on a distinction of two understandings of how utilitarianism is to apply to actions:

(1) Act utilitarianism holds that on each occasion, the right (or anyway, morally best) thing to do is what would, on that occasion, have the overall maximum utility in the long run.

(2) Rule utilitarianism says that no, on the contrary: the rightness of individual acts is to be determined by their relation to general rules, while it is the business of the principle of utility to tell us which rules to have. (There is an analogue of this in Hare's view. Hare distinguishes between the reflective, critical morality of the "Archangel" and the intuitive, gut-level moral responses of the "prole," who doesn't think about moral theory much. Is this the same thing?)[25] Alas, we don't have time to go into this distinction at length. But I just note that it is very difficult to produce a solidly defensible version of rule utilitarianism, especially if you refrain from helping yourself to just the sort of "moral" utilities I've been talking about here.

Thus, consider the readiness with which young men have responded to a call to arms to defend their country, even when they

---

[25] Hare, *Moral Thinking*, ch. 3, "The Archangel and the Prole."

must have known that a great many of them would be killed. They do this, and their actions are widely approved, because they, and we, think they are defending themselves, their families, and other citizens of their country from unjust aggression, and that we have a right, even a duty, to do that. They don't decide whether self-defense is justified on the basis of a general utility calculation. They don't consider whether perhaps the sum of the whole world's happiness might be greater if their own side were to just lay down its arms and surrender. What they think is that they have a right (perhaps a duty) to fight, general utility maximized or not. But so many of them think so that perhaps the total utility of allowing people to fight on this basis is greater, after all![26]

Assessing Utilitarianism (II): Utilitarianism and Moral Foundations

Can utilitarianism be "refuted" in the sense of shown not to have any foundations—any good reason for accepting it? I think so. (Note: I was once a strong proponent of the theory, so this is not said lightly.) Remember that a rationally justified morality is, according to the arguments given earlier, a sort of rational agreement among everyone. Would the principle of utility be what everyone agrees to? If they were behind a veil of ignorance, I think then they would indeed "agree" (they'd have no choice!). But as real people? Not on your life! We don't propose to let people do things on the basis of whether those things would, taking everyone's utility in a lump, give us a larger lump. We want to know where *we* come out in the deal. And in principle, it seems, utilitarianism cannot easily deny that awful things done to me might make for great benefits to others, and that those benefits might, on their principle, outweigh the awfulness of what is done to me. The important point is that I, as an individual, am not about to be impressed by such facts, even if they are facts, even if they can be proven, ever so clearly! In short, considered from our separate points of view, it's hard to see how utilitarianism could be the best deal for each of us.[27]

---

[26] Moore, *Principia Ethica*, ch. 5, "Ethics in Relation to Conduct," reasons in just such a way to come to the conclusion that we should always do what the local moral code approves. . . .

[27] See Russell Hardin, *Morality within the Limits of Reason* (Chicago: Univ. of Chicago Press, 1988) for a sophisticated and well-informed sympathetic treatment of utilitarianism.

'Consequentialism'/'Nonconsequentialism'—A Note on a Bogus Distinction

One of the most frequently invoked distinctions in ethical theory has to do with the question of whether what is right and wrong is so "in itself" or instead is so because of its consequences. If a view has it that the former applies, it is said to be a "deontic" theory, or a "formalist" one; if the latter, then the label is "consequentialist." A great deal of ink is spilled on behalf of this distinction. Few ethical texts these days don't include a claim that ethical theories divide broadly into those two categories.[28]

Unfortunately, this is a distinction that has very little going for it, and certainly not enough to sustain anything like a claim that there are "deontic" basic theories and then there are "consequentialist" basic theories. We will pause here to re-appreciate why this is so, using the example of murder. Is murder wrong "in itself"? Or is it wrong "because of its consequences"? The answer is—that depends on what you mean by 'its consequences.'

To describe an "act" is to draw a sort of line around a bit of the world, separating it from everything else. Outside that line lie (1) surrounding items, past, present, and future, that are simply irrelevant, (2) background items that may be relevant (such as the motivation to the act, the circumstances in the actor's background that may have influenced him in doing what he does, and so on), and (3) consequences, that is, items *brought about* by the performance of that act.

Now, where do we draw the required line between the act and the consequence? Our example is murder. So consider the designation 'murder.' To describe an act as one of 'murder' is to do the following:

(a) to impute a bringing about of someone's death by the agent in question

(b) to impute intentionality to this doing

(c) to imply that the doing in question was morally wrong, that this was not a case of justified killing. Thus if it was self-defense, say, and we think self-defense is legitimate, then we must take back the description of the act as 'murder' and replace it by the more neutral 'killing.'

Now consider (a): In killings, the death of someone is an effect of another person's actions. But is it an *effect* of *murder*? Well, no, actually.

---

[28] For example, a text arrives just today, whose opening chapter on moral theory discusses six theories, the first of which is "Consequentialism."

It's an effect of, say, shooting the victim, or stabbing him, or whatever the means was. But the word 'murder' logically implies that there is a victim, and that victim is dead. It is not a *further,* open question *whether* there is some "consequence" *of the murder* that makes *it* wrong. What's crucially wrong with murder is basically that someone ends up dead: no death, no murder; and if there is no death, then the wrong of murder, in that case, has not been committed. If it's the death that makes murder wrong—as it obviously is—then what it makes wrong is, for instance, a shooting or a stabbing or a poisoning or whatever. And it is not true of any of those acts that *they* are wrong "in themselves." It is quite possible to shoot without killing, and in some cases where shooting is killing, it may be a defending of all that is good and true and right (as in the case of defending against the Nazis by killing soldiers in World War II), and so on. Thus the 'in itself' terminology is very misleading here. It makes it sound as though no sort of effects or consequences of anything matter here. But if murder is wrong, and yet is murder because of the death it involves, then that simply isn't so.[29]

An important moral thesis is that we are not to do evil that good may come. That has strong support from the social contract, as I will be arguing in the next part of this book. Giving people rights, especially, is intended to block such undertakings. But that they can be blocked absolutely is another matter, especially when, in desperate situations, we must choose among evils.[30]

Are all wrong acts wrong because of *their* consequences? Relative to ordinary-language descriptions of acts, obviously not. Lying, cheating, stealing, murder, rape, arson, fraud—all of these are wrong "in themselves," in the sense that to describe an act as one of these is already to specify that certain evils occurred, and were caused by a certain agent. In each case, however, one can revert to a more neutral or primitive level of descriptions relative to which what was done was wrong because of its consequences and not in itself. To slander is wrong "in itself," but to move one's lips isn't: yet to slander is to move one's lips, or one's pen, or whatever, in such a way as to impugn someone's reputation. Similarly with *all* the rest. (Try it.)

You will read in the philosophical literature much talk about "consequentialism," whether it is true or adequate or whatever.[31] This little

---

[29] See Jan Narveson, "Formalism and Utilitarianism," *Australasian Journal of Philosophy* (May 1965): 58–71. Recently reprinted in Jan Narveson, *Respecting Persons in Theory and Practice* (Rowman & Littlefield, 2003), ch. 1.

[30] Elizabeth Anscombe, "Modern Moral Philosophy," in *20th Century Ethical Theory*, ed. Steven M. Cahn and Joram G. Haber (Englewood Cliffs, NJ: Prentice-Hall, 1995), 351–64.

[31] Example: Michael Stocker, "The Schizophrenia of Modern Ethical Theories," in *20th*

analysis should make it clear that all such discussions are suspect, for the issue is basically bogus. Every wrongful act can be analyzed into acts which are not wrong in themselves, acts relative to which what is wrong with them lies in their consequences; alternatively, anything claimed to be wrong because of its consequences can be redefined so as to incorporate those consequences, and then the newly defined act will be wrong in itself.

To move three steps to the left is not wrong, but to do so when there is a foul line one step to the left may be to cheat, which is possible only when there is an agreement that we will abide by certain restrictions, the rules of that game. The harm this brings about, if undetected, is a function of the structuring of our activities by these agreed-on rules. So we cannot maintain that only "consequences" make things wrong unless we reckon consequences in relation to the understandings of the participants in the situation in which the act takes place.

Some "anticonsequentialists" might claim that such things as intentions and mutual understandings are relevant to the appraisal of acts as well as consequences. Such theorists are thinking of consequences as one thing, intentions and understandings as other things. If so, they are right. On the other hand, some anticonsequentialists might hold the position that (1) lines can be drawn around acts in a way such as to demarcate them strictly from other events which are consequences, and (2) that at least in some cases, no further consequences are even relevant to the moral appraisal of acts. Such "anticonsequentialists" would seem to have a hopelessly implausible view. The attitude that one must do x, literally no matter what, must be dismissed as fanatical. On the other hand, the view that we can simply weigh the losses we impose on others against goods for ourselves and our friends, without restraint, is the death of morality.

Rawls

John Rawls has been more widely read among nonphilosophers than any other academic Western philosopher of the twentieth century, at least in the English language (and his main book has been translated into many others, too.)[32] Rawls bills his theory as a sort of modification of social contract theory, his central idea being that the rules of justice are the prin-

Century Ethical Theory, ed. Steven M. Cahn and Joram G. Haber (Englewood Cliffs, NJ: Prentice-Hall, 1995), 531–40.

[32] Rawls, *A Theory of Justice*.

ciples that rational beings would choose for regulating their mutual relations forever (more or less). Rawls, however, attaches two other ideas.

1. One is a methodological one, which has been widely taken up by others in the philosophical profession. Called "reflective equilibrium," it consists in, on the one hand, trying to retain those of one's moral intuitions that are the most strongly held; and on the other, deferring to theoretical considerations when they seem stronger. If there is tension between them, then we go back and forth, modifying one or the other until we get a package we can live with—"equilibrium." Since there is no sort of principle supplied regarding how this process is to be controlled, we have to classify it as intuitionist, insofar forth, and so suspect on that account.

2. The other idea is that this choice whose making is what founds the principles of justice is to be made "behind a veil of ignorance"—we are to be shielded of knowledge of our own position in the society whose principles we are meditating about. Rawls claims to be ringing subtle changes on the social contract idea, and he often sounds that way.[33] In the genuine social contract tradition, we are trying to find principles on which all moral agents would agree—their individual reasons persuade them to accept the result. Does Rawls retain this? Unfortunately, it is impossible to say. For Rawls thinks that in order to get the job done fairly, we must reason in a way that excludes what he claims are biases—in particular, the effects of differential genetic and other endowments. How to do that? His answer is: Step behind the "veil of ignorance." This is a fairy-tale way of saying that when we reason morally, we may not employ premises that would give us a bargaining advantage over others. To sidetrack this possibility, we stipulate that *nobody knows who he is.* We know that we are somebody, but we don't know *which* somebody we are. We must, then, reason from the general point of view. Is this restriction workable? Does it make sense? Is it the right restriction?

The Veil of Ignorance: Two Views

Just what is the meaning of the "veil of ignorance" idea? We come now to a basic split between two extremely different ideas about how the "veil" is to work.

(1) On one view, the veil makes a vast difference to what we would decide. It makes this difference because we are genuinely choosing on the basis of values very different from those we have in real life. We are,

---

[33] Rawls, *A Theory of Justice*, 3: "I . . . present . . . a theory of justice that generalizes and carries to a higher level of abstraction the traditional conception of the social contract."

namely, choosing from the perspective we would have if, somehow, we really were nobody in particular, had no particular abilities, or any other resources.

(2) On the other view, though, the veil is a mere figure of speech, designed to show us what sort of considerations real people would have to use in order to arrive at an agreement of this type.

Once we see this difference, then there is a powerful argument against view (1). To wit: suppose people would make a certain agreement when they were behind the veil. But now they aren't—they're back in the real world. And there they make decisions on the basis of what they know about themselves, their circumstances, and the people they deal with. Why should they care about what they would have said in those weird conditions, if it differs from what they could work out in the here and now, given their situations?

I believe that this argument is conclusive, in fact. The alternative way of construing it, view (1), has a problem. For the "social contract" was originally the idea that the rules of morality are in effect the kind of rules we would all choose to live by, provided that others lived by them too (about which we will be saying much more shortly). But the effect of this construal would be to cut off argument about the contents of morality by, in effect, arbitrarily defining it as having a certain content. That is surely contrary to the contractarian idea. On behalf of view (2), the following can be said. Remember, we're trying to choose the permanent, ultimate, most fundamental principles of justice, the principles we will appeal to ever after in the settlement of disputes with our fellows. So those principles can hardly be about local and concrete matters, which vary widely. The very fact that people and concrete matters do vary widely means that a very far-reaching agreement of this kind must be very "thin." The values and assumptions about human conditions that are the premises of the argument have to be valid for humans as such, in their "essences," as philosophers say. For otherwise, if they depended on some varying condition, then they would not be convincing to those who are no longer in the conditions we have assumed.

I shall shortly argue that the most plausible candidates are really only two—neither of them Rawls's own professed view: libertarianism, which holds that our only fundamental duty is to refrain from harming others, and utilitarianism, as discussed previously. The first interpretation will, I think, give us libertarianism, which in effect discards Rawls's second principle. The second interpretation of the veil gives you utilitarianism, which presumably amounts to discarding the first principle.[34] In any

---

[34] An enterprising utilitarian might argue that Rawls's system, despite his continual

case, the veil may be of no substantive significance compared to the general idea of the "social contract." If, as Rawls suggests, the motivation is to ensure fairness, in the sense of not loading the dice against anyone, then the fact that in the standard theory *everyone* is to agree surely does that whether or not people "know who they are." But if it is supposed that the idea of the veil has some real effect on the outcome, then we have another major problem. For we are not behind veils—we are real people who know who we are (more or less!). It is for us real people that the theory is to work, and if the veil condition is unrealistic in the sense that its results are not what real people would go for, then the veil is a mistake.

Rawls often calls his theory "justice as fairness" (which indeed is the title of one of his earlier essays, and much later of a book, *Justice as Fairness: A Restatement* [2001]). That title is very "grabby"—we all want to be fair, after all! Presumably it is supposed to invoke some of our moral intuitions—that we should always be fair to people and that justice has something centrally to do with this. But how do we expound the idea of fairness at this level? There are two ideas here—two very different ideas, arising out of such contexts as games:

(1) We all operate by the same rules—nobody is to be favored by the rules
(2) Our chances of winning are about equal—playing against the big guys is "unfair" unless they are given some kind of handicap to equalize our chances. (More on this shortly.)

Which conception is relevant for social justice? We have already accepted the first. But we certainly should not accept the second. That idea has to be rejected because, after all, we *are* different. Some people really are a lot better at playing the piano than others, some at financial investment, some at washing dishes—who knows? Insisting that these people all be levelled in terms of what their various specific abilities and personal qualities might get them is far from obviously fair. If anything, it is obviously *unfair*.[35] I will be criticizing Rawls for, in effect, incorporating the second idea under the guise of the first.

---

complaints about utilitiarianism, can nevertheless be squared with it. See my "Rawls and Utilitarianism," in *The Limits of Utilitarianism*, ed. H. Miller and W. Williams (Minneapolis: Univ. of Minnesota Press, 1982), 128–43.

[35] See the devastating criticism of Rawls on this kind of point in Robert Nozick, *Anarchy, State and Utopia* (New York: Basic Books, 1974), 195 (and more generally, 183–231).

Let's start by recognizing what ought to be a perfectly obvious point here: Society *isn't a game*. We do not and cannot choose to belong to society, but we do choose to play games. Nor is there anything in social life necessarily analogous to "winning" or "playing." Society isn't a competition, though it contains many and various competitions. But basically, society is just a lot of people, living their various lives. Some are competitive at something in relation to somebody, much of the time—but most, at any given time, are not competing against anybody in particular, or at all. The entire syndrome of "competition" is inapplicable to the basic structure of society.

Suppose we are playing a game, or engaging in a competition for fun. We presumably wouldn't play a game that we know in advance we couldn't possibly win—at least, not if we played with a view to winning (which we don't always do, to be sure). In some games, like golf, the stronger players are given a "handicap": they have to make the next hole in fewer strokes than their weaker opponent. If we do our handicapping just right, then the probability of the stronger player's winning the game will be the same as the weaker player's. That will induce many more weak players to play, no doubt. It may also induce some strong players not to play. Again, if we are cutting a cake for two hungry children, we might be concerned to make the pieces equal—especially if they are *our* children, whom we know to be quite jealous of each other's shares. But the trouble with using such ideas as models is that justice is for *everyone*: it is to regulate everyone's general activities in real life. Most people are not playing games in life, nor are they children—especially, not children of the same parents. Thus we should be leery of the idea that they are entitled to equal chances of "winning" or to equal amounts of "cake" or of anything, come to that, just by virtue of being what or who they are. If people aren't playing games, then many interesting conditions specific to games will not apply. For example, we do not choose to live—we simply are alive; but game players, as I say, must choose to play. So the rules of life aren't necessarily rules giving everyone an equal chance to do something called "winning." In fact, they don't even define what winning would consist in; ideas about that are highly variable among people. One person's successful billionaire is another person's disaster as a human being.

One major shortcoming of the metaphor of 'winning' is that winning in games is normally a matter of coming out ahead of the other player(s). But we must not assume that that is the purpose of everyone's life, or anyone's. We should assume that people are the way they are, not the way some trumped-up theory would like them to be. And as to the other analogy, bear in mind that while we were children once, we do grow up, and then things are different. In particular, we can't hide behind our mother's apron any more, nor expect anyone to play the role of infinite sympathizer, bottomless purse, or, for that matter, stern taskmaster for us. As adults, we are on our own, and we must take that into account in dealing with the rest. We cannot assume that we are "brothers under the skin," say. There are a lot of people out there who really don't want you for a brother or sister, and your proposing to become such won't necessarily be received as glad tidings.

Rawls's "Two Principles": Problems

According to Rawls, we emerge from our deliberations behind the veil with two principles:

(1) a liberty principle, providing that everyone is to have an "equal right to the most extensive total system of equal basic liberties compatible with a similar system of liberty for all;" and

(2) "Inequalities are arbitrary unless it is reasonable to expect that they will work out for everyone's advantage, and provided the positions and offices to which they attach, or from which they may be gained, are open to all."[36]

In his major work, *A Theory of Justice*, this second one evolved into the "maximin" principle, which has it that social and economic goods are to be distributed in such a way that *those who get least get as much as they can:* if we try to give them more, we will fail, and they'll end up with even less. Equality is demanded prima facie, but if both parties can do still better with an unequal arrangement, we select that unequal arrangement which is *maximally advantageous to the less-advantaged party.*

Rawls is also famous for holding that (1) is "lexically prior" to (2). This is supposed to mean that until the first is fully satisfied, we don't even consider the second. So, no one's basic liberties can be abridged in order to get more TVs for everybody, say. Presumably, then, we can't invade people's liberties in order to promote "public benefits." *Everyone*, he says, must benefit. If this is right, and violating someone else's liberty makes him worse off, then the maximin principle is also infringed. Let's have a quick look at each of these two by now very famous principles.

A first and general point to make is that there seems to be a major problem in that the two principles are not, on the face of it, compatible with each other. The most extensive system of basic liberties possible

---

[36] Rawls, *A Theory of Justice*, 60–61.

would seem to include economic liberty, the liberty to use one's resources as one will, respecting only the right of others to do likewise. Isn't that possible? If it is, though, it would clearly be a violation or restriction of this liberty to be subjected to requirements that you skew your efforts so as to be maximally advantageous to the least advantaged, however we interpret the latter. What if you don't particularly want to spend your life feeding the poor? Why would real people give up the advantages available from application of their superior abilities and energies? Even if they weren't superior in those respects, why would some quite ordinary peasant who was slightly better off than his neighbors give up his hard-earned goods? How can morality presume to make people do this?

I should quickly add that there is another region of morals besides what is absolutely required, and that is what is morally recommended. Helping the needy and the unfortunate can plausibly be regarded as highly virtuous activity and recommended as such. We'll discuss such things later. But for the present, remember that Rawls purports to have a theory of justice, not charity. So this apparent implication of his second principle is intended as a demand, not a recommendation. But if the liberty principle states a demand that we respect everyone's liberty, then the problem of incompatibility is with us in full force.

Rawls's later formulation of the "second" principle, the maximin principle, says that we are to distribute other "social and economic goods," goods other than liberty, in such a way as to maximize the share of the worst off. Does he really mean this? In any case, what does it mean? That is very problematic. Apparently we are to understand that the second principle allows infractions of the first, provided the results are better for all, and in particular for the disadvantaged. But how can it do this, if the first principle is supposed to be absolute, as Rawls always later said? He later arbitrarily hacks off economic liberties from the scope of the liberty principle—with no explicit justification. And then, how can a violation of somebody's liberty be *better for everybody*? Clearly it is not better for the person whose liberty is suppressed. From his point of view, he can't think he's better off as a result of someone else not allowing him to do something that is perfectly compatible with a "like liberty for all."

The depth of this problem might be appreciated more if we contemplate a point I have developed elsewhere.[37] There I note that Rawls makes equality the benchmark of just distribution. If it is, that should mean that unequal distributions need some kind of moral justification.

---

[37] Jan Narveson, "A Puzzle About Economic Justice in Rawls' Theory," *Social Theory and Practice* 4, no. 1 (Fall 1976): 1–28. It is reprinted as chapter 2 of my *Respecting Persons in Theory and Practice* (Lanham, MD: Rowman and Littlefield, 2003).

Equality, in other words, is a "prima facie duty," to use Ross's terminology. But if it is, then how would inequalities be justified? What he says is that inequalities could be justified either by the requirements of training, or by incentives. Now the former are not a problem, since they aren't primary goods anyway—more schooling for those who can be doctors and engineers is fine, since the purpose is to enable them to produce more for the poor. But incentives are another matter, for they are ways of inducing greater production by increasing take-home pay—the primary goods of the inducee. But equality says he isn't supposed to keep that extra pay for himself, since he's supposed to divide it equally, in the absence of the special justification. But how could the sheer fact that I *want* more count as a special moral justification? And if it does, what is the use of the difference principle? How, then, can Rawls think that maximin justifies unequal income distribution at all, in principle?

Rawls is universally thought to have justified what American middle-class intellectuals want: the progressive income tax and the welfare state. But he has done nothing of the sort. What he would justify if anything, so far as I can see, is pure egalitarian socialism—unless you take the priority of liberty seriously. But if you do that, then he justifies pure capitalism, and the difference principle can be ignored. Not a happy outcome for a theory.

*   *   *

This part is a review of many of the major popular (among philosophers!) theories about ethics. These are understood as general *normative* theories as distinct from the metaethical theories of part 1. Normative theories are supposed to provide guidance, to provide reasoned information about what really is good and bad, right and wrong. We looked at many of these theories: moral relativism, egoism, religious views, conscience, convention, law (first the sense in which law is "legislated," and then the idea that law might be "natural"), moral rationalism, especially as expounded by Immanuel Kant and his theory of the "categorical imperative," and intuitionism again, viewed as a source of ethical knowledge; then, an idiosyncratic idea known as "particularism," a look at the role of sentiment, and then the very influential theory of utilitarianism, concluding with some observations about the complex recent theory provided by John Rawls and his two principles of justice. Criticisms of all these views were quite wide-ranging (after all, so are the theories!), and so hard to summarize. However, the most general fault of all these theories was found to be a failure to capture central aspects of morality satisfactorily:

namely, that it is both to be an appealing theory, one about which we can understand why it is the object of so much concern, and at the same time designed for the regulation of interpersonal conduct among people, that is, the *social* function of morals. Thus, moral relativism simply abandons hope of reaching accord among diverse people, since each, according to it, has their own set of rules which really are the ones they should be using, even though when there is interaction with others of different customs, we are obviously headed for insoluble conflict. Egoism, for similar reasons, makes no sense whatever in social contexts, where we would each be committed to an indefinitely large number of conflicting goods, or else to our own, damning, as it were, all the torpedoes. Virtue theory has it that the rules for society are really ways of advancing the quality of the agent's life; but why and how it would do this, unless some other theory of how those rules work is adopted, is puzzling. Religious and other authority theories either turn morals into the dictates of some allegedly super-powerful persons, sacrificing any idea that morals makes rational sense for the persons who are to be governed by it, or else it is hopelessly circular, defining the authority in terms of the very ideas, goodness and rightness, which we are supposed to be explaining. The idea that moral rationality is "innate" likewise evades the issue of how something that is merely "innate" can also be interpersonally rational. Kant's theory, while brilliant as an exposition of the general shape of morals — namely, as rules that are rational for all to adopt—becomes unintelligible when we ask why we should act on those rules. Particularism sees that moral rules, below the absolutely fundamental level, are always imperfect; but it either leans on the very universality it claims to reject, or makes it impossible to understand how ethics can apply to actions generally, as it surely does and must. Moral sentiment has the same structural problems as moral intuitionism, despite having some appeal as a picture of how people in society actually get on together. Utilitarianism, the view that the fundamental criterion of moral good is production of the "maximum sum" of happiness for all on a basis of cardinal measurements of each person's good or ill, literally summed over all, has huge problems of a conceptual kind, about the needed measurements, and also again loses track of the motivational problem for people, who after all are individuals and not cells in a big organism. A kind of important general comment on how moral theory has lately been done is provided in the discussion of the alleged distinction of "consequentialism" and "deontology" which is argued to be fundamentally bogus. And the much celebrated theory of Rawls is shown, similarly, to have problems of intelligibility, plus problems of motivation. All this leads to the need to re-expound morals in the (hopefully!) right way, which is the project of part 3. But it also shows the need to distinguish sharply between moral theory in the narrow sense in which it concerns interpersonal regulation of general conduct, and the theory of the *good life*, which of course must underlie all of morals but is by no means identical with it. A look at that fundamental area is reserved by the final part of the book, part 4.

PART 3

Normative Morality: A Theory

Introduction: The Defining Features

We now turn to the project of constructing a moral theory, in the sense in which that is *not* the same thing as ethical theory generally, working from what we have learned so far from the preceding rather longish review of various well-known theories. Let's start by reviewing the main metaethical points about morals.

(1) A morality is a set of rules.

Why "rules"? Rules tell us what to do. In particular, the idea of a rule is that it can overrule tendencies to the contrary. I do not intend here that any rule in this context is necessarily going to be simple to formulate. Nor need it even be a "rule" in the sense of a specification of a particular sort of act that is called for. It might instead be a socially supported picture of how to live, or a list of virtues. (But bear in mind the doubts about coming on strong about virtues that have been voiced above.)

(2) These rules are intended to be complied with by everyone.

Moral rules are addressed to everyone. Those to whom they are addressed are people capable of responding to them—agents, who are rational beings. They have interests of their own, they make judgments about what to do, and if the rest of us are going to try to tell them what to do, every now and then, they will, very reasonably, want to know why they should accept the advice or comply with the orders in question. Rational beings act on *their* judgments, and try to achieve *their* goals—to promote what *they* see to be valuable.

(3) Everyone is to encourage everyone to comply with moral rules.

The idea is for the rules to be a universal canon for all. But it is not to be assumed that people just automatically know these rules. So everyone is to act as a publicity agent for the rules as well.

(4) Moral rules are not legislated.

That is to say, no select persons, and especially no few persons, think them up, and there's no such thing as "passing" a moral rule. They are informal: no one's property, and everyone's. Over time, the content of the rules is refined, and hopefully improved; but there is no central agency to lay down the rules, either originally or in the process of evolution.

(5) Moral rules are not centrally enforced.

Everybody enforces and reinforces the morality of a society; just as everybody, from his or her own individual actions, "creates" morality.

(6) Moral rules claim to be reasonable.

When someone—let's say Jane—advances a moral claim, she is supposing that we will all see the point, will all find reason to agree with her verdict, or alternatively show that she's in error in some way. If some moral judgment turns out to be arbitrary, biased, or whimsical, those are fatal criticisms of it. Morals are not immune from criticism.

A tribal morality might look to us outsiders to be quite violently unreasonable. The insider will think otherwise, though still be unable to explain the rule's rationale. And of course, the tribe might be wrong, too. But it is this aspect in particular that opens the door to philosophers and moralists, who may claim to be able to improve things. Perhaps they will, perhaps not. A major error of intuitionism is that intuitionist theory enshrines rules without allowing criticism.

(7) Moral rules must be impartial.

From features *(1)* through *(6)* we can infer that *the moral rules must be impartial.* They must be for everyone's good, not just a select few or for that matter a select many.

In view of all this, are there good ideas about what a rational morality might be like? To answer this, we have to have a general view of what people are like, in the respects that would lead us to see the need for a set of rules of the kind depicted. Part of that view is already mentioned above. A set of rules can only work for people who can understand them. And compliance with them can be expected only if their motivational systems can somehow be engaged by the set of rules presented.

Those motivational systems govern a set of beings with the important feature that they differ enormously from each other. We all have bodily constitutions of fairly similar structure, but some are far stronger or faster than others. When we include skills and psychological powers, the range is much greater still. Further, the variety of specific interests and aims of these diverse people make it rather likely that they will come into conflict. We have *conflict* when individual A's achieving her aim would make it impossible for B to achieve his.

As we saw in discussing Kant's idea, a necessary condition for a proposed moral rule M's being acceptable is that it be possible for everyone to succeed in complying with M. That is, if M tells an individual to attempt to do x, or to bring about result R, then it is possible for that individual to do x or achieve R in the circumstances in question. But since morality tells everyone this, it has to be possible for *all* to do that. The rule has to be compatible with universal compliance with it.

Example: The rule, 'Don't kill, except in self-defense!' is one on which everyone can act successfully: A's not killing anyone doesn't interfere with anyone else's efforts not to kill anyone. We can all succeed at this perfectly. By contrast, the "rule," 'Kill your enemies (but stay alive yourself)' has the problem that if A and B are mutual enemies, then either of them acting successfully on this rule automatically entails that the other fails to act successfully on it. (Another example: 'Play games only if you will win!' makes it impossible for two people both to follow the rule. Note that "play only if you are sincerely trying to win" is another matter. The loser, if he has done his best, has fulfilled the rule as well as the winner. Kant's idea does not rule out all conflicts. It rules out those to which all participants could not agree from their own points of view.)

Where interests conflict, it is, obviously, impossible for everyone to succeed in achieving their interests as they stand. A morality will need to say, in such cases, whose interests are to be permitted to be acted on and whose not; or alternatively, to dictate some sort of scaling-down of aims so that the aims everyone is permitted to act on can be accomplished. But that requires at least some modification of egoism, as we previously saw. How to do this is the great question.

Universalizability has loomed very large in moral theory, both in recent years and as long ago as Kant, Hume, and Hobbes. What is its status? Why should we accept universalizability as a constraint on our practical reasoning? Why should we bother to get into the business of accepting such rules, at all? When do we have a good morality, as moralities go?

A plausible inference from the list of defining properties of morality is that morality should promote the good of everyone equally, or alike. But we must be careful to note that, in this context, 'equally' does not mean that the person ends up with the *same amount* of some good as everyone else. It means, rather, that morality as such favors no person relative to anyone else; that the contribution to a person's good made *by morality* be the same in each case; that if we all live up to its rules, then we can all expect to come out better than if there were no rules, or than with some other set of rules, though better, no doubt, to very varying degrees.

This idea has a long pedigree. It is at least implicit in Plato and Aristotle, and gets excellent explicit formulation by St. Thomas Aquinas, who, as was observed much earlier, proposed that law is "a directive of reason for the common good."[1] 'Common' implies what the phrase 'good of everyone alike' brings out: that no one may be left out, sacrificed for anyone else. Morality isn't to be idiosyncratic; it is to be both universal and positive. That idea has caught on in the past couple of thousand years, and rightly so.

The formula is that we can all expect to come out better than if there were no rules, or than with some other set of rules. The 'if' clause in this last is critical, however. For these rules, like most, have the property that they can be exploited by the unconscionable, those who are willing to take advantage of others. That is a hazard we need to be concerned about.

Moreover, there is an important qualification. Morality aims at cooperation. And some people do not. Morality will be hard on those people. Nietzsche criticized the morality of his time as "herd morality." But since morality has to be for everyone, it had better be a "herd morality" if it's to have any chance of success. The idea of universality, however, also goes beyond the herd. If there are extraordinary people, morality should make room for them as well; its benefits are certainly not to be confined to ordinary people. What morals won't tolerate, though, is people who are "extraordinary" *at the expense* of others. Superman *non grata*!

The "Social Contract" Approach to Moral Theory

The idea that morality is, somehow, a sort of "agreement" now presents itself as an interesting analysis of morals. People are a diverse group, whose members, possessed of varying powers, each go on their own sets of interests, make their own judgments about what to do, and do not necessarily care much about others. If we think that they *should* care about others, that will require argument. We previously criticized some moral theories, such as utilitarianism, for requiring an assumption that people should ignore the differences among themselves and, as it were, meld themselves into the group. That is not a plausible thing to do. It would make morality into a special interest, rather than a universal canon: which group to "meld into," and whether one has any interest in such melding, will obviously be highly variable among people. The interests in question need to be tamed, made compatible with others.

What all this suggests is that we look for sets of rules that all can agree on because they are seen, considering the realities of social life, to be useful for everyone, that is, to *each* person *given* the rest being the way

---

[1] St. Thomas Aquinas, *Summa Theologia, Treatise on Law*, Q 90.

they are, despite their differences. The set of rules to be accepted also has to have a claim to *necessity*: if some see that they should ignore or circumvent the rules when that is how they are generated, that's bad, since it will undermine the point of the system. Whether this can be achieved is the question.

Our depiction of egoism in the preceding made it clear that everyone's simply going it alone, without any modification, is a bad idea. Thomas Hobbes is famed for depicting a "state of nature" in which, he supposed, things would go very badly indeed for everyone. Hobbes intended a *political* state of nature, but our interest here is not in how things would go without government, but how they would go with no *morals*—no sets of rules, acknowledged by all and appealed to for the settlement of disputes when they arise and the prevention of them before they do. Whatever the plausibility of Hobbes's depiction of the political state of nature, the corresponding result in a "moral state of nature" looks very plausible indeed. If no one takes anything to be wrong, then no one will be criticized for the most drastic incursions into other people's lives. Taking that idea seriously is a good way to appreciate the centrality of morals in human affairs.

Why is the social contract idea interesting? The reason is fundamentally metaethical. The fundamental challenge presented by ethics is grounding or deriving the ideas of morality from ones that are not themselves moral. But here we are interested in *morals*, not just *ethics*. Broadly speaking, in part 1, Metaethics, I supported the general conclusion that value is indeed a matter of how things relate to our wants, very broadly speaking. Morals present a different problem. People's wants do not as such necessarily include the desire to be virtuous, or to do right, in the moral sense. Morals are rules that can and very likely will overrule our wants, on occasion. We act according to our interests and wants, by nature (to put it somewhat misleadingly); but if some people happen to want to refrain from killing each other, that's apparently a matter of luck. Feelings, desires, wants, are not reliable that way—they range widely, and certainly range beyond the limits that anything recognizable as a morality would impose. So that's why there is a problem about morals.

This is a problem that cannot be solved by talking about primitive and innate moral senses, or external authorities. If we are going to accept anything like what morality purports to be, the acceptance has to come from within; but within us, there are only our various desires and interests. ("Needs" too, if you like. But people may or may not recognize a need as such, and in any case they are perfectly capable of wanting what they do not need, even wanting what they need not to have. To move to 'needs' for this purpose is evasion, not solid theory.)

But morals are essentially about our behavior in relation to each other—in society, in groups; and especially, in the largest group of all, which is all people in general. (Not all *animals* in general. That brings up special issues, and again tends to invite question-begging affirmations. Those who like steak are unlikely to be moved by those affirmations.)

We can pose our problem in very general, but still relevant, terms. Each person has a set of interests or wants or desires, the sum of which we can call that person's "values." Whatever your particular values may be, I get to assume that what you want most generally to do is the best you can do according to your own values. And you can assume the same about me and my values.

Turn now to the subject of *other people*. What do we want of them? Various things, of course, at the level of particulars. But in general, it is safe to put it in these terms: we want our relations to others to be maximally beneficial in terms of *our* values. At the risk of inviting a charge of "egoism" of the kind refuted above, we may say that we want to maximize the value of the impact of others *on us*. The way in which this is misleading will be addressed shortly. Meanwhile, it is obvious enough that what other people *do* makes a difference to us. People can benefit us, or they can harm us. What we want is the former, not the latter. Again at the risk of being misleading—this time by making it sound much more precise than it is—we may say that what A wants from B is *maximal net positive impact* of B on A. Positive *to A*, that is— not necessarily to B.

Naturally, A and B are just arbitrary variables here. Everyone is A, and everyone is B—which is the point. Whoever our fellows may be, we hope to emerge from any transaction with any of them as well off as possible, taking the good along with the bad. Since we can't just presume that we love people, and cannot presume that we have any antecedent moral views—contrary to intuitionistic views, which we have dismissed as pointless for purposes of moral theory—the situation is that if there are to be any sort of rules capable of restricting our own behavior in one way or another, those rules are going to have to be due to the things other people can *do* to or about us, as well as what we can do to or about them. For what distinguishes people is that they are independent, autonomous, rational, self-motivated beings, and beings equipped with considerable powers.

Those powers, or rather their exercises, are classifiable into three general sorts here: those that don't matter to us one way or the other, those that do us good, and those that do us harm. Our problem is, how do we get them to make the former predominate?

There would seem to be just three possibilities here:

(1) they're just nice anyway, so we don't really have a problem
(2) things we can *offer* can induce them to make their actions toward us positive or at least nonnegative
(3) things we can *threaten* them with will induce them to do that.

Idea (1) may be dismissed for this purpose: we wouldn't have a subject of morals at all if it were always applicable. As we know, too many people are not "nice" in the required ways. So we need to move to one of the others.

The second is very promising. But is it the case that all the various things they can do to us are of a type that will enable us to confine their impact to beneficial ones by offering some positive inducement? Or might we need to resort to force or coercion? Again, it is not obvious that we can rely on diplomacy, as it were, rather than war. Some people out there are not like that. They are ready to threaten us with death unless we do what they want—and sometimes even if we do. A determined person of that kind is going to be a major problem.

At this point, two generalizations can be invoked. One is due to Hobbes: "as to strength of body, the weakest hath enough to kill the strongest." That is to say, that from the purely physical and general psychological point of view, virtually any of our fellows could, if it comes to that, not merely harm but actually kill us. The other is implicit in Hobbes, but we will make it explicit: virtually any of our fellows can likewise benefit us. Nonviolence is itself a benefit, and a huge one when we compare it with violence. However, the usual baseline of comparison is not murder, but indifference. Almost all people on earth are doing nothing at all that will either benefit us materially or harm us significantly in the near future. (Yes, there may be long-run general problems: overpopulation leading to this or that kind of shortage, say. Again, though, any such problems are not confronting us tomorrow or the next day.) As compared with that state of *noninteraction*, the type that makes me better off than the status quo is possible for almost anyone, and as well, the type that makes me worse off is also possible. It is because of those serious possibilities in the case of virtually anyone that we might find moral rules coming in handy, if we can get them formulated plausibly. Remember, the idea of morals is to be a rule for everybody. If we can find plausible rules of that kind, then when we interact with miscellaneous people, there will be a strong presumption that those rules are going to be acceptable as prevailing among us.

Now to return to the idea of the social contract. The beauty of contracts is that they lead to self-obligation, obligation that is nobody else's doing but yours, and that, if all goes well, is *in your interest to take on*. In the normal contracting situation, neither of us had any prior obligation to make the offer that leads to acceptance or not. If we make it, it is because we envisage a benefit from its acceptance and successful accomplishment. You want my money; I want your gasoline; or whatever. So: you give me the gasoline, I pay. I am better off even when I pay, given the gasoline, than if I don't pay and don't get the gasoline. And you are better off with the money and somewhat less gasoline than you would be with less money and more gasoline.

In both cases, however, there is a catch. For if I would be better off with your gasoline and without my money (in the relevant amount), I would be still better off—wouldn't I?—if I had *both*. And the same with you. Perhaps the best move would be to "take the money and run"—or, in my case, drive off; in yours, to have me drive off without your gasoline and with you in possession of my cash.

The kind of problem this generates is familiar to a couple of generations of inquirers under the name, "prisoner's dilemma." We must pay some attention to that now.

Prisoner's Dilemma

In recent times,[2] many thinkers have become aware of what are now called "prisoner's dilemma" problems, as well as with various others we'll say a little about later. For those who don't know the original story, here it is: two crooks, A and B, in the course of their nefarious activities, commit two crimes—a minor one and a major one. The district attorney[3] can convict both for the minor one, but not the major—for that he needs at least one of them to confess. He claps them both in prison, out of communication with each other, and makes a deal with each, separately: confess, and if the other doesn't, then you get off with no penalty; if neither confesses, both are convicted of the minor crime—one year in prison; if both confess, both get consideration for cooperation, but get socked with five years each; but if one confesses and the other does not, then the latter gets the full penalty—ten years. What is a rational prisoner to do? Prisoner A reasons that if B confesses, then he, A, had better too, for otherwise he spends the maximum time in jail. On the other hand, if B does not confess, then he, A should confess, for in that case A gets zero years—best of all. Of course, B then gets ten, but we are assuming that

---

[2] In the philosophical world, the foremost among these is surely David Gauthier, whose book *Morals by Agreement* (New York: Oxford Univ. Press, 1986) is widely admired and studied. Gauthier's work, in fact, provided the impetus for my own turn from utilitarianism in this direction.

[3] This will be the Crown Attorney, for Canadian and British readers.

A, who is a crook after all, doesn't care about that. The upshot is that it looks as though each prisoner, reasoning clearly and proceeding rationally, will choose to confess—and each will then end up with many more years in prison than they could have had if both had instead kept quiet. The title 'dilemma' is appropriate, then, for it seems that a certain general (and highly plausible) view about practical reason leads to the result that rational people will do what they can see will be worse for themselves.

The prisoner's dilemma has received an enormous amount of well-justified attention in the past fifty years or so, since it was first formulated. We may restate and generalize the problem as follows, for a two-person case: A and B are so related that

(1) A's best outcome is B's worst and vice versa;
(2) There are intermediate outcomes, second and third best, such that their interests are identical as between them: A's second best is the same as B's, A's third the same as B's;
(3) If either party attempts to get his best, then the other party's best response is such as to make it worse, and both acting on this perception brings about third best for each; and finally,
(4) Both parties have as available options actions that would secure second best for each.

Here is a generalized diagrammatic depiction of prisoner's dilemma situations. Each agent must choose between only two options, x ("cooperate") and y ("defect"). Both doing x gets each his second best; both doing y gets each his third best; one doing x and the other y gets the person who does y his best outcome and gets the person who does x his worst outcome. Where A's ranked outcome is the left number in each box, B's the right one, the situation is this:

	B	
	x	y
A x	2 , 2	4 , 1
A y	1, 4	3, 3

The profound problem posed by prisoner's dilemmas is this: if each prisoner acts with a view to achieving his best outcome as independently assessed, then each will in fact achieve his *next-worst* outcome as so assessed. For each prisoner reasons as follows: "If the other does y, then I should do y, for otherwise I shall come out worst; but if the other does x, then I should also do y, for then I come out best!" Yet if both do reason that way, each will achieve only his third best (next-worst). It's a "dilemma" because it seems paradoxical to say that everyone's doing his best action won't get anyone his best result, or even his second best—when getting the best possible result was the whole point of performing the action.

We can restate the case against moral egoism in these terms. Why is egoism susceptible to the prisoner's dilemma problem? Because in such situations, interestingly enough, we do not do best, individually, by performing our individually-considered best actions. Aiming at maximum self-interest defeats the achievement of maximum, or even second-best, self-interest. When the resultant *third-best* outcomes include death and utter poverty, for example, the importance of abandoning the out-and-out egoism that we may take to be our natural heritage becomes very clear indeed.

The Assurance Problem

Prisoner's dilemmas require a certain discipline for their solution. A and B may agree with each other to do x rather than y. But how does either know that the other will in fact keep his agreement, since after all it will pay him to cheat if you keep your end up? And if I don't know he won't cheat, my best response, even if I would otherwise have been prepared to go along and do my bit, by doing x, is to head him off and do y myself. We need assurance, that is, trust. Can we get it, though? Or are we fated to endure the horrors of the amoral condition?

That question is evidently answered, somehow, at the empirical level, for while humankind has endured plenty of horrors, most of us are indeed doing pretty well. That a great deal of this is due to the fact of morals is a plausible hypothesis. That it can do still better is to be hoped; but meanwhile, the assurance problem cannot be literally an insurmountable obstacle to cooperation, since cooperation frequently does happen. That problem must somehow be alleviated, avoided, or resolved. How?

Morality's Contribution to a Solution

If our problem is one of prisoner's dilemma, what should we do about it? The Hobbesian solution was to appoint a powerful referee, the state (or "sovereign," as he called it), and adopt this as our rule: Do what the sovereign says! The problem with that idea is, in a nutshell, that sovereigns are untrustworthy and expensive. These are serious problems. Regarding the first: what is to keep the sovereign from becoming a despot? Why will he be concerned to enforce good rules, best for each of us, instead of rules that work to his advantage and against ours? (History shows that, indeed, he often does.) And as regards the second point, about expense: just consider that if we had simply each taken the cooperative option to start with, we could save the costs of having the enforcer around to make us take that option. The international nuclear arms race was a major example. Each party reasons as follows: "Should I have nuclear arms? If the other guy does, I'd jolly well better too, or he'll be able to crack the whip over me. But if he doesn't, I should anyway, for then I'll be able to crack the whip over him!" So both develop nuclear arms, which are very expensive and very dangerous. Each could have saved an enormous amount of money and frayed nerves by not having nuclear weapons in the first place.

But how do we achieve this? The *form* of the "solution" is clear enough: by *agreeing*—that is, by consulting with each other, seeing what is in our mutually best interests, indicating to each other that that is what we will do—and then doing it. That is the rub, of course. If we didn't trust each other, what would we do? Go home and do just the opposite of what we said—thus putting us back in the arms race? Perhaps. So we need trust, somehow. And where is this to come from?[4]

Part of the answer in the nuclear case was the capability by each side of checking to see whether the other side was in fact abiding by the agreed-on terms. Such vetting procedures are sometimes available, as in that case, and often not, or not until it's too late. And the procedures are sometimes expensive, sometimes not. When they are, their costs can sometimes be assessed primarily on the offending party, and sometimes not. In all of the cases where they can be, our problem is essentially solved. Where they can't, it remains, and there the mechanism of morality, with its internalized monitoring, needs to take over. It often works, though sometimes not.

Another and more substantial answer lies in *iteration*. That is the technical term for the situation in which the participants are playing not just one prisoner's dilemma game, but an indefinite number on into the future. When that happens, A can threaten B with noncooperation if B doesn't cooperate, and make it stick. The strategy called "tit for tat" tells us to cooperate in the first place, and thereafter do what the other player does, whichever it is. If he insists on defecting, and we reply in kind, and so on, we will then be in the situation of the famous Martins and McCoys, the feuding mountain boys who respond with continual violence instead

---

[4] See Russell Hardin, *Trust* (Cambridge: Polity Press, 2006).

of cooperation. This leaves them, after a century or two, at least as poverty-stricken as when they started, whereas their wiser counterparts make an agreement early on and stick to it, leading to bourgeois wealth for both. Iteration makes it highly rational to cooperate rather than the reverse.

In society we don't often get into prisoner's dilemmas with the very same persons over and over again. Rather, we participate in a sizable community the members of which see familiar faces who see other familiar faces and so on. Thus, with lags, what goes around comes around: a bad move by one gets both reported on by others and its effects reduce cooperation with many, including eventually the original defector. But A's benefits to B set up B to benefit C who . . . and eventually, someone benefits A. None of these is foolproof, but what is clear is that this is a community that will do a lot better if its members generally and habitually cooperate. Perhaps the way to achieve that is to instill in everyone, and ourselves, the attitude of foregoing self-interest, aiming instead for the optimum rather than the maximum. The optimum is the best we can *mutually* do. In that sense, it too is a "maximum." The person who aims for his independently considered maximum is the problem. But cooperation is the proposed outcome of self-interest when we take the rational responses of others into account in our practical reasoning.[5]

The content of morals comes from consideration of our general relations to each other. But the idea of morals is that performance comes *from within*: people are to equip themselves with conscience, an internal sense of what the reasonable rules have to say about this and that case, and an internal enforcer, a prod that tells us to do or to desist accordingly, without further discussion and without assessing the probability of enforcement from without. A group that is well provided with these will perform better than other groups, and that benefit redounds to each individual in the group.

Rational Morality as the Best Mutual Agreement

We now have a criterion of rational morality to suggest. A rational moral rule fulfills the condition that it directs people to do what is best for each person, *if* each other person does it too. Morality imposes a uniformity, which is also uniformly advantageous if everyone complies with it—by

---

[5] David Gauthier, who among contemporary philosophers is the modern prophet of the social contract, uses the nice phrase for morality, "constrained maximization." Its sense is exactly right: we constrain our tendency to seek maximum benefit without regard to others.

comparison with the case where no one complies. This does not mean that it gives each person an "equal share" of, say resources—that issue lies ahead. What it does mean is that each person does better than he or she could do in the absence of any rule, or in the presence of general noncooperation (which comes, we may suppose, to the same thing.) This, in short, is "morals by agreement"—the title of David Gauthier's book expounding the theory.[6]

The agreement to which this idea refers is not, however, literal. People do not get together and sign up for morality. What, then, do they do? The short answer is that they "dispose themselves," as Gauthier puts it, in a certain way. Namely, they are ready to cooperate with those who will cooperate—and not with those who will not. If this works, we will indeed gain the benefits of cooperation. And these are expectedly very great.

It is easy not to appreciate how great they are. That is because of two things. First, it is easiest to look only at relatively modest, specific agreements. Our gains from these may be quite modest. And second, people do not normally include in the idea the most important single thing, which is the tendency, or agreement, to *refrain from violence*. We all owe our lives to this, however. Why hasn't anyone murdered me or you, as yet? There are a few sensible answers. One is that probably nobody we know would think he or she would have anything to gain from doing so. Perhaps people we don't know would, though? (At the time of writing this, anyone will think immediately of religious fanatics—terrorists.) Perhaps some of those people are induced to refrain by the presence of police and the other institutions of government. Perhaps. Moreover, even those we know may feel they have nothing to gain from such things because they've never even considered the subject. A large factor in the bringing about of that happy condition, surely, is that everyone we know thinks murder is wrong, and wouldn't even think of resorting to it in any remotely normal circumstances. Their thinking it to be wrong and their refraining from it go hand in hand. And thus you and I walk the streets in considerable confidence that we'll get home in one piece, insofar as the possible causes of our not doing so lie in the dispositions of our fellows.

People may even perceive that the general habit of refraining from violence really is a huge benefit in social living—since, after all, that is pretty obvious. But they do not first calculate the expected return of murdering someone, then rehearse game theory a bit and conclude that they should stifle their impulse. For they don't get to the calculation in the first place—so effective is their negative attitude toward murder. If we know

---

[6] Gauthier, *Morals by Agreement*.

anyone who reacts in the first way, the effect is chilling. They are happily few.

Such factors, very likely, fuel the intuitionist engine. The sense that something is wrong and not to be done tends to be immediate and unreflective. But it does not follow that no rationale can be supplied. On the contrary: some of us will do the above calculation and reflection, and come up with the conclusion that to behave in the unreflective way that most people do is in fact optimal, and to be pretty generally encouraged.

Nielsen's Critique: Why Should I Be Moral?

A familiar skeptical case against morality is put by the contemporary philosopher Kai Nielsen. His question is, "Why should I be Moral?"[7] If this question was addressed to a pure conventionalist morality such as moral relativism, then it would be a good question and the answer might often be: you shouldn't! But instead he's asking this of the best moral theory we can imagine that is still recognizably a moral theory and not something else. Does Nielsen cast real doubt, then, on the claim that we ought to "be moral" if this means that we ought to live up to the principles of a rational morality? Nielsen in fact has Gauthier and others of the social contract persuasion in mind, so we are right to assume that he is trying to do just that.

He correctly points out that the 'should' in his question cannot usefully be regarded as a moral 'should.' There is no sense in asking whether *from the moral point of view* one should be moral. But there is, he thinks, sense in asking the question, "But why should I adopt the moral point of view?" And he is perfectly right in thinking so. He rightly notes that we can free ourselves from superstitions and compulsions. It would be no good if we can only conclude that morals is merely a bundle of taboos with no rational basis.

He thinks there is a general conflict between collective interests and individual interests. His skeptic "recognizes the plain value of moral institutions for us." But "he is asking, 'Why should I be moral?', not 'Why should *we* be Moral?'"[8] Nielsen thinks we can ask this question, but that we don't have a good answer. It's important whether he's right about that.

---

[7] Kai Nielsen, "Why Should I Be Moral? Revisited," in *Contemporary Ethics, Selected Readings*, ed. James P. Sterba (Englewood Cliffs, NJ: Prentice-Hall, 1985), 98–105. Originally published in *American Philosophical Quarterly* 21, no. 1 (1984): 81–91.

[8] Nielsen, "Why Should I Be Moral? Revisited," 100.

He also puts it in terms of why we should take the "agent-neutral" versus the "personal" point of view.[9] But then the question, Why should I take an agent-neutral point of view? is open. Is he right about this? Is there such a contrast, really? Do you need to take a special point of view to see the merits of constraint? The short answer is that we had better not need to. For morals, I have insisted, is for everybody. That's what it's *all about.* Therefore, we can't have the rationality of morals being a function of your *particular* value commitments. Morality can't be good only for some of us.

The Marxists contemptuously referred to "bourgeois morality" and "ideology" as if morals and justice loaded the dice in favor of the bourgeoisie. If they were right, that would be a serious indictment of morality. Nielsen imagines a "classist amoralist" benefiting from a class-biased morality, and asks, in effect, why that person ought to adopt a neutral point of view, which he thinks would entail equal treatment for all. (Just what it does entail is a question for normative ethics, which we will get to, somewhat, later on.) Nielsen's conclusion is that "Whether or not it is in your true interests to be moral depends on what sort of person you happen to be."[10] It is important that this be false. Let's consider further.

Nielsen asks us to imagine an "immoralist" who denies the benefits of morals. Such an immoralist will (and will have to) be an "adroit free-rider. He will have an interest in other people being moral . . . and . . . an interest in the effective enforcement of the principles and precepts of morality."[11] Interesting! But *how* effective does he want this enforcement to be? Not one hundred percent for in that case the immoralist himself would be one of those caught in the net of enforcement.

Alan Gewirth's Argument: Does It Avoid the Social Contract?

We take an instructive interlude here by considering a well-known argument by Alan Gewirth, who thinks to have solved the "real" is-ought problem[12]: to have demonstrated in a non-question-begging way that there are certain moral "oughts" which are prescriptive, egalitarian,

---

[9] Nielsen, "Why Should I Be Moral? Revisited," 101.

[10] Nielsen, "Why Should I Be Moral? Revisited," 101.

[11] Nielsen, "Why Should I Be Moral? Revisited," 101.

[12] Alan Gewirth, "The 'Is-Ought' Problem Resolved," in *20th Century Ethcial Theory*, ed. Stephen M. Cahn and Joram P. Haber (Englewood Cliffs, NJ: Prentice-Hall, 1995), 500–518. Originally delivered as the Presidential Address to the Western Division of the American Philosophical Association, 1974.

determinate, and categorical. By 'moral' he takes to mean that they take "positive account of the interests of other persons." 'Determinate' means that they actually tell us what to do in some moderately concrete way: they show us that, at least broadly, some recognizable kinds of actions are right, others wrong. And 'categorical' means that one can't escape them, one has, so to speak, no coherent option but to accept these results.[13] Thus he denies Nielsen's thesis: morality is rational, in the sense that to deny it is irrational, self-contradictory.

Gewirth proposes to show that a very general and, indeed, the fundamental moral principle can be established, in the sense of noncircularly and nontrivially deducing it from what are clearly not evaluative premises. This principle is that we ought to concede and respect certain general rights on the part of everyone, and not just our selves—that we ought to actually concede that they have rights, and not just ourselves.

For this, he proposes to use a strictly "dialectical" procedure: that is, to show anyone that that person must accept this principle just by virtue of what he has to admit from the bare fact of being someone at all. The foundation of this is to be, simply, human action. Gewirth tries to show that action has a necessary normative structure, which is "logically implicit in action," and that there are certain moral judgments, which entail a supreme moral principle.[14]

Gewirth bases his argument on the "generic features of action"—the features any action must have in order to be an action at all. The procedure is to start with a type of claim that all actions presuppose and which, therefore, anyone who is acting must accept, and then try to show that his acceptance of that also commits him to accepting the supreme principle of morality.

I shall sketch his argument here. (I have put asterisks by the ones that Gewirth claims to follow logically from some previous one or ones.)

1. To act is to do something in order to secure some or other end: I do X for end E
2.* Therefore, I must also accept E as good [to do something for an end is to assume that that end is good.]
3. Obviously, however, two conditions are necessary to perform this act successfully, whatever it may be: Freedom and some minimal level of well-being [I will refer to these hereinafter as 'F&W']
4.* Therefore, my freedom and basic well-being are "good as the necessary condition of all my actions"—that is, they are necessary goods; i.e., I *must* have F&W

---

[13] Gewirth, "The 'Is-Ought' Problem Resolved," 508.
[14] Gewirth, "The 'Is-Ought' Problem Resolved," 508.

5.* Therefore I have *rights* to F&W

Now: the agent asserts he has these rights on the ground that he is an agent ('R'), and nothing more. In other words,

6.   I have the right to F&W because and only because because I am R

But rights are universalizable: if A and B are alike in the relevant respects, that is, the ones that ground rights, then if A has them, so does B.

7.* Therefore, all prospective purposive agents have rights to F&W
8.* And by virtue of the correlativity of rights and duties, it follows that I must accept the principle of respecting everyone else's F&W.
9.* Conclusion: everybody must, by virtue of being an agent at all, accept that he ought to respect equal rights on the part of everyone else.[15]

Critique of the Argument

First, consider the "necessary goods" of claim (4)—a point fundamental to the whole argument, since it is what grounds the step to (5) with the consequent move to (9). We might ask, in what sense are his freedom and well-being necessary goods to someone who is, say, suicidally despondent? Or does he count as an "agent"? One could try to make him out not to be rational, but how would one do this without assuming certain values—values which, quite possibly, not all agents have? And what is the character of this 'must' in line (4)? That, as it turns out, is a decisively important question.

The real question is how we get from (1) to (4). Suppose that having rights to F&W is, indeed, necessary in order to have F&W. Then if you must have F&W, you must have those rights. True. But why must you have those rights? Perhaps you'd prefer to get along without them and take your chances. Is that a live option? The trouble is that it might be, for all we know.

What the rational actor wants is freedom—that people not interfere with him. But it needn't be the case that the only reason they don't interfere with him is that they think he has rights which they want to respect.

---

[15] Summarized from Gewirth, "The 'Is-Ought' Problem Resolved," 510–16.

Perhaps they just don't care, or see no reason to interfere with him—or perhaps, noting the size of our rational agent's biceps, they fear to interfere. To some extent, surely, we can defend ourselves without invoking rights. But, would "having" rights in fact make us safer? Only if others acknowledge and respect them, and then only if they did this *when they otherwise wouldn't.* Gewirth seems to overlook these points altogether.

Gewirth maintains that talk of rights and duties is all *universalizable* in the following sense: that when I claim rights on the basis of some property P, then I must grant that anybody who has P has those rights. So far, so good. But why must I claim them on the basis of some general property, a property that everybody else has as well as myself? Why claim my rights on the basis of the fact that I am a rational agent (one among many)? Why not claim them on the basis of the fact that I am this particular rational agent—Jan Narveson (or, Joanna Jones, or whoever you are)? Why must I choose a universal property as the basis of the right I want? Unfortunately, Gewirth doesn't really tell us that. I believe he thinks that anybody who tried to claim this wouldn't be sincere, somehow. But why not?

We may agree that *if* that's how one claimed it, then you could cheerfully agree that everyone who had that property would have that right. But only one person has the new property I am suggesting—Jan Narveson, in the example cited; or Joanna Jones, in her case; or whoever the particular person is who goes through his exercise.

Note that there may be—indeed, there *is*—a terrific reason why other people should not accept your particular claim. (It would, not to put too fine an edge on it, be stupid for them to do so.) But the point is, such a reason is *needed*: Gewirth cannot just say, in the abstract, that assertions about rights must appeal to properties as general as the one he cites, namely, being a rational agent as such.

Remember, we are only talking about the claims an agent must make, qua rational agent. Gewirth hasn't yet shown us why he must make the grandiose general claim that gets our agent into the hassle of morality, instead of the much slimmer one that will merely get him the benefits of morals (rights) without also landing him in the costs of morality (the duties). For duties entail costs. To have a duty is to be subject to a requirement to do what we don't necessarily want or like to do at the time when we are called on to do it: we must do it anyway.

What fatally upsets the apple cart is the next point. Gewirth, like many moral philosophers of old, proceeds as though we simply have to accept (*2) and are therefore stuck with whatever follows from it. But if p implies q, that doesn't mean we have to accept q. It means that we must *either* accept q *or* we must reject p. Now, our wily prospective agent may well reason as follows: If I have to accept universalizability in Gewirth's sense, then if I accept these rights—which would be very nice to have, no doubt, provided that others actually respected them—then I also have to accept all these duties. The duties are the price of the rights. But is it a price I'm willing to pay? Maybe not.

What seems to be needed is something that would induce people to accept these rights *at the price* of taking on their correlative duties. Does anything suggest that this would be a sound bargain? If there is no bargain, Gewirth's case simply cannot succeed, for if the individual can get along without these rights, he won't need to pay the price in terms of duties, and since he would clearly be better off if he could do that, he rationally won't pay it.

The point, then, is that at the crux of the argument we require a social-contract kind of move: that is, we require that individuals would find it worth trading in some of their liberty to do whatever they please in return for acquiring the kind of security that others, and only others, can provide. One way to get that security is to offer a bargain. Another would be to be able to crush all opposition and ignore torpedoes. We humans are in no position to take the latter option. We will therefore do much better to take the former—to embrace morality ourselves *provided that others do likewise*. And they in turn will reason just the same way.

The Hobbesian Premise

The essentials of this view of morality were set forth—definitively, perhaps—by Thomas Hobbes, who points out that people are roughly equal in one very crucial respect: (virtually) anybody can kill anybody, if he or she has a mind to do so. It doesn't take a lot of strength, and we are all equipped with enough reason to figure out how to do it.

Are we all interested in staying alive? Almost all of us are, and in a sense, those who aren't don't matter. (Just what this "sense" is will be considered shortly.) What does matter is that all of us are highly dependent on the dispositions of others in this respect. For whatever we may think of death, it is a "stopper": once we're dead, we can accomplish nothing more. (Some believe that this is false—that death is merely the entryway to another, maybe better and certainly longer, life. Such people also present a problem. Again, we'll say a little more about it, below.)

The Hobbesian premise makes it extremely plausible to think that *if* we could get a dependable bargain, *and* we *needed* to do that, then it would be worth it, because *not* having it would then leave us without protection against others who just might want to wield the Hobbesian club in our direction, and who, if they do wield it, can do us ample, including mortal, damage. So we can put it this way: If I can greatly improve my chances of staying alive a lot longer if and only if I both sign and live up to an agreement to grant everyone else rights, and respect those rights, then I would rationally sign up.

So the question is: *do* I have to "sign up"? And do I have to keep the agreement if I do? It is unclear, at this point, where Nielsen stands on these questions. He is evidently replying to the second one in the negative. Whether his answer to the first is also negative is much less clear—partly, to be sure, because it is unclear just what signing up consists of here. At any rate, the case for the Hobbesian idea is as strong as the case for the thesis that we do have some prospect of gaining from entering into this arrangement. Question-beggingly, I will, like Nielsen, call it "the moral arrangement." Some will dispute that that's what it is, and so the tag should be taken as just that, for the moment: a tag to briefly identify the proposal, in terms of what it is attempting to do—namely, be the best fundamental account of morals.

Unpacking the Metaphor of "Signing Up"

What, then, constitutes signing up? For obviously we do not literally sign anything, and there could not conceivably be anything like a general meeting of society in which these things are discussed. But still, there is a decent answer. That answer is that signing up consists in whatever is involved in accepting a practical proposition, adopting a practical attitude, a general stance or disposition to do things in the way specified. Getting the point, seeing the rationale, having the penny drop—these are things that can and do happen to people, under the influence of experience and thought. Notice that what each person adopts, in the contractarian view, is itself *conditional*. Thus the individual does not need to engage in prior bargaining. He does need to size up those he's with—something we are all familiar with in life. Is this person trustworthy? Just how we make those judgments is not easy to say, but what they are judgments about is easy to say, and that we can do this, more or less well, is clear enough.

We are under considerable pressure from those around us to be the sorts of persons who will adhere to the principle or principles in question. People teach morals to their children, and often succeed. They put moral pressure on themselves, and sometimes succeed. And when they do wrong, they frequently are redressed for it by others. Nothing is perfect in human life, but all these devices do work, moderately well. Thoughtful people can see why this is a good thing. No rational person can deny the benefits of the principle of free exchange among people.

Negative versus Positive Rights and Duties

Gewirth is right that rights entail duties. I take this to be a purely conceptual point: all we mean by a 'right' is a status entailing duties for others in relation to the putative rightholder. A right is a claim that, in view
of some fact or other about the agent and his relation to the others
involved, those others have duties regarding his doing or having whatever he's claiming the right to do or have.

But, what kind of duties? These duties have to be to do or refrain from
things whose effects are in some way beneficial for the rightholder. That
individual must be better off for having these duties respected by those
upon whom they fall. After all, if they weren't, then Gewirth's idea that
we *want* these rights wouldn't make sense.

Now, there are two and only two ways in which this could be realized. One kind of duty might be to *allow* or *permit* the right holder to do
what the right is a right to do. The benefit to the rightholder is, in brief,
freedom in the sense of one's not being prevented from doing that thing.
Since people do things in order to improve their situations, the result of
this is a benefit to him relative to the condition in which he lacked that
freedom, that is to say, in which other people might not let him do those
things.

The other way is provided by "positive" duties. These would be
duties, not just to refrain from interference but also to *help* the rightholder
do whatever the right is a right to do. Thus if it's, say, a right to walk and
the rightholder couldn't do this without a prosthetic, then a duty on the
part of others to provide him with the needed prosthetic would be a benefit to him—in this case, a very considerable one!

Gewirth, unfortunately, fails to appreciate this distinction. Does that
matter? Let's consider.

Negative duties are observed by *not* doing certain things. In general,
notice, it is quite easy to comply with a request not to do something. We
can fulfill these while we are asleep, for that matter. If we very much
wanted to do the thing we are required not to do, then fulfilling the duty
may cost you, indeed. But even while it hurts, it won't involve positive
effort.

On the other hand, *positive* duties cannot be fulfilled while asleep. If
Jones has a right against me that I keep him from starving to death, I may
have to feed him, and that will cost money, which means work—at least
for most of us; but for anyone, it will mean parting with valued things—
whatever we could get instead with the money in question.

Negative rights are rights entailing negative duties on the part of those
against whom they are rights. Positive rights are rights entailing positive
duties on those people. Note that if a whole lot of people have positive

rights against me, then there is a problem about my resources being equal to the task. If I must feed everyone in the world—well, I simply can't. On the other hand, even as I sleep I fully observe my duty not to kill anyone at all—I fail to kill a single soul, out of all the currently six billion potential victims. And it's a snap. In general, negative rights are *less costly* than positive rights. The commitments they generate are much easier, in a wide range of familiar cases, to fulfill. Moreover, positive rights presuppose negative ones. It makes no sense to suppose that I have a positive duty to relieve the negative effects of things I do to others, and yet no duty to refrain from causing those effects in the first place. With that kind of yawning difference looming between negative and positive, it seems that this distinction should not be ignored.

Recent writers on ethics have tended to throw cold water on the distinction, citing special cases in which the difference between doing and refraining is very tiny.[16] We'll discuss those marginal cases a bit, later. But we should appreciate right now the implausibility of this philosophical gambit as a reason for dismissing the distinction itself. On the contrary: in order to appreciate the importance of the distinction, we should be looking at the kind of perfectly typical cases I have cited above, rather than the marginal, borderline cases in which the difference is minute. Perhaps some writers who have criticized this distinction are multimillionaires to whom the difference between merely doing nothing in relation to someone else, and doing what costs hundreds of thousand of dollars to do, is simply trivial. For the rest of us more ordinary mortals, the difference is positively stunning. And the "rest of us," after all, count. Morals are made for everybody, not just for tycoons. Just as hard cases make bad law, here they make bad philosophy.

Thus it is clear that (1) Gewirth's procedure, so far as it goes, does not guarantee that we will take on any rights at all; (2) when supplemented, as it must be, with a proper accounting constraint, then it looks as though we will want negative rights to freedom, but that (3) we will not all want positive rights, *even to minimal welfare*. Not just like that, anyway. For the cost to one person of providing even minimal welfare to another may be considerably more than the first person thinks it worthwhile to pay, even when weighed against the benefit to her of the very unlikely case in which others provide that welfare to her in return. I am not going to collect my return from the millions of near-starvelings in today's world, ever. If they collect it from me, on the other hand, it will cost a lot. That's a bad bargain, on the face of it.

---

[16] The classic case is put by James Rachels in "Active and Passive Euthanasia," *New England Journal of Medicine* 292 (1975): 78–80. It is very widely reproduced.

Yet that is exactly what Gewirth is fishing for: he thinks he can jump straight from my *wanting* freedom and minimal well-being to my having a *right* to it. Of course we reserve the possibility that we might make a separate, much more local deal with some few other people that each of us will feed the other when in real distress. There's no need to deny this at the present juncture. On the contrary, to be free to make whatever deals other actual people are ready to make with us is a major part of what we want from morals. But the question here is not whether we have a *right* to get into welfare arrangements in various specific ways with various specific people. It is whether we have a *duty* to attend to the welfare of anyone and everyone whom we might happen to be in a position to benefit. Since Gewirth thinks his proof is a straight deduction from start to finish, the preceding observation vitiates his main argument, so far as its logic is concerned. But since our present concern is precisely the rational status of morals, that's important.

The moral of the story is that there simply is no option to thinking in social-contract terms. Gewirth doesn't want to be an intuitionist, but as things stands, he's either stuck with that option, or he should be converting, as it were, to the contractarian idea. That's exactly the dilemma I faced upon first acquainting myself with David Gauthier's work. I concluded that Gauthier is right—the social contract is, literally, the only game in town![17]

Counting the Cost

The rational agent, realizing this, will now ask: is it worth the cost to me to claim rights against everyone else? If I have rights against everybody, so do they all against me, and I will have to go to the trouble of fulfilling my responsibilities. (This is if I'm sincere—an obviously important, but for present purposes, separate issue. For just now, we're merely trying to evaluate a proposed deal, rather than addressing the important question of how to administer it once it's made.)

Now, the right to freedom is one that it's pretty easy to believe would be a good deal to "buy" from virtually everyone, in view of Hobbes's observation. If indeed almost everybody in the whole world *could* kill me if they felt like it, while I could kill perhaps one or two of them, or maybe a few more, too—well, it only takes one of them being successful, and that's the end, folks! Clearly my interest in remaining alive is much greater

---

[17] See Jan Narveson, *You and The State: A Short Introduction to Political Philosophy* (Lanham, MD: Rowman and Littlefield, 2008).

than my interest in being able to kill other people when I like. It's highly plausible to suppose that we will all accept a deal with each other, the terms of which are for all to refrain from killing the others. And that is in considerable part because nobody would accept a social contract, the terms of which called for persons like himself being eligible to be killed at will by members of some other specified group. (Or is it "almost all"? What about contemporary suicide bombers in the Middle East? We will address those below.)

Does this apply to all manner of restrictions and costs that some people can impose on others? These now vary a great deal. Still, in every single case, and by definition, each of us has a general interest in not being prevented from damage or injury, and more generally restrictions of our desired activity in *any* significant way. And in every case, we *don't* want them to. Hobbes's thesis that all could kill us can be generalized: anyone can make life difficult for anyone else, should they really want to.

Freedom, remember, does give us the option of reversing this immunity in cases where we want to agree to that—as when, for example, we enter the boxing ring. That is what makes the principle of general liberty so attractive. It makes our lives and activities insofar as compatible with the lives and activities of others a baseline, from which particular people can voluntarily depart if they wish.

The situation with positive rights, however, is altogether different. If I need food, say, and have freedom to use my abilities, then maybe I can grow some or find some and keep myself fed. In that case, I won't need a right against others that they feed me if I'm hungry. On the other hand, if I do have such a right, then I will also have the duty to feed any of those other people who might get hungry. Not so good! It doesn't look like an obviously good deal: the able and industrious and lucky will be highly disinclined to sign up for a package of positive rights. And the idea of the social contract is to be universal. Any failure of universality is a failure, period.

The Hobbesian "Law of Nature"

Hobbes himself seems to have seen this clearly. He proposes as his first and fundamental principle of morals—which he calls the "Law of Nature," simply that we are all to keep peace with each other, and to use violence *only* for self-defense against the attacks of others (including the defense of others under attack who voluntarily enlist our aid in helping them). His claim is that this is not only the "first" in the sense of being at the top of the list, but more importantly that it is fundamental in the sense that it is the one from which all the others follow.

There are, depending on how you count, another dozen or so more detailed ones in Hobbes's formulation.[18] We do not need to dwell much on details here, except to note that he places prominent attention on the next two laws especially. Law Two says that we are to "be content with as much liberty against other men as he would allow other men against himself." Law Three tells us to keep our "covenants," these being two-way agreements in which there is a possibility of one of the two losing out to the other because that one acts first. That is so typical that we won't go far wrong to read it simply as a general requirement to keep one's agreements. (The agreements have to be fully voluntary, and thus, for example, not involve deception or coercion.)

The significance of this structure is that the second and third laws are claimed to be deductions from a fundamental rule of "keeping peace," which is conceived as nonaggression. Insisting on more liberty from others than you will allow them is aggressive, because liberty is nothing more than other people's nonaggression. And cheating on properly made agreements is aggressive because it leaves the cheated party worse off than if he hadn't made the bargain in the first place. That is just what aggression can be seen to consist in: "invading and despoiling," in Hobbes's words: that is to say, treating others in such a way as to make them worse off when every person is concerned to make himself as well off as possible, and certainly not worse off.

What about the Terrorists?

One familiar criticism of the contractarian idea is that some people just won't sign up, and so the universality that I said was a sine qua non will not be forthcoming. Contemporary terrorists do not regard their own (earthly) lives as important enough to make it rational for them to accept a general principle against killing. So it is said.

There are two general points to make against such criticisms. To make these more effectively, let's distinguish two versions: the specialist and the dead-end versions. They are importantly different. What I call the "specialist" version is exemplified by terrorists, who think they have the right to blow up persons of the "wrong" religion (or political identification, or whatever), and who are quite willing to sacrifice their own lives for the purpose. "Deadbeats," as I call them, on the other hand, are nihilists in effect: they care about nothing, and instead of trying to reserve the *right* to kill selected others, simply don't bother about morality at all.

---

[18] They are found in Hobbes's *Leviathan*, chs. XIV and XV.

The first case is dealt with by asking terrorists whether they would like, for example, to be blown up at breakfast time before they embark on their last suicidal journey. Do they think *that's* okay? If their proposed suicidal mission is for a purpose, then they must suppose that whatever would frustrate that purpose is bad. The rest of us will promptly do our best to frustrate that purpose. The suicide bombers are at war with the rest of us. But the point is, they can't think that it is rational for the rest of us to let them win that war, and they can't think it rational for themselves not to care whether they do. And that's the end of the story. The point is not that war is impossible, but rather that it's impossible to tell a moral story that will justify the aggressors. Warlike activity cannot be justified for any cause other than defense.

What about the people who profess supreme disinterest in anything as boring as morality? A modified version of the above is all we need for them. If they are sincere, then as soon as any of the rest of us find this out, and if we are serious, then their life expectancy is just about nil. If such deadbeats simply don't care how they treat anyone else, then we needn't care how we treat them. And since it appears that such people are lethally dangerous to all, the way we should treat them is by rapid extermination. No doubt we are too nice to do that, and will, at least nowadays, just lock them up instead, or try to provide them with psychiatric help. But as a matter of principle, Hobbes has it right: in the Moral State of Nature, as I call it, people have *no* rights. If that bothers them, then they're welcome aboard—but only if they are willing to pay the price in terms of respecting the rights of others.

Is Morality Rational? The Score Card

The general characterization of morality given back in the part on metaethics makes it quite possible for a society to have a not very rational morality. Moral codes thoroughly permeated with witchcraft, mumbo-jumbo, and assorted prejudices are frequent enough. The very thesis that there can be a *rational* morality can be questioned. That seems to be what Nielsen is claiming. Let us see.

Just what would it be for a morality to be rational, though? Here are two ideas about this: (1) rational action and (2) rational administration. The first idea, rational action, would literally identify moral behavior with rational *behavior*: if act x is rational for person A to do at time t, then x is *ipso facto* what is *moral* for A at t.

A second idea, rational administration, is very different. On this view, we will attend to more features of morality than just the feature of action in relation to the set of requirements. That is one main aspect. But it is not the only aspect. For a society to have a morality is for there to be a general disposition to approve or disapprove certain things, and not just to do or not do certain things. Indeed, we expect a society's institutions of expressing disapproval and approval, and also of more substantial kinds of punishments and rewards, to have quite a lot of influence on the behavior of its members. We might call this the "administrative" aspect of morals. The general purpose of what I am calling administration is to get people to comply with the various proposed rules. Indeed, what it is for a rule to be a particular society's *moral rule* is for the people in that society, in general, to engage in activity aimed at stimulating people to do what that rule calls for. Note that, as one would hope, this implies that the moral rule in question need not be *stated* at all. The visiting anthropologist might have to *infer* from tribal behavior what the "rule" is. Codification of a society's moral code is fairly likely to be something that few in the society attempt to do, if any. Professors of philosophy concern themselves with such things, but normal people probably don't.

Even so, it is possible to assess the rationality of those engaged in this behavior. Are they trying to get people to do things that are rational to want done in that society? And, are they trying to do this in ways that make sense?

Roughly, the latter question will be answered by considering whether the sort of thing that people do by way of inducing compliance is likely to succeed in so inducing it. The former question, however, is answered by seeing whether people are likely to *do better* by virtue of being subject to such a rule or set of rules.

In all cases, 'doing better' is taken to be measured by the person's own evaluations. It is rational for me to pursue *my* values (or "utilities") just because they *are* mine, in the end. It is not that my assessments of my own condition are necessarily *right*. It is that I have no intelligible option but to act on what I take to be my best assessment of that.

In light of this distinction, let's return to Nielsen's critique(s)—echoed by so many other writers. Nielsen himself agrees that his hypothetical immoralist will not go about advertising his immoralism. More precisely: Nielsen assumes that morality calls for *cooperation*. I think I have shown that this is true. In view of the preceding analysis, this cooperation is going to consist predominantly of reliable nonviolence. People will deplore aggression, and will approve those who pour oil on troubled waters, are helpful and generally polite and kind instead of the reverse, and so on.[19] Other people will note that our hypothetical immoralist does engage in that kind of behavior. He too, like us, professes to

---

[19] They will not disapprove of defensive measures, on the other hand—they are not pacifists.

deplore violence and so forth. And yet, says Nielsen, he will not actually *be* nonviolent. Beneath his cloak, he will be ready to do evil whenever it pays.

Well, first—when *does* it "pay"? People out there are disposed to return kindness with kindness, to refrain from violence to those who are not violent themselves, and in general to make good people feel good about being so. They will smile at such people, for example, and be ready to relate to them in various good ways. Our hypothetical rational immoralist presumably puts on such a good act that he collects quite a lot of this kind of psychological payoff. Then, one fine day, we presume, he—what? Robs a bank? Breaks somebody's arm for no particular reason? Lies? Cheats? But of course, this has to be done in such a way that people are unaware that he is doing it. A part of our response here is to point out that this will not be so easy.

A more speculative point stems, approximately, from Plato, who holds that justice is the "harmony of the soul." That somewhat romantic-sounding idea is actually capable of being fairly plausibly explained. Our souls are in harmony if part A and part B don't clash: one part of me doesn't insist on doing something that another part roundly deplores, for example. Now, one who goes about being a total hypocrite may have a problem along this line. He lets on to all that he disapproves of various kinds of behavior, all the while being perfectly ready to do it himself—and knowing that people have very good reason for being very peeved at people such as himself. Or worse, of course. For in the case of the more seriously evil kinds of behavior, we will not stop at verbal expressions of disapproval. If our immoralist gets into bank robbery and assassination, we will do our best to track down the doer of such deeds, and punish him severely. Disharmony of soul doesn't consist in being punished. But it *can* consist in doing what you know perfectly well deserves the punishment in question, along with the fear and apprehension, and constant concern to cover one's tracks, that the hunted are inevitably going to have to be involved in. It is, for such reasons, not obvious that genuinely immoral behavior is rational, under the circumstances. It is not at all surprising that there is a common perception that criminals aren't very bright, and a suspicion that people who engage in a good deal of very antisocial behavior may be in not very good psychological condition.

As I write this, there are newspaper accounts of a young man who walked into a shopping mall and killed several people with a shotgun; his five-minute session ended with himself being killed by police. His parents and the parents of some of his victims were interviewed to the same effect: they did not understand this boy's behavior, and regarded him with pity. Rightly so, surely—what a miserable way to spend a life!

But what we must really ask is—what are the *terms of reference* here? What are philosophers obliged to prove along this line? It is impossible to "prove" that no person will ever do evil. We cannot, after all, prove what just isn't so. It is also impossible to prove that it will never even appear to anyone that it is sometimes rational to do what a rational code of conduct would disapprove. Critics advancing this line seem to forget that the whole reason we have anything like morality in the first place lies precisely in the fact that often an individual *will* have reason, in terms of his own perceived interests, to do the kinds of things that morality pronounces against. Robbing someone *could* be beneficial to the robbers, and so on. Anyone who thinks that a moral theory is disproved by the fact that it does not demonstrate that immoral actions can't possibly ever pay, in any terms whatever, is crying for the moon. That can't possibly be what we are supposed to be showing.

But it is possible to prove that having a working social institution of the moral kind is a really good idea, and is so from *everyone's* point of view. And it is possible to prove that this institution should be organized around certain general principles, most generally the social support of cooperative behavior, and more specifically the avoidance of violence.

The relations among people on whom these results are founded are perfectly real and objective. There is no serious room for doubt about them. And so we are perfectly justified in pronouncing various kinds of action to be wrong, others to be right. That they are so will not certainly bring it about that each and every person will always be moral. They do make it highly likely that by far most people will.

There will be exceptions to worry about. I have mentioned the suicide bombers, for example. They act under the influence of religious beliefs, let us suppose. The points made above about religious morality have, probably, never occurred to them. And the beliefs they have induce them to suppose that their own deaths are a good thing rather than the reverse. Against such people, what is there to do? Unfortunately, the main answer is to hope that we can catch them before they succeed in blowing us up. But philosophically, that is a *sufficient* answer. It is not true that morality is shown to be wrong when people with beliefs of this kind think themselves to be rationally justified in immoral behavior. What is true is only that (a) they are not justified in any sense implying that the rest of us have no reasonable complaint against them, and (b) alas, the world is not a simple place, and life is not without problems.

Morality: The Carrot and the Stick

The basic output of the story so far is that we are all under a general obligation to refrain from imposing sizable costs on our fellows. That single general principle needs to be refined, to be sure. Some of our fellows deserve to have sizable costs imposed on them—the murderers, for example. At much humbler levels, we will contemplate ways of appropriately getting back at people who do us small evils.

Nor is that all. There will be times when it is impossible not to inflict sizable costs on innocent people. At such times, there may be large, and possibly intractable, problems about just who should bear those costs. A morality that says such things can never be justified at all is likely to cost lives. A principle of minimizing such costs is more plausible, though not as easy to memorize or to apply.

The question in many readers' minds, very likely, will be whether the social contract, as depicted here, is not too narrow in its output. Do we really owe our fellows no more than nonviolence? For example, if it's pretty easy to save someone's life, do we not have an obligation to do so?

The short answer is yes, we do. But that answer is very short. There are billions of people out there, and many millions whose lives are probably in peril unless someone does something. How much of our time and effort are we *obligated* to spend in locating and helping, so far as we can, such people? The reasonable answer to this, surely, is—very little. Urgent needs of persons in the immediate neighborhood, and such that we can help a lot without great expenditures of time and effort, are no doubt needs we ought to try to help with. But those cases are necessarily rare.

Note the point: they are *necessarily* rare. What is meant is this: if there were a great many such cases in the immediate area, the sense that we had a compelling moral obligation to help them all would dissipate. Help to any one is unlikely then to be easy, and help to very many would take over one's life. We are not obligated to expend our lives in that way. The Mother Teresas of this world may feel that way, and no doubt we should hold such people in high esteem. But the claim that each of us is obligated to be like her in that respect is without plausibility. Morals is for everyone, not just for heroes.

Mutual Aid

We can formulate a reasonable principle of mutual aid to cover such cases. It will, as it must, be stated approximately and roughly, but the point, I think, will be clear enough. The "social contract" on mutual aid will ask when it is to everyone's rational advantage for persons who do not know each other and have no prior special duties but who are reasonably presumed to be innocent of evil intent to *expect* each other's assistance.

The first condition on this must be that the cost of rendering the assistance, to the person who provides it, be quite low in relation to the expected benefit of his assistance to the other. Both will vary greatly. We all help each other with volunteered minor but useful bits of information, for example. The cost of supplying it, if we have it, is very low—a few words, for example: "It's just down the street, on the left-hand side." But if our acquiring of this information would cost five minutes on a computer or twenty minutes on a trip to the library, that's another matter. In cases where life is at stake, a higher cost is reasonable. But how high? Being ready to put my own life at serious risk in order to help a stranger is too high a price to expect all to pay, in anything like normal circumstances. We'll be disposed to praise the person who does that, perhaps, but insisting that all be like that, in any but extreme circumstances, is going too far.

Secondly, we render help in regard to understandable things— things which we could envisage being in need of ourselves. We all need to eat, to be in ambient temperatures compatible with continued life, and to have limbs and such repaired if repair is possible. It could happen to me—even if I were Bill Gates. And even he could possibly stand in need of someone's help, though almost certainly he would be in a position to buy the help when needed. The point of this condition is, again, to make the moral rule a reasonable proposition from the general point of view. If I know that condition X can never befall me, for whatever reason, then when someone else suffers from X, the case for my agreeing in general to be responsible for rendering help is lessened. Naturally, there are many values of X, and quite possibly I could be in need concerning Y, which would never happen to the X-afflicted person. Thus it might be a good deal for me to be ready to help you with X provided you are ready to help me with Y, in case of great need. That is a good reason for leaving the mutual aid principle stated loosely, in terms of need and assistance.

The principle is rational to support if my expected gain from it in the long run exceeds my expected costs. Where rendering help is easy and not costly, benefits are great, and there is a real possibility that I myself might stand in need and would greatly benefit if help is rendered, then the case for rationality is good. Where any of those conditions is not present, the case is considerably weakened.

In any case, there is a serious question whether the mutual aid principle is enforceable. May we threaten with punishments those who fail to be helpful when they could? To make it so is, I think, too risky. Better to leave this at the level of admonishment rather than punishment.

Charity and the "Social Contract"

But here we want to explore a very different point: that morality is not confined to rules of the type that are to be enforced by imposing costs on noncompliers. A good part of morality uses the carrot instead of the stick. We should be ready to reward, with praise and encouragement especially, certain people whose behavior is especially helpful to others. There are small favors we can do to many people which we do well to be disposed to do; often those are enjoyable enough anyway, and where not, the case for doing very many of them again dissipates rapidly.

Why should we all be disposed to praise and encourage good deeds done to random strangers? In fact, the case is easy to make. Praise is pretty cheap, and the benefits to be had by the people whom helpful people will help are considerable. We may ourselves be the beneficiary of someone's charitable disposition. Where the benefits are modest and ordinary, indeed, it is extremely likely that we will benefit, on occasion. Benevolence is a virtue we do well to encourage.

Moreover, we can here call on Hume's idea to advantage. Hume supposes we all have a streak of sympathy for our fellows. That is at least pretty close to the truth. The case for regarding charity as a virtue leans on this streak. When we encourage people to be helpful, we can be confident that our message doesn't fall on deaf ears, for as fellow humans, they are equipped with a fair amount of human sympathy and fellow-feeling anyway.

Thomas Hobbes's Fourth Law of Nature calls for gratitude to those who benefit us. We don't, he explains, want to discourage those who, with no prior obligation to do so, do us a good turn. He has a point. When people put themselves out on our behalves, we ought to make clear that we appreciate the kindness. That tends to stimulate more of such behavior, while ingratitude tends to extinguish it. Biting the hands that feed us is not rationally to be commended.

All this is undone if instead we insist on turning charity into a duty of justice. Will the rational person, not assumed to be conspicuously benevolent but knowing that it may be possible to benefit from the assistance of others, agree to a rule compelling everyone to do this? No. The cost of compulsion is too great. Those who wish a higher level of assistance, after all, are always free to arrange this with willing others. For example, we could join an insurance group that would provide higher levels and be obligated by contract to do so.[20]

---

[20] An interesting working-up of some of the general ideas proposed in this book can be found in G. R. Grice's *The Grounds of Moral Judgment* (Cambridge: Cambridge

Moral Complexity

The basic idea of morals has been frequently articulated in such ways as this: *don't do evil* and *do good*—in that order, meaning in particular, that we are not to try to do good to some people *by* doing evil to others. This account agrees with those of Hobbes, Kant, and many others.[21] The rationale behind it is clear from the preceding. Self-directed people don't want to be deflected from their pursuits; if they want help, they'll ask for it. A general principle purporting to direct the behavior of all concentrates especially on our capacities and tendencies to pursue our various goods at the expense of others, abjuring us to desist from the latter. But once we are secure from each other's possible depredations, cooperation in specific ways with specific people is only to be expected, since we have so much to gain from coordinated action with the right other people. Being left free to seek those people out, rather than being subject to coercion in the course of inducing us to work for and with all and sundry, like it or not, is sure to be more productive in general.

If we suppose that each person is the authority on what is good or bad for that person, then the nonharm principle will be identical with a liberty principle: since person B defines, in B's case, what is "harmful," A respects the intent of nonharm by simply confining herself to actions relating to B that B agrees to, and refraining from those he doesn't. But the two aren't necessarily the same. For one thing, people are sometimes unable to express themselves, for any number of reasons. For another, we all have bodies and minds complex enough that we don't understand them very well, and sometimes others understand them better. Doctors, for example, know much more about my interior organs than I do. Nevertheless, this does not justify overriding of individuals' wishes regarding themselves. The doctor must still get permission from his patient, if it is obtainable, when he proposes significant incursions into that patient's interior. Still, permission is not always obtainable; sometimes the permission is manifestly given or withheld on the basis of wrong information; and occasionally the patient will be in such bad shape that it is unclear how to interpret her utterances as actually conveying permissions or denials. A good deal of moral judgment concerns such things—deciding whether to interact with someone in ways that ordinarily would be clearly wrong or clearly right but in the circum-

---

University Press, 1967). His terminology differs from mine, but in the main the account is interesting.

[21] This formulation in essentials is found in St. Augustine: see his *City of God*, bk. xix, ch. 14.

stances are not clearly anything, is a considerable part of life for most of us.

In any case, when our principle is as described, we assume that we know where a given individual leaves off and someone else begins. I am not to harm *you*, but just what constitutes you? There will be your body, usually relatively easy to keep off. But how about your property? And what about your various engagements and undertakings? Many of them are in turn involvements with still others, whose selves and therefore freedoms are also to be respected.

Equality and Egalitarianism

Morality must be impartial. If it deviates from impartiality, it loses the support of those who are hard done by. But many writers of recent times have been enthusiasts for *equality*, not just *impartiality*. The two are very different. Impartiality supplies benefits and awards penalties on the basis of performance, independent of anything else, such as race, sex, tastes, lifestyles, and religious opinions. But different people will have greatly varying needs, wants, budgets, and capabilities. If we stick to our basic nonharm rule as the fundamental principle of morals, we will not expect that people will come out equally well at the hands of others. In any case, they will have very different genetic endowments, which will, for example, dispose some to horrible diseases while others live long lives without ever visiting the doctor's office. Genetics—so far as we know—will also see to it that some are whizzes at mathematics, others scarcely able to work with single-digit figures. All of these facts make it enormously unlikely that different people of widely varying kinds will enjoy equal incomes, or equal health, or equal happiness, or equal anything of significance. "Equality before the law," which we may reasonably be said to be entitled to, certainly won't entail any of those.

I am taking *egalitarianism* to be a view about *justice*: that is to say, a principle about what we get to compel each other to do. Egalitarianism is not merely a preference for some or other kind of equality, a view that it is a good thing. Instead, it is the theory that *compulsion* may legitimately be used for the purpose of making people more nearly equal in some respect (to be specified by the theorist).

We have previously considered Rawls, who is thought to be something of a champion of equality, but whose system, so far as I can see, provides no plausible case for equality in any sense in which it is not just a misleading word for impartiality or universality. But we can benefit from some consideration of a professed champion of equality. I select for this purpose the work of Kai Nielsen, again.

Nielsen argues for equality of condition as a right. "The goal we are seeking is an equality of basic condition for everyone . . . everyone, as far as possible, should have equal life prospects, short of genetic engineering and the like . . ."[22] By this he means that they have a positive right to these things. It would be pretty close to meaningless to defend equality of condition as a negative right—would that be the "right" not to be made any worse off than one is now, if one is less well off than the other person? But if this is to have teeth, we must assume that the idea calls for coercion against those above the line, in order to bring about the wanted equality with those below it, or at very least that coercing for such purposes is permitted by the theory. But that is just about what positive rights are: rights imposing enforceable duties on others.

Nielsen identifies inequality with "some being in a position to control and to exploit others."[23] But those are hardly the same thing. One would have to inquire what sort of control and exploitation is envisaged here, if it's to be compatible with everyone respecting everyone else's general liberty. For as those terms are normally used, person A controls or exploits person B only if A is able to threaten B with some harm for not complying with B's wishes—but that is exactly what the absence of liberty consists in. That is very different from inequality as such.

Included in the list of conditions he wants equalized is "autonomy." But this is combined with the condition that "everyone alike, to the fullest extent possible, has his or her needs and wants satisfied."[24] Well, who is to satisfy them? Evidently the "autonomous" people who, apparently, do not have a choice whether that is what they shall do.

"Where we have conflicting wants, such as where two persons want to marry the same person, the fair thing to do will vary . . . in the Marriage case, freedom of choice is obviously the fair thing."[25] But why is it? What if marrying Joe will fulfill her needs and wants more than marrying Sam—whom she would rather have? Suppose Sam can have any girl he wants but Joe can get only you, if anyone . . . then what? Why isn't it now your duty to marry Joe anyway?

It will help to become clearer about the notion of equality. To say that x is "equal" to y is to say that *there is some respect such that x and y can vary in degree in that same respect, but that in this case the degree is the same.* In order to talk sensibly about equality, it has to make sense to say that people can be equal or unequal in that respect, and therefore that

---

[22] Kai Nielsen, *Equality and Liberty* (Totowa, NJ: Rowman and Littlefield, 1985), 283.

[23] Nielsen, *Equality and Liberty*, 287–88.

[24] Nielsen, *Equality and Liberty*, 283.

[25] Nielsen, *Equality and Liberty*, 283–84.

some kind of metric, however vague, can be employed. If it is also true that they can be *made* (more nearly) equal by appropriate actions of others, then the egalitarian can be characterized as holding that people ought to be made equal in those respects or at least, more nearly equal.

Are some ways of making people equal better than others, in the egalitarian's view? Suppose there are a few blind people and lots of sighted ones. We cannot restore sight to the blind, but we could put out the eyes of all the sighted ones, thus making their condition equal to those of the blind. The egalitarian is presumably not in favor of that. Why not? Nielsen suggests that "*ceterus paribus*, where questions of desert, entitlement and the like do not enter, it is only fair that all of us should have our needs equally considered, and that we should, again *ceterus paribus*, all be able to do as we wish in a way that is compatible with others doing likewise."[26] But these modifications leave us with *no theory at all*. For the libertarian agrees entirely with this last clause, except that he sees no "other things" that could be "equal" enough to outweigh liberty. And Nielsen's reference to "desert, entitlement and the like" would have the effect of completely eliminating any room for maneuver. Once those who made things get them, and those who are given things by others who are entitled to them get those things, there would seem to be nothing left to distribute, equally or otherwise.

Since liberties and equal opportunity are at odds with each other, a principle saying that we have "an equal right to the most extensive total system of equal basic liberties and [emphasis mine] opportunities"[27] means absolutely nothing. Compounding the problem, he says, "The equality of condition appealed to in equality as a goal would, if it were actually to obtain, have to contain the rights and duties enunciated in those principles."[28] Still later he refers to "fair terms of cooperation" along with rights to noninterference. But how are terms of cooperation fair if some parties are forced to equalize the situations of others? And what happened to these "rights" of noninterference if the sheer fact of inequality is enough to justify infringing them?

Nielsen shares a widely held view that somehow wealth entails power. But just because I have lots and lots of money, do I get to force you to do things? How? At the time I began what turned into this book, there were two elderly men in Toronto living in a dilapidated house in the middle of the city. Wealthy people and corporations were positively queuing up to acquire their property, offering enormous sums—but the

---

[26] Nielsen, *Equality and Liberty*, 287–88.
[27] Nielsen, *Equality and Liberty*, 289.
[28] Nielsen, *Equality and Liberty*, 290.

old men liked it there and just didn't want to sell. Those men are quite poor. Where was the "power" of the wealthy? What is pretty obvious is that virtually anybody, of whatever level of wealth and resources, can use those for good or for evil. Having much does not entail that one will go for evil. It is not even more likely. Indeed, if anything, given the track record of wealthy people in, say, America, it looks as though wealth goes along with increasing philanthropy, much more than it incites the exercise of coercive power over others.

Arguments for Equality

Where does the idea come from that we have to treat people "equally" in the sense of bringing it about that they have equal amounts of something, for example, by taking some from somebody else and just giving it to them? The question of just what we are supposed to bring about equal amounts of is obviously crucial. Popular candidates are: welfare, opportunities, "shares," and "access to the means of production." But so too should be the question of why we are supposed to do anything about it.

Sometimes people deserve equal amounts of something. For this to be the case, there needs to be

(1) some reason why those who get whatever it is should be given anything of the kind; and
(2) evidence that the reason in question applies equally in the cases in question.

Any such system also implies that those who deserve *un*equally should get *different* amounts.

If I value someone's services—they do me a service, make me better off—then I may well have reason to reward that person. If I value something that is not a person, say a garden, there may be things I would need to do to keep it in a condition such that is valuable to me. It might degenerate without my attention. So might persons in my environment. If one pays insufficient attention to one's spouse, he or she may leave; to one's children, they may turn into juvenile delinquents; to one's employees, they may quit. In all these cases, when the person or thing does well, one has an interest in seeing to it that it continues to do so. Transferring to them things they need or value is often called for. But suppose one does *not* value them? The obvious response in that case is indifference. Indifference is not necessarily neglect. If one has reason to value them and doesn't, then lack of attention is to be criticized and counts as neglect. But what if one does not?

Some philosophers think that all humans have "inherent" value—are valuable just by virtue of being humans, despite doing nothing to earn our attention. But those who say this effectively short-circuit argument. If the value is "inherent," then apparently no account of it is needed. They don't, on this view, need to do anything to deserve our attention and effort. We are to reward them on the basis of simply being people. This would seem to be a pure emotional response, an affective response, such as we might have to a beautiful scene, say. But the trouble now is the same as with intuitionism, of which this would seem to be a species. What if we don't respond that way? Then the egalitarian will call us bad names, to be sure. But where are the arguments? If it's a matter of taste, then the old adage that there's no disputing about it has an obvious point. Some like Mozart, some like rock music, some hate music altogether, some like people, some don't. *Chacun a son gout.*

In the obvious cases, the desert basis is also obvious. Here is someone who does valuable work for you, on terms specified in a contract. But beyond the contract, there is the fact that she does it really well—better, suppose, than the contract calls for. She indeed deserves a reward from you: it is in your interest to pay her something extra. But if this is our model, then the trouble is that most people have done nothing for us, nor did we make any contracts with them; while among those who have, deserts differ greatly. In any case, this smacks of something the egalitarian needs to disavow: "meritarianism." Since people will surely differ in their merits, those who merit more should get more. This is antiegalitarian.

The theorist might insist that people do not differ in their "merit." But what would he mean by 'merit,' if so? For a major part of the concept of merit is that it is subject-specific. A merit in context C is of no interest at all in context D. Being a terrific ground-ball fielder in baseball counts for nothing if your project is composing a paper on functionalism in biology, say; and vice versa.

The problem with theorists of the type that egalitarianism represents is that they think of merit as residing in the person whose merits are under consideration independently of their bearing on any interests of the persons bestowing the rewards of that merit. But that is unintelligible. Desert and merit simply can't be assessed without an evaluative background, which the putative distributors of the good in question will have to be interested in.

In short, egalitarianism converts the impartiality of morality into a morality requiring us to be totally indifferent to relevant differences among people. But there is no logical necessity that morality should be like that. A moral rule can say, "within the following domain, everyone may do as she pleases." If someone pleases to prefer some people to others for some purpose, that's okay. The moral *rule* doesn't prefer her to others; it says to them all, impartially, that they're welcome to be as partial as they want to be in the areas in question. Morality's impartiality is entirely compatible with extensive personal partiality. Our loves and hates, our connections with all sorts of particular people such as children and friends, are all partialities—and they are also, for most people, the stuff of life.

Not only is the impartiality of morality compatible with much personal partiality, but it really entails it. To disallow humans preferring some to others for any number of reasons, and treating the ones they prefer better than they treat others, would be about as severe a violation of persons as can readily be imagined.

The Two-Variables Fallacy

There is a familiar theorem in mathematics: you can't maximize two independent variables. Suppose we are told to maximize good F and also good G: but what if more F means less G? Or what if one action produces both, but at different rates? If the rate at which we would get more F by doing x gives us a lesser increase in G than if we do y, which would get us more G but a lesser increase in F, which should we do? Nielsen speaks loosely of maximizing equal welfare, equal opportunity, and so on. But these are all different things, and different policies will produce different amounts for different people. How are we to choose? Notice that F and the *equality* of F are also independent variables. Suppose plan X gives everyone a small amount of F, while plan Y gives everyone more F than the first plan, but gives some people a lot more than others. Which is the "radical egalitarian" to opt for?

David Hume observed long ago that egalitarianism's potential for tyrannical politics is enormous.[29] The problems just noted are compounded when we have even more than two variables, as Nielsen certainly does. The mathematical problem mentioned assures us that there is no natural sense to the notion of the "right mix." Someone will have to decide, and his decision is bound to strike some as arbitrary. Who is going to decide which mix is the right mix? Who, and with what kind of budget for deliberation—and how much clout? Who is paying their salaries while they thus deliberate? Unfortunately, we know too well the answer to that one: *we*, the people taxed by the central committee, will pay. And it won't help much if that committee is elected by a "democratic" procedure. Many people cannot know what is unknowable any more than few.[30]

---

[29] David Hume, *Enquiry Concerning the Principles of Morals*, sec. III, pt. 2.
[30] See Larry S. Temkin, *Inequality* (New York: Oxford University Press, 1993). See also

Morals and Politics

Libertarians tend to harp on the iniquities of government. That is because governments do step in and order us around, whether we like it or not; and because they do so with regard to things that are not obviously for any sort of common good. An obviously interesting and important question about politics is how morals bear on it. As expounded in this book, the assumption is that the principles of morals should apply to all persons, in whatever capacity they may be acting. No one is immune to them. So if the view advanced is about right, then complaints of a moral kind are simply complaints about certain kinds of actions, whoever might be performing them. It is fundamentally a moral thesis, but, because it applies to all actors, and therefore political ones as well as private persons, it is, at least apparently, a thesis with rather restrictive political implications. However, following these out takes us beyond the confines of this book.[31]

Virtue, Again

Here we address a quite different set of moral terminology than that of 'right' and 'wrong', the categories in which we have mainly been carrying on our considerations thus far. What are virtues and vices and what is their relation to rules and to right and wrong? Virtues and vices are "in the soul": they are traits of character, which reside "within" a person. However, they don't just sit there, for they essentially affect action: our character is our set of tendencies to act in morally significant respects, or, perhaps, the set of internal states of the soul that issue in those tendencies.

There is a lengthy tradition, going back to Aristotle at least, of philosophers who consider virtue to be the primary subject of ethics. Philosophers attracted to this idea claim that it is at least misleading and mostly just wrong to make out that ethics is mainly a matter of rules or principles. Those who say this, I suspect, tend to deny that a strongish distinction is to be made between the larger, more general subject I call 'ethics' and the narrower one I have called 'morals.' In previous sections, I have rejected the claims of antifoundationalism and particularism, insisting that instead there is a rather narrower and special subject of morals with principles of its own and peculiar to it. Morals are based

---

my discussion of that book, in *Philosophy and Phenomenological Research* 16, no. 2 (June 1996): 482–86.

[31] Narveson, *You and The State.*

on the fact that there are other people in this world, and that they are different from each other. The fact that these are independent minds, with distinct and greatly various sets of values, interests, goals, aspirations, plans, and so on, makes a difference. Indeed, it makes *all* the difference. The principles of morals look fairly absurd when self-applied. There are those, no doubt, who impose various rules on themselves, but the interest of others is concerned about the fact that Jones is about to murder someone.

"Virtues," says Philippa Foot, are "in general beneficial characteristics, and indeed ones that a human being needs to have, for his own sake and that of his fellows."[32] But this is only a start, since there are other qualities with that characteristic, perhaps, that are not accounted virtues—or anyway, not moral virtues.

The notion of 'virtue' is applicable well beyond the bounds of morality. Business people, engineers, basketball players, and so on, can all have general dispositions that are highly valued within those trades but are hardly to be accounted 'moral'. It is part of the idea of morality that its rules and precepts—and its lists of virtues—are capable of being displayed by essentially anyone; they are all-purpose useful traits. Hume defends the thesis that virtue is "a quality of mind that is useful or agreeable to self or others"[33]; this is not so far from Foot's definition—she leaves open the possibility that there might be benefits other than agreeableness or usefulness, though I don't think that's an essential part of her picture.

Though she doesn't discuss the concept of "cardinality," Foot lists the virtues as the classic cardinal four: courage, wisdom, temperance, and justice. Note that three of those have no special connection with morality as such: one can display courage or temperance, or wisdom in non-moral contexts, and worse yet, they can be displayed by people in the course of villainous activity; and there are certainly no moral rules requiring one to be courageous, temperate, or wise—only justice seems to have that feature, and that because it is as such moral. (Though to be sure, we do talk of "doing justice to Maisy's apple pie.")

Nevertheless, these are virtues of moral interest because morality makes requirements on us that we may be unable to meet if we lack these qualities. It takes some courage to be just, intemperance can get in the way of duty, unwisdom can make it impossible for one to do one's duty effectively.

---

[32] Philippa Foot, *Virtues and Vices* (Berkeley: Univ. of California Press, 1978), 3.

[33] Hume, *Enquiry Concerning the Principles of Morals*, sec. IX. More precisely, it's "personal merit," but throughout this is equated with virtue.

Virtues are tendencies to act. But if the acts in question are not good, how can the quality that gives rise to them be so? It is clear that what makes the virtues virtuous can only be a logically antecedent judgment that certain kinds of action are desirable, others undesirable. And having said that, we then have to point out that there are all sorts of interests in terms of which to rate various actions as desirable or undesirable. What is a virtue in tennis won't be so in chess, if it is even interpretable in chess. We are here talking about morality in particular, and for it, as I along with so many others have argued, the relevant interests are the effects of others' actions on our general good or ill. Thus virtue for moral purposes will be suitably described in, say, Hume's terms: "that personal merit consists altogether in the possession of mental qualities, *useful* or *agreeable* to the *person himself* or to *others*."[34] Hume's characterization is far too broad for morals in our narrow sense of the term, however. Doing what is agreeable or useful to oneself is not something we have any direct interest in promoting; we presume that people are trying to do those things, but we don't demand it. It is the category of what is useful, or especially the reverse, to others where morals comes into its own.

To be sure, we can distinguish between someone's happening to do what is required by morality, and his doing it because it is the morally right thing to do. Kant, notoriously, makes such a distinction—between acting *in accordance* with morals and acting *from* morality.[35] He holds that we get no moral credit for any action done for any other reason than the latter. But this brings up a paradox. Aristotle holds that the truly just man loves justice; if he acts purely because the moral law requires him to, Aristotle would give him fewer points, but Kant apparently would give him more, or rather, he would give Aristotle's just man no points at all. That is surely a mistake. Nice guys rate our support, just as do those who do right on principle and despite inward temptation.

A different account of virtue is offered by Alasdair MacIntyre, who holds that virtues are essentially related to "practices," which are "any coherent and complex form of socially established cooperative human activity."[36] Such practices generate "internal" goods, that is, goods that are internal to the practice in question: a high batting average is an asset within baseball, say. Is this true, though? Some virtues don't seem to be applicable only within practices of any particular kind: charity and justice,

---

[34] David Hume, *Enquiry Concerning the Principles of Morals*, sec. IX: Conclusion, part I.

[35] Kant, *Foundations of the Metaphysic of Morals*, sec. I: "I also set aside those actions which really conform to duty, but to which men have no direct inclination, performing them because they are impelled thereto by some other inclination."

[36] Alasdair MacIntyre, "The Nature of the Virtues," in *20th Century Ethical Theory*, ed. Stephen M. Cahn and Joram P. Haber (Englewood Cliffs, NJ: Prentice-Hall, 1995), 622.

to take two conspicuously important cases in point, don't seem so. You could try making out that the general morality of a community is itself a "practice." But this is misusing the term 'practice.' Morality is all-encompassing: it applies to all the actions of everybody in a community. No matter what our practice may be, we are not to lie, cheat, steal, and so on. I don't see, then, that MacIntyre is right; Foot's account seems much preferable. And both are inferior to Hume's. With Hume, we understand the point of the virtues: they are qualities of mind that are useful, or agreeable, to self or others. In the case of morals, the "others" are the primary things: what can the rest of us reasonably ask of you, the individual? Your response, if everyone's homework is right, will be, indeed, to acquire the tendencies to act which the rest of us want of you in those respects, and which you agree are reasonable demands, considering your own interests and capabilities.

Virtues and Rules

There are those who believe that there is a general contrast between "rule" theories and "virtue" theories. Rules are bundles of sentences telling us what to do. Virtues are qualities of person, specifically of character. What are virtue theories going to have *in place of* sets of rules? Presumably lists of virtues. These lists name the desirable states of character in question. Temperance, industriousness, honesty, reliability, affability, loyalty, politeness, civility, and a whole lot of other such things have been claimed to be virtues.

But is the supposed contrast real? In particular, do we have to take our choice? This is not obvious. After all, we do, normally, go in for a fair amount of both. We frequently issue rules of morality such as when we say, "Don't cheat!" and so on; but we also make reference to virtues, such as when we say, "A is a very nice person" or "B is really brave." So why must we take our choice?

We would if we were looking for what is fundamental in morals, and if we supposed that only one or the other could be literally fundamental. And one would be fundamental if one of these categories presupposes the other, and not vice versa. Is this the case? No. For the trouble is that a rule is psychological: in purporting to guide us, tell us what to do, a rule necessarily presents itself as something we respond to from the inside. It doesn't rewire us—it asks us to regard the context in which it operates and to appreciate that a rule of this kind is needed, called for, able to improve things. The disposition to do the things that the rule asks us to do is, surely, precisely what following a rule is. And so the connection between virtues and rules is intrinsic, and intimate.

But *morality* is essentially about interactions with other beings, and it's what those other beings reasonably ask from you in the way of behavior that affects them that forms its essential subject matter. So moral virtues logically proceed from outer to inner—not from inner to outer. The moral agent needs to have the resources for responding to moral requirements, and these are indeed virtues. But what makes them virtues is the sort of required action that they require. We saw earlier that Aristotle's account is essentially a logical cop-out: the "right amount" of passion x is neither too much nor too little. But too much *for what?* In the case of the strictly moral ones, in our narrow sense of the word, too much is when you've been prompted to do some wrong thing, such as murder somebody; too little is when you aren't moved to do what you ought to in such cases. Appraisal of what is done comes first; attribution of virtue to the tendency to do it is derived from that.

Fuzzy Edges and Approximate Principles: Rules and the Real World

Jeffrey Olen notes that few of us strictly observe most of the general rules of morality.[37] We will lie and cheat a bit for our friends, for instance, even though we have no doubt that lying and cheating are wrong. How much this proves is a very interesting question. Especially, we need to ask, first, whether it casts doubt on the status of moral "rules"—does it provide fuel for the particularist or perhaps the virtue theorist after all? And second, it prompts us to ask whether there are built-in vaguenesses in the theory itself. Aristotle famously insisted that we must not expect too much. "We must be content, then, in speaking of such subjects and with such premises to indicate the truth roughly and in outline, and in speaking about things which are only for the most part true and with premises of the same kind to reach conclusions that are no better."[38] Mathematicians, and even engineers, need to be and can be precise; moralists, maybe not.

It is hardly surprising that Aristotle's dictum is widely and approvingly quoted. Yet it must also be pointed out that sometimes we will have to be very precise indeed, and the inherent imprecision of the subject will be no excuse for not providing it. In a given case someone might be entitled to precisely 50 percent, say, and reasonably feel cheated if instead

---

[37] Jeffrey Olen, *Moral Freedom* (Philadelphia: Temple Univ. Press, 1989).
[38] Aristotle, *Nichomachean Ethics*, bk. I, ch. 3.

he gets 49.5 percent. And a scientist might fail in a moral duty by being imprecise about something about which he could have been precise, and where it matters precisely what is going on.

We also have to point out that the "secondary axioms"—or as we might say, the theorems— of morals are inherently incapable of being rigorously universal. Should we never lie, cheat, steal, or kill? No. But firstly, that's because it is sometimes right, for reasons that can be made quite clear and be recognizably moral, to do those things. And secondly, in many matters, degree really is important. Are we really not even to *touch* our fellows on the bus? The point of morals is largely protection of individuals. But damages can vary from enormous to trivial, and when they are trivial, it is not reasonable to insist on people refraining assiduously from inflicting them. The office employee who takes home a few paper clips or rubber bands is reasonably ignored. Cases such as pollution are more difficult, but a hundred million times some very tiny quantity may add up to a very significant amount; and so on. In general, we need to ask: is the kind of damage we are concerned about such that *this case* amounts to a significant infliction of it? The answer is often in the negative. Moreover, while we do not live in Hume's imagined case of life among ruffians, we do live among varying kinds of imperfect people, many of whom will tolerate more than would various other groups. The fundamentally liberal point of view of this book is such that those things make a difference.

Concluding, though, that morals isn't a matter of rules at all is, I think, misguided. What matters is to know why a given case is an exception, rather than assuming that there can be no exceptions because there is no rule in the first place.

Moral Luck

The man who rescues a young girl from a fire in her twelfth-floor apartment is regarded with more admiration than the man who, alas, despite his best efforts, drops her twelve stories to the ground. Why is this? It seems that very often our actions are morally appraised in part on the basis of what is purely accidental, out of our control. The child runs into the path of our car, whose brakes we have failed to check; we feel perfectly awful and are blamed, whereas the next driver, whose brakes he also has failed to check, happens never to do anything terrible because of it. There is a sound basis for in general being guided by events rather than intentions. The latter are hard to get at and appraise independently of actual results, and it would be intolerably easy to convict this or that person of ill intent if there were no need to point to real effects. It isn't only in the law that the rule of habeas corpus is a good one.

This problem threatens to become philosophically serious when we note that no matter what we do, there will be elements in our action for which we could not have been responsible: our genetic endowment, circumstances of upbringing, plus various happenstance events such as the aforementioned. This can lead us to the gloomy conclusion that we are never morally deserving of praise or, perhaps, of blame. That way lays the problem of "freedom of the will." Perhaps our actions are entirely a function of circumstances over which we have no control at all? We are quite unable to believe that, however. And praise and blame do make a difference to people's behavior. That is why concepts of responsibility are nevertheless useful, despite these philosophical doubts.[39]

To be "morally lucky" is fortunate; to be morally unlucky is sad, sometimes tragic. But those facts give us no reason to think that our principles are wrong, nor that our general practice, of rewarding with praise those who do good and discouraging or punishing those who do evil, is mistaken. We are doing just about the sort of thing, given what we know about life and people, that we should.

The "Existential" Factor

One further point: Life is short, and calculation of consequences is long. So is the process of making sober decisions, be it calculative or not. At some point, we must act. How much deliberation, how much calculation, is the right amount? There is no easy rule about this, but it is clear that these things, like everything else, can be excessive. That is one very good reason why a morality that imposes some fairly definite and strong constraints on us, but otherwise leaves us free to pursue our lives as we will—and free to take the consequences—is surely, for most of us, preferable to one that monopolizes our lives, either by filling it chock-a-block with duties or by making our duties so difficult to determine that it fills it instead with agonized moral calculation. That is a further objection to the "radical egalitarian" program, for example. It is highly oppressive, requiring a great deal of us; and its principles are so indeterminate, even while being very demanding, that monopolization of our lives is inevitable. This, surely, is not a rational aim of morality.

---

[39] For a very sensible and perceptive discussion, see Joseph Ellin, *Morality and the Meaning of Life* (Ft. Worth, TX: Harcourt, Brace, 1994).

Personal Concerns versus Moral Requirements

Bernard Williams takes Kant, and some others—notably utilitarians, at least in general theory—to be incapable of adequately appreciating the personal factor in life. On their view, moral requirements are loftily abstract and general and impartial, having no sympathy for or insight into the character of personal obligations, as to spouses, friends, children.

Take the case of the man who must choose between saving his wife and some stranger. In Communist China some time ago, we read a story (possibly apocryphal) of a man who had to choose to save either his family or the local Party Chairman, and chose the latter on the grounds of political duty! Is it possible that he could find this a genuine problem? Or that he could accept a duty to randomize over the two? Incredibly, it was. However, I, and surely almost all of us, think that such purely personal preferences, based on "morally arbitrary" characteristics—such as the color of her eyes, or the particular style with which he plays the guitar, or whatever—are perfectly reasonable and perfectly acceptable. Morality, on the contractarian view, is entirely a matter of trying to optimize benefit from interaction, with the benefit being estimated in the light of our own different understandings of what is good. We are not concerned to advance some massive "total sum of good" in which we or our spouses and comrades count as mere digits in the sum. That is, actually, one of the main things that makes the contractarian view so superior. Realistically, it asks each of us to sacrifice no more, to depart from guidance by our own preferences no more than what would constitute a sort of investment, to be repaid in the course of general interaction with our fellows. One reason we want a rule against murder is that we don't want our friends to be murdered—it's by no means solely a matter of our own skins. Most morally significant relations are person-to-person, and all persons are individuals, with unique histories of their own. Generalization is unsafe, adjustment to individuals often called for. None of this undoes the general viewpoint advanced in this book, that there are indeed foundations of morals, and that they eventuate in a very general principle of refraining from harms to our fellows, together with a disposition to encourage those who are also helpful, and to be helpful ourselves. But just how to help *this* person, just what *would* significantly harm that one—these can be very difficult things to discern, indeed. Given the differences among people that are so much the stuff of our experience of life, why wouldn't they be?

Unchosen Personal Obligations

We don't make social contracts with our children, do we? We don't choose to have this particular set of parents, yet we often feel obligated toward them. The tribesman feels a strong sense of obligation and loyalty to his fellows, despite never having joined that tribe. But does this really prove anything? These particular kinds of obligations are not ones that hold for everybody in the world; they hold for fellow members of that tribe, say. And while they are not chosen, we can certainly say that people have the right to exit from such relationships if they can; no one has the right to hold an unwilling participant in his clutches—neither an individual nor a tribe—nor, for that matter, an ethnic group or clan, either.

Once we distinguish between the acquisition of a relationship, which may well not have been voluntary, and exit from it, which always in principle should be voluntary, we can avoid the misapprehension that the liberal point of view in morals would be fatal to the flourishing of personal relationships.[40]

*   *   *

The project of part 3 is to expound the basic principles of morals in view of their rationale as it emerges from our earlier discussions. We start with a general exposition of what has come to be known as the "contractarian" theory of morals, according to which right and wrong are conformity or violation of rules that are essentially *agreements* among all persons, for mutual benefit. Obviously these are agreements that are not literally negotiated or signed; the theory is named in a somewhat metaphorical manner. However, its basic idea is straightforward: that there will be no reason for one person to modify his or her own behavior in relation to others, in ways that go against his or her interests, unless others are willing to do likewise. Moral behavior, then, is *cooperative*—it is good for each provided that all observe the rules in question. This raises a basic and much-discussed question: "why should I be moral?" A sharpened sense of that question enables us to see that in general it is because we will do better if we are all moral, but that it is easy to see why individuals in particular situations would nevertheless be tempted not to conform. This leaves us all with a familiar project: to habituate each other to the

---

[40] For further treatment of this issue, see Jan Narveson, "Collective Rights?" originally in *Canadian Journal of Law and Jurisprudence* 4, no. 2 (July 1991): 329–45. It is reproduced in Jan Narveson, *Respecting Persons in Theory and Practice* (Lanham, MD: Rowman Littlefield, 2002, ch. 13, 225–42.

basic restrictions of morals, general success at which would certainly make life better for all. But what, then, do the fundamental principle(s) of morality call for? The proposed answer, familiar from a lengthy stream of the major moral philosophers of the past, is that there is just one fundamental principle of justice or "strong" obligation (the kind that can be enforced)—and that is the principle that everyone is to respect everyone else's general freedom. But there is another side to morals, where we are not proposing to compel compliance, but rather where we are *recommending* practice. Here charity and benevolence rule: we are each encouraged to do more than the minimum, to benefit others well beyond that merely respecting their liberty calls for. Along the way, views such as egalitarian ones, and virtue theories, are put in their proper places.

Happiness, Living Well, and Doing Well

Introduction

What are we to do in life? Are there some general purposes that we should be aware of, and organize our lives around? Are there some special virtues we simply must cultivate and display, on pain of living a bad life? Is there meaning in life? The point of view of our preceding section, part 3, is that these matters are at least largely personal. Many have thought otherwise. Among those many are quite a few who have, as I think, confused what I have been calling morals (or morality) with what I call ethics. It is not surprising that such theorists could not regard these questions as "personal"—we don't want murder to be a matter of taste. But once we make that distinction, it will be much less obvious that there must be a philosophically correct master theory about how to live lurking in the background. In this concluding short section, we will look at a few of the major ideas in this area. Good books have been written about it, and readers keen on more are referred to them.[1]

Generally speaking, we can divide theories on this general subject into two groups, or perhaps three depending on what you count.

(1) One group of theories base themselves on the claim that there are purposes *inherent* in our natures; these, as it were, set the stage for our lives and tell us what we should be doing.

(2) Another group, which might be regarded as a variant of the first, has it that these purposes come, somehow, from *outside* of us, for example, from God, or perhaps from society.

(3) But a third view has it that individuals have a very wide range of choice what to do with their lives, and which ones they choose not only is but *ought to be* entirely up to them. Again, there is a subdivision possible.

(3a) *Hedonism* is the view that the thing to do in life is maximize pleasure, or more specifically *net* pleasure. But what do we get the pleasure from? Are there good and bad pleasures? Some will say yes, some no. If the criterion of a "bad" pleasure is that the pleasure in question will make for pains later, or will crowd out other and greater pleasures, then the view stays within the perimeter of pure hedonism. If it's something quite else, however, then the view is not purely hedonistic.

(3b) Other theories are nonhedonistic, or claim to be. These might be called "ideal value" theories. Some of those will in effect be versions of the self-realization idea. In our brief treatment, we will look at the latter

---

[1] For one interesting example, see Raymond Belliotti, *Happiness Is Overrated* (Lanham, MD: Rowman and Littlefield, 2003). See also the excellent chapter on "The Meaning of Life" in Ellin, *Morality and the Meaning of Life* (Ft. Worth, TX: Harcourt, Brace, 1994).

first—at the idea that the good life is what "realizes our natures." This indeed is what many of the ancients would have understood by the term 'naturalism,' rather than its modern metaethical meaning.

The idea that life might be "meaningful" and how it might be so, and why that's a good thing to try to achieve, will occupy us first. We will then look at hedonism. That will lead fairly naturally to what we may call the "liberal" view—that there is no end of ways to live a good life, and the criteria for considering it so are personal. Finally, we will ask what the point is, after all: why we might gain anything from thinking about this subject.

In all this, by the way, the reader must bear in mind that we are not directly addressing *morality*, which, as you will know from the previous material, is a fairly special kind of value-domain.

Human Nature

All of us humans were born of two human parents, and are equipped with bodies of a recognizable and distinctive kind—two arms, two legs, we walk erect, and so on. The 'and so on' takes in quite a range. All of this gear *functions* in various ways: the eye enables us to see, the legs to walk, and so on. How far does this 'and so on' take us? Enthusiasts suppose that everything in the human body was designed for a purpose. Those who think so have a problem with, say, the appendix, which appears to do nothing except sometimes to cause enough trouble that we will need an appendectomy, thus providing an income for surgeons—or meet an early death, which no doubt might be useful in a few cases. But more seriously, there is the question of in what sense we may attribute "purpose" to things like hearts and legs. Note that the term 'function' would commit us much less than 'purpose.' That a thing functions a certain way is a fact about it, and if you want to use the thing, you're likely to have much better luck if you use it so as to take advantage of its functional capabilities. But in which way do we do so? It is the function of the cognitive part of the mind, say, to think—but think *about what*? Insofar as we're just talking about function, it could be anything. And it often is: very evil people sometimes make very effective use of their brains, enabling them to be much more evil than if they were not so bright. On the other hand, there are the Mozarts and the Newtons of this world. They too use their brains, but to very different and far better effect. If we propose to say that the criterion of goodness in life is the "realization of our natures," then, the problem is that just to say that someone is utilizing his or her personal capabilities is hardly to say that what that person does is admirable. What he or she uses them for is what matters, and that seems to be entirely underdetermined by talk of function.

While we are making distinctions, there's an important one to invoke at this point. It could be thought that the nature we are to realize is that of a human being in general: one template, as it were, for all. Alternatively, though, it can be held that what Sheila Smith ought to realize is the nature of Sheila Smith, and not a human being in general. There are two questions here. One of them is on what this talk of "realization" comes to at all. The other is on just what we would focus our self-realization efforts, supposing we could make something of it. We'll take the first one first.

"Realizing" the Self

The idea seems to be that, lurking within us somewhere, as it were, there is this thing—one's self—trying to get out, and we are to help it do so. This might sound a bit crazy (and indeed, as I shall argue, really is so). But I put it that way in order to focus on the central issue. To "realize" is to "make real," on the face of it. But so far as reality goes, there is a problem, as it were, of generosity. Suppose I have to choose between doing x and y—can't do both. And I choose x. Now my life will include a doing of x—that will now be "real," and the life in which I choose y will not happen, so it won't be "real." Is there any way to escape the consequence that—alas, for this theory—the idea of self-realization is completely useless? For no matter what we do, the person who does that, rather than anything else he or she might have done instead, will be *real*. We can't *help* realizing ourselves! The self you realize will inevitably be *you*. As you live, you assemble, so to say, the material of your autobiography—the good, the bad, and the ugly. The idea of "aiming" at doing this is without meaning, since there is simply no sense to the idea that you might fail to achieve *that*.

Those wanting to avoid this must say, somehow, that some lives we might have lived are more real than others. Or better, that they are "the true you." If you go one way, you live the wrong sort of life for a person such as you, and you'll do badly; live the other and you'll do well. The question is, do we derive the criteria for appraisal of our results *from* the idea of self-realization?

Now, the idea that some of our possible selves might be more real than others offers something we want: namely, the sense that we can do better or worse, and that we can have enough access to the criteria of saying one or the other that we can be reasonably confident about the judgment. Yes: but the question is, is the relevant criterion that of *real-*

ity? If we do better rather than worse, will it really have been *because* this "more real" creature wanting to get out did, happily, manage to do so— or not? Alas, it doesn't sound promising.

Desire

Theoretical life regarding the role of nature becomes a lot easier if we help ourselves to the notions of desire, want, interest, aspiration. Given those, a promising idea would be that we do well when we succeed in living the sort of life we *want* to live, and do worse when we don't do that. We all have desires, after all, and these automatically entail criteria of success and failure: for desires have objects, which may either be achieved or not. Typically, they can not only be "achieved or not" but also achieved to greater or lesser degree, and even in different ways. Think of being a big success in a lesser league or a minor team player in the National Hockey Leagues. Or of switching from hockey to "ringette," and becoming a dazzling success at that when one was merely so-so at full-up hockey.[2]

One way to go with self-realization, then, is to take it that the realization of "self" is actually the achievement of what the self in question *desires*. Then one question would be whether there are some very basic objects that everyone desires, and such that a "better life" is one in which *those* objects are obtained. But another obvious option is that different people have different desires, even down to quite basic levels. Thus Joanne would realize herself by doing entirely different things than Lorna or Alistair.

In either case, this kind of theory again runs into a severe problem. When we act, do we not always act for some or other purpose? Moreover, don't we always do what we *most want to do at that time?* If so, what is this about "real" desires that we might be more or less successful at achieving? How can there be any such thing?

And if somehow there is such a thing, then why do these things have normative weight? Suppose I can choose between one of my "real" desires and what I merely feel desirous of right now—which is something quite different, as it happens. Why should I be sorry if I suppress the former and go with the latter? It must be part of the idea here that the desires that are "real" are somehow also the more substantial ones. But if they

---

[2] "Ringette" is somewhat like hockey, but a lot safer, played with a rubber ring instead of a hard puck. See http://www.whockey.com/ringette/. For American readers, no doubt similar comparisons can be made with types of ball games (baseball, softball, slow pitch softball).

are, presumably they would tip the balance against the short-term ones. Or if not, why not?

A desire is a desire for something, a certain kind of outcome. Why do we want what we do, though? Do we evaluate the outcome, and then on the basis of that desire the one with the best outcome? If so, what's driving our practical theory is not desire but the value of the outcome, which then, apparently, must be assessed differently.

And then there is the very serious issue, how do we know what we want? Or might we not know this crucial thing? And how do we find it out if we don't? People are said to have spent years searching for what they really want in life.

There appears to be a big difference between desire and value.[3] Or is there? Suppose we claim that some possible outcome has a high value—but we *don't* desire it. Then what? Value should guide our choices, but if it isn't desired, it won't and can't. We do what we most want to do; if upon inspection we don't want something, we don't go for it. Or at least, not unless we distinguish other motivational states from wanting. For example, someone might feel conscientiously driven toward doing x, even though he characterizes the situation by saying that he would much rather do y, which doing x precludes. But how is a conscientious drive different from a peculiar but very strong desire?

It is a claim of this book that in the case of morality, at least, there are discoverable principles at work that enable us to put our desires at any given time in perspective. Still, what drives the whole project is our interest in, thus our desire for, the sort of things that morality helps us, in social contexts, to achieve. What distinguishes moral motivation from the rest is not that it is a uniquely different thing from desire altogether, but desire in light of various subtle considerations of interaction. Moral desire is reasoned desire in a way in which desire for chocolate is, very likely, not. But it's still broadly of a piece with other desires.

There are other differences among desires. We can have whims, we can have stable, long-term interests, we can have medium-level projects that we desire to get accomplished, and so on. Meanwhile, we have all these various desires because of the way we are. Something about me is what makes it the case that I want this or that rather than the other. But the idea of "self-realization" seems to be that we should undertake a study of ourselves in order to see what we do really want. Is that possible?

---

[3] See, for example, E. J. Bond, *Reason and Value* (Cambridge: Cambridge Univ. Press, 1983) where it is argued that value has nothing to do with desire—except that once we know what is good, we also *want* it.

Health as a Model

Health is a good example of a value that virtually everyone holds. At times we will trade off a certain level of health for something else that we think is worth more, all things considered. Still, health is a major item on the agenda of most of us, in the sense that when it is threatened we will do a great deal to attempt to get it back at a good level. That level varies a lot: some people devote large parts of the day to exercise, avoid many foods that they might find quite delicious, and avoid many enjoyable activities that they believe will lead to ill health. There is a question of the "mean"—the degree of alteration of otherwise desirable activities that we should put up with in order to improve, or prevent a further deterioration, of health.

Of particular interest is health's amenability to science. Humankind at large now knows a great deal more about health than in previous eras. Progress is being made at defeating major diseases such as cancer. And almost all of us will follow advice of our doctors on the ground that the doctor knows better than we do what is good for our health—in contrast to previous millennia, in which following doctor's orders was likely to hasten one's demise. The knowledge we can have about our health is, usually, objective.

Or is it? Doctors are notoriously fallible. They are not always right and are, uncomfortably often, seriously, even fatally, wrong. They disagree to a disconcerting degree among themselves. All this may be granted, but still, we plausibly think that health is to a very substantial degree amenable to knowledge. Why is health desirable, though? Is health an intrinsic value? The short answer to this last question is—not *mainly*. The answer is not merely no, for health is a plausible intrinsic value, in its place: it's something one doesn't need to look further to justify wanting it. A sense of health and vitality is a good thing to have, indeed—but to rest there is to commit a sort of intuitionist error. We don't need to look further into its intrinsic value, because there is a general, background case for thinking health will be extrinsically desirable: namely, that its absence gets in the way of almost anything we might do, and its extreme absence is fatal. Health is an odd intrinsic value because when we have it, we mostly don't notice it. We just go ahead and do all those things that good health enables us to do. On occasion, we will *feel* healthy: vigor, a sense of well-being, are doubtless nice states to be in. But they are also rarely felt, especially by people who exemplify them outstandingly.

Health puts the idea of realizing one's nature in perspective. Our natures enable us to do all sorts of things, and being in good health mostly enables us to do almost anything we might want to do better than if we aren't in good health. But that still doesn't get us to health as a value above all else. We might have good violin-playing genes, as it were: we might be well suited for excellent accomplishment at this or that. But does it follow that we want to do those things? No. Does it even follow that we *ought* to do them? No. What does follow is that we might want to consider doing those things, since there's a good chance that we might succeed if we do.

To see this last, consider two sorts of cases. One obvious one is that we might have great assassin genes, too. We might be such that we would be brilliant at some thoroughly evil activity. If we were to find out that we would be, should we then get into the murder biz? For excellent moral reasons, we should *not*, obviously. "Fulfilling one's nature" is not necessarily the way to go. The other sort of case is where doing something that you might be really good at just leaves you completely cold. You might be excellent at mathematics, but somehow it just doesn't appeal to you. Is that a defect? Suppose that you have a talent that could earn you a very large income. You'd like that large income, too. But doing the things well that this talent enables you to do simply doesn't interest you. You prefer, perhaps, cooking and oil painting, though you aren't very good at either of them. Aristotle seems to have neglected this possibility, or perhaps thought it impossible. But most of us know people who exemplify it in some way or other—very likely including ourselves. We should not regret not having spent our lives doing something we really wouldn't like very much, if instead we did something we *did* like very much even though it left us in "genteel poverty." We could regret that we didn't like doing those things we would have been so good at—that's another matter. But the regret shouldn't bother us very much.

And *that* might be what's "in our nature." Is there any way to know this, or find it out if you don't know it? Most likely, the way is the way of experience. It's not very efficient—but it is probably the only way. That, as they say, is life.

Virtues—One Last Time

We've looked at the idea of virtue twice already. This last glance concerns its potential for telling us how to live a good life. Aristotle thought that the happy person is the one who exemplifies maximum virtue, and he has many followers in this. Is there anything to that idea? We have to try to separate two questions here. The first is whether the virtues are to be regarded as things that make it likely that their possessor will be happy— or are they, instead, what literally *constitutes* happiness, so that there simply can't be any question that virtue and happiness are correlated? The second is whether happiness is what fundamentally matters? Or is it that virtue is so important that if one literally had to choose between virtue and happiness, one should prefer virtue? Neither of these is an easy question.

Before proceeding further, there is an essential cautionary note about the discussion. For there is a tendency to equate the category of virtue in general with that of *moral* virtue. This may be confusing—well, indeed, it *is* confusing! Part of the confusion is due to the ancient identification of the moral with the department of self-control, rather than with my much narrower notion of rules for the group. Group rules do call for self-control in certain respects, as I have argued; but the converse does not hold. Society has no business in calling upon you to observe the mean in regard to many things that have little or no effect on the well-being of your neighbors. Nevertheless, those things are, quite possibly, very important to you personally. For example, consider obesity. The medical people tell us, with good evidence, that this is a likely cause of diabetes, heart attacks, and other maladies, and on that account to be avoided. Aesthetically, there is a preference, at least currently, for slim rather than fat figures too, and the slim person is likely to enjoy the appreciation of her or his fellows—no small matter in many people's lives. Still, it is not, in my narrow sense, *immoral* to be fat, even if it is a bad idea personally.

But now, to return to the first questions distinguished above, we have the issue of whether people might be fat but happy. If they are, is overeating even a vice at all? Or if it is, then is the happy fat person wise in having little use for that particular virtue? If virtue really is logically a distinct matter from happiness, then what makes a virtue a virtue?

Here again, there is an idea that the virtue of an acting entity, as we might call it—one that *does* something or other—is, as Plato has it, that which enables the thing to do that something *well*, or even, in the limiting case, at all. The champion NBA basketball player is very likely to exemplify such virtues as coordination, speed, quickness at selected cognitive skills such as sizing up the pattern of play by his opponents, and a few others. Possession of these virtues is likely to make him an excellent player, which in turn may earn him a very high salary, the appreciation of millions of fans, and hopefully his own exhilaration at being able to do those things so well. Will they make him happy? Maybe, maybe not. Will they make him *morally good?* Again, maybe, but not at all obviously. Front page news about the foibles and sometimes the misdemeanors of highly talented athletes are not rare in contemporary newspapers.

I concentrated specifically on basketball-playing virtues in order to bring out two points. One is that just made: not all virtues are moral virtues, or even have very much to do with those. The other is that it is quite possible for people to be not very interested in cultivating or even possessing many such virtues. I am sure I wouldn't *mind* having the more important basketball virtues, but I have no intention of doing anything to bring it about that I have them, at least insofar as they are specific to that sport, and the fact that I lack them generally does not, I must admit, bother me overly, or at all.

The story with moral virtues isn't quite like that. Can we be indifferent to *them*? Philippa Foot famously remarks that she can know perfectly well that cowardice is a vice, courage a virtue, and know that she lacks the virtue quite utterly.[4] That Foot can say this about courage is interesting, and plausible. But here again we have the familiar confusion threatening the discussion: that courage is a "moral" virtue is a familiar view, and plausible, in one sense of the word 'moral': but when it's a question of the morality of the group, it is not quite so plausible. We do think courage may be needed for some moral purposes, and on that account to be recommended. In ancient Greece and many other places and times, courage was especially needed because of the high likelihood of typical men being put to work as soldiers in wartime, and there courage is the classic virtue. But do we really think it's in general your moral *duty* to *be courageous?* It would not be easy to say the same thing about, say murder: "Hey, I know murder is wrong, but I know perfectly well that that wouldn't keep me from murdering anybody!" There would be serious question what someone who said that meant. For example, as some have unhappily been known to say, "Oh, I know there's this quaint custom in our society, that we shouldn't kill people, but we Supermen are above that sort of thing . . ." (or whatever). People like that need to be scrutinized to see whether they're serious. If they are, the rest of us need to worry.

We come, I think, to the same conclusion as before. If it is claimed that virtue promotes happiness, that will be because one selects the particular set of virtues, whatever they are, that will promote the kind of happiness that *you* can and want to have—not because happiness consists in being virtuous. And morally, the virtues are recommended because they are tendencies to do things that are independently assessed as right. Virtue as the fundamental variable drops out.

Accomplishment

The general idea of self-realization is frequently close company to the idea that we humans should be "doing something" instead of just going on from day to day with no particular ends in view. Just why it should

---

[4] Foot, "Moral Beliefs."

be thought that we are, somehow, "fulfilling human nature" if we spend our lives working for charitable causes, say, or achieving positions of great importance or power, or making a lot of money, or becoming great actors or musicians, rather than living the life of a ne'er-do-well or a hobo is not entirely clear. It is clear that the achievers are useful to the rest of us. We benefit from their activities, usually, and if we don't, there's a problem. (Was Al Capone an "achiever"?) And it is generally clear that achievement is useful to oneself.

It was a familiar theme of the Protestant ethic that we should be spending our time doing good works of various sorts, including commercial works, the idea being that the Lord would look with particular favor on accomplishers. That idea, indeed, was important enough that we had better devote some attention to it in this book; we'll look at religious ethics shortly. Meanwhile, if we detach this idea from religion and simply ask what it has going for it, we really don't lack for decent answers. Accomplishments of various kinds make life interesting, challenging, and, with luck, satisfying. The sense that we are being useful to other people is characteristically part of it, and a perfectly good part at that: why *shouldn't* we devote a good deal of our lives to making other people's lives go better? Sociobiology no doubt will add a few things about this, but we needn't have pretensions to "science" if we observe that people who are involved in various fairly specific projects, who devote much of their time and energy to them, and who are at least fairly successful while they're at it, are living good lives.

Meaning

Jokes abound on the "meaning of life"—images of gurus on mountain tops uttering solemn platitudes or weird formulations about wet birds and rare air and such. Still, there seems to be something to the idea that life can be meaningful, and that if it can, it should. But the first question must be, what is the meaning of 'meaning' in this context? We have a decent idea of linguistic meaning, but it is not clear how that applies, if at all, to life as such. The meaning of life does bring up the question of the meaning of 'life'—the word, that is, rather than the thing. And there the trouble is that many more organisms besides humans have life. If life as such has some sort of meaning, it is something we would share with snails and alligators, for example. And what might that be? There is an answer, of sorts: plausibly, what all life does is to reproduce itself.

This, actually, provides a nice test case for the idea of "meaning of life." People engage in sexual activity for the sake of reproduction, frequently enough to staff the world, currently, with around six billion specimens, up from less than half that number at the start of the twentieth century. True: but also, people engage in sex with no intention of reproduction, and indeed they take great care to avoid it on, probably, most occasions when it occurs. How does that fit in with the idea that the meaning of life is reproduction?

We can imagine—we don't even need to imagine, since they do exist—some who assert that those who engage in sex with contraceptives carefully in place are somehow doing something *wrong,* contravening, say, the intentions of Mother Nature. That requires that Mother Nature have some intentions, which is problematic enough; moreover, it requires that her intentions are the "right" ones and ours, if different, need correction—which is even more problematic. Perhaps it is thought that Mother Nature's intentions are prior because she must, so to say, win out in the long run. But that would bring up the question why we should prefer the long run envisaged there—very long indeed—to the benefits of engaging in highly pleasurable action in the short run. For after all, in the long run, as the apt and frequently quoted saying of Keynes has it, we are all dead. And while it may be intriguing to say that all life aims at death, to take that literally is to indulge in great nonsense. We will die— we hope it will be later rather than earlier—and just how we die is a topic of interest too. But death, as Epicurus put it, is where we are not, and to aim at death is to aim at nonexistence, nothing. Seriously doing that undermines all activity, making it meaningless, not meaningful.

No doubt some sexual activity may be put down as meaningless; but in the sense in which that is clearly true, there are plenty of cases in which it is equally clearly false, even though these are not cases where reproduction is envisaged. Couples often engage in sex out of strong affection. The couples in question feel wonderful about this, both during and after. They provide paradigms of one kind of humanly meaningful activity. But there are innumerable others, and most of them seem to have scant connection with reproduction. There must be people to enjoy and appreciate the products of many meaningful activities, but that makes reproduction a necessary background condition for these, rather than their *point.* And that, indeed, is the point here: the evolutionary "goal" of man may be reproduction, but my goal in reading an interesting novel, or yours in playing tennis, or someone else's in solving a tough problem in mathematics, is obviously not. We can enjoy listening to Brahms or playing chess, or for that matter taking a nice hot shower, with no thought of reproduction. The *meaning* of the claim that the meaning of life is reproduction is what is called into question here. Either the connection to literal reproduction is so distant and obscure that there seems nothing to the claim, or it is just obviously silly, as a generalization about the meaning of all human life.

This is all in addition to the rather fundamental point that reproduction seems an oddly bad answer to the question, 'what does it all mean?' Recall Aristotle's famous observation, that if everything is valuable only as a means to something else, then all action is "empty and vain." If the point of life is said to be, merely, *more* life, we should feel cheated. For one thing, there's good life and bad life, and if we are to talk of "point" and "meaning" then we should surely be claiming that life can be and often is, and as often as possible should be, good rather than bad and good rather than indifferent. Reproduction for the sake of reproduction doesn't suffice as an explanation of that.

I noted that linguistic meaning seems to be the paradigmatic sort of 'meaning'—the kind where the word 'meaning' is most at home. Whether that is right or not, we can pick up one aspect of linguistic meaning as constituting a contribution to the question of the meaning of life. Words mean by their relation to things that are *not* words. Typical words mean by virtue of reference: 'cat' refers to cats. If others do not—'to' does not "refer" to something called "to"—they nevertheless have their meaning by the way they contribute to meaningful sentences which, as wholes, convey something about the world apart from words. Does a meaningful life have meaning by virtue of its relation to something *else*, something outside of life altogether?

Again, there can be stories about molecules and such, working away in systems, which in the end turn out to be you and me. Yet our lives do not *refer* to such things; they are merely *dependent* on them, if modern science is to be trusted—as we will presume it is. Not only can we take in, and admire, a string quartet with no thought of neurons and DNA or whatever, but to be thinking about the latter at the time would be a major distraction. Something has gone seriously awry with the idea that life has meaning if reference to something else outside of it is supposed to be its essence.

The same goes for religious interpretations. People sometimes think it's great if we are cogs in a grand scheme of the gods, but let's face it: Bach's religious music is a great deal better than, say, one of his minor fellow composers, despite the sameness of subject matter. There is boring religious music and inspiring religious music. Reference to the gods just isn't enough to do the job. And if the sopranos are too busy thinking about how great god is, at cost of sufficient attention to pitch and dynamics and tempi, the results will not be good.

Lives do, however, get devoted to various goals. Some people devote their entire lives, as they see it, to pursuit of one, very large goal. We might well say that, in those cases, the goals in question provide meaning for that agent's life. But what about those who don't organize their lives in that way?—which is by far the majority of us. We pursue many goals, but our lives are not dominated by any one of them. Are we making some major mistake? It's hard to see how this could be proven, or even very seriously argued for.

Moreover, the one-goal view has a further major problem if it is to be brought in at the level we are discussing this. Is this a goal we could change, or not? My intended examples above are of people who pursue one goal throughout, say, their mature lives—but a goal that many other people do not pursue, and a goal that the goal-pursuers themselves did not always have and must have come to adopt over time. Now, suppose we ask why the ones who pursue it do so, and why those who do not do not? Can we answer this question? The single-goal person might claim that what he pursues is *the ultimate* goal, the one inherent in everybody's nature, somehow. If he does claim that, he could easily be right so far as his own case is concerned—but why, then, don't these other people pursue it too? Why does it not even appear to them to be very attractive? Are they deluded?

There are two ways they might be claimed to be. First, it could be claimed that they really are pursuing it but don't know it. Or second, it could be claimed that they admittedly are not pursuing it, but in that they are making a big mistake. But in both cases, there are strong replies—to my mind, definitive. To the first one, we can say that if this is a goal we can be pursuing without knowing it, then the sense in which we are "pursuing a goal" is being tinkered with. One good way to win an argument in this area is to redefine your position so as to be compatible with that of your opponent. But it is a pointless maneuver. Unless some sense can be given of the notion of pursuing a goal without knowing it—especially when it's a goal quite different, even opposite, to the ones we are quite sure we *are* pursuing—then this claim is without substance.

The claim that we are making a big mistake has the familiar problem of begging the question. "You are making a big mistake because, as you can see, you won't achieve goal G if you go on as you are!"—so says the pursuer of goal G. But if the reply is that I don't *want* to pursue G, and thus am not at all bothered by the fact that I'm not achieving it, then this reply bounces off—it's just irritating, not a real reason. Unless it can be shown that the goals we are pursuing will, say, be frustrated by the fact that we are not pursuing G instead of the ones we are pursuing, or some such thing, this kind of argument is bound to be ineffective. And at worst, it's arrogant: it comes to just insisting that others do things *my* way, even though I can produce no reason why they should. The major point is that many people lead happy lives despite lack of a single all-consuming goal. And for that matter, some who do pursue such goals do not impress us as being particularly happy.

That leads us to the subject of happiness. Is it everything? Or is it, even, very much? We will look at this large subject at least briefly. But before getting to it, let's draw some conclusions about meaning.

David Wiggins observes that the modern world view is not conducive to the old religious-based ideas that we have a "place" in the world, set by the gods.[5] The atoms and the planets don't care one way or the other what we do. But does it follow that we should feel lost or insignificant, say, by comparison with the immensity of the astronomical universe around us? Indeed not: this is a mistake; that kind of "size" is an irrelevancy. Meaning has nothing to do with size in that sense. But what does it have to do with in the century of the naturalistic fallacy? Wiggins very shrewdly observes that taken at face value, the naturalistic fallacy has a bizarre implication: that there is no way to ground any of our preferences in the facts of life—that, as it were, underneath it all, everything is arbitrary and thus absurd. Wiggins constructs, in terms that are probably incomprehensible to most readers, a semantic apparatus designed to restore room in the world for values of a sort. Rather than being irrelevant to values, facts are underdeterminative of them: many different evaluative constructions are compatible with similar factual arrays. Nevertheless, this is good enough, he thinks. The upshot, in more prosaic terms, is that the meaning of life is not just whatever you choose to make it, but on the other hand, that it has a lot to do with what you do and choose. There is no simple formula for drawing a given sort of meaning from a given segment of life, but still, some sorts of life clearly have more meaning than others, and of those that are meaningful, each has its own particular sort of meaning.

If we refrain from putting too much weight on the specific term 'meaning', talking instead simply of the value, or valuableness of life, then values to live by are not far to seek. Almost all of us have them, and one has no idea what to say to those who profess to see nothing there. Perhaps they have not looked hard enough. Meaning might be found, for example, in the aesthetic aspect of life, taken broadly: not just the properties of paintings and operas and such, but of leaves in the pathway, sunsets, the sound of our neighbors' kids playing, and so on. These examples also suggest that we needn't look in grand projects, nor even any projects, to find meaning; though there is potential meaning in all of them.

---

[5] David Wiggins, "Truth, Invention, and the Meaning of Life," in his book *Needs, Values and Truth: Essays in the Philosophy of Value*, 3rd ed. (Oxford: Clarendon Press, 1998). Reprinted in *20th Century Ethcial Theory*, ed. Stephen M. Cahn and Joram P. Haber (Englewood Cliffs, NJ: Prentice-Hall, 1995), 541–72. (Citations are to the reprinted work.)

A Note on the Religious Life

Many, many people profess to find meaning in life by embracing some religion or other. This raises complicated issues, since many of those same people think also that their religion has something to do with morality. To think so is, I have argued, mistaken. But that still leaves religion, for many people, as a source of emotional support, and as providing an array of symbols, rites, and forms within which to live one's life. We outsiders shouldn't knock that. What we do have to worry about, however, is whether religion doesn't have a serious liability, a serious disadvantage, in that it appears to be very closely involved with a set of beliefs, or at any rate, attitudes that look very much like, or appear to presuppose, beliefs. Are these *genuine* beliefs? That is a difficult question. In form, though, it looks like it, even to the point that religious people often claim that this or that historic event or might-have-been event actually provides *evidence* for the truth of their beliefs. To that, doubters will reply that the historical claims in question are either false or badly garbled and when clarified, actually provide evidence *against* those beliefs. Different believers will point to various different facts as providing evidence for their own particular doctrines—though each doctrine is incompatible with all the rest.

The worrisome issue for religion, then, is whether the attractions of that particular religion's way of life are undermined by the epistemological situation regarding their beliefs. But perhaps this is only a worry for intellectuals. Again, very few religious people take courses on the philosophy of religion; most accept their beliefs "on faith" without further ado. They don't worry about its possibly shaky foundations, if 'foundations' is even the right term to apply here.

Moreover, it's possible to take up a stance such as that of the famous American-Spanish philosopher George Santayana who seems to have regarded religion as entirely aesthetic. His attitude toward the content of religious belief seems to have been entirely skeptical, saying for example, "That fear first created the gods is perhaps as true as anything so brief could be on so great a subject."[6] The sensible response is to dismiss the stories as irrational and take it from there. Where? Well, one way to go concerning the religious life, or something near to it, is to drain it of its theoretical commitments, as do, nearly, the Unitarians. There is a famous quip: that Unitarianism is "the belief that there is at most one god."[7] The Ethical Culture Society, an American group,

---

[6] George Santayana, *The Life of Reason: Reason in Religion* (New York: Scribner's, 1905), 28.

[7] Attributed by some to Alfred North Whitehead, but I do not know the source, if so.

eschews any official religious belief,[8] yet holds service-like meetings in buildings that look like churches, some of them very attractive. All this lends some support to the idea that religion is more nearly a social than an epistemic phenomenon, and that its attractions are as much a matter of bonding with others as anything else.

Let's leave it that it is possible to distinguish different aspects of religion, some of which would explain its attractions even to persons who are left cold by the theological claims in which most religions claim to consist. Few lovers of music would not miss the music of Bach, which might never have happened without his robust Lutheranism. We can be impressed at the lovely dignity of a Quaker meeting-house gathering, or the solemn rituals of the established versions of Christianity. And few, alas, can fail to be impressed at the level of fanaticism achieved by too many religions. Violent intolerance is a cross that many religions bear. It needs to be discarded—and retaining the good features of the religions that generate it while simultaneously shucking its antihuman and inhuman features is no easy job for would-be believers.

We have to conclude that religion as a credible version of the good life is riddled with problems.

Hedonism

The view that pleasure is the good is called *hedonism*. Hedonism has rather a distinguished history, and its popularity is hardly surprising. But we must begin by distinguishing two versions: that pleasure is *a* good, and that pleasure is *the* good. The first is far easier to defend—if defense is even needed—than the second. One objection to it is that there are *bad* pleasures. If that is true in any very fundamental sense, then it is not clear that we can even count pleasure as a good at all, since something's being a pleasure is compatible with its being bad.

But there is an obvious account of bad pleasures that would reconcile it with the narrower thesis. Bad pleasures can be, in Bentham's terms, *impure*:[9] they can lead to pain in future. In that case, the fact that these pleasures are bad would not be due to their being *intrinsically* bad, but to their external effects. A hedonist does not need to maintain the implausible thesis that pleasures never lead to pains. Quite the contrary: the archetypical hedonist Epicurus held that *seeking* pleasure is a mistake, because the kind of pleasures you can get by seeking them always turn

---

[8] For more, see http://www.nysec.org/sitemap/about-ethical-culture/.
[9] Jeremy Bentham, *Principles of Morals and Legislation*, ch. 4.

out to have negative effects.[10] The thing to do, he thought, is simply avoid pains, and then pleasure will take care of itself.

Epicurus's hypothesis is evidently an empirical one, and it seems to most of us clearly false. Many pleasures are relatively "pure" and do not lead to significant pains in future. Plato and others supply good examples. Music, for instance, is pretty unlikely to do this, as is a quiet afternoon's reading, conversation with a good friend, and many other things. Epicurus may have had in mind wild parties, about which he does have a point. But even there, we can play our cards right and avoid, say, drinking to excess, or getting involved with shady characters, and yet enjoy the party greatly.

What about the sadist, who simply enjoys torturing people? Even there, it is not hard to argue that the trouble with sadism is that it is *immoral*. That is quite compatible with its pleasures being, taken *purely in themselves*, good—but since this is a good that is impossible to have without the production of major pains to others, the moral case against taking it in itself is overwhelming. In this part of our inquiry, we are not talking as such about morality—but we are allowing for the reasonable presumption that some acts really are immoral and that their being immoral is a major point against them. We will table that issue here, therefore. We won't table the issue arising from a claim that if the hedonist really does get absolutely his maximum pleasure from torturing others—assuming that the others don't like to be so treated, anyway—then it would be rational for the sadist to engage in those activities. The response to this is simple: if there are really people like that, we'll have to deal with it by severe measures, including a major reduction in life expectancy for the sadist.

Provisionally, I propose to take it that pleasure is indeed *a* good, and that it is so at a quite generic level. But the word 'pleasure' calls for some explanation, and a query that will take us to the root of the matter in considering whether the stronger thesis of hedonism, that pleasure is not merely *a*, but indeed *the* good, is plausible.

Consider, then, a specific gustatory pleasure: the taste of a fine wine or a fine chocolate. And compare those—if you can!—with the pleasure of dancing, say, and then of proving a theorem that has eluded you for long. The question arises whether we even *can* usefully "compare" them. What do they have in common?

Here are two components, which add up to a plausible answer insofar as there is one. First, if we are interested in the *pleasures* of these

---

[10] Epicurus. *Letter to Menoeceus*, and *Principal Doctrines* are the brief classics expounding his ideas. There are numerous editions.

things, then we are referring to the *felt* aspect of them, the "immediate experience." The benefits of your mathematical proof may redound for long in the halls of mathematics, and perhaps lead to advances in certain sciences, and so on. But the *pleasure* of proving this theorem will be in the *sense*, the *feeling* of having at last solved this thing. The pleasure of dancing will be in how it feels to be doing so, and not, say, the health or further social benefits of successful participation. Secondly, in calling it pleasure we are in all cases identifying these feelings as "positive."

Can positivity be explained without invoking the very concept—good—that we are attempting to underpin here? I think so. Pleasure is "positive feeling" in the sense that it is the sort of feeling we want, and would seek out. People do not need antecedent explicit value-terminology to recognize these things. Indeed, the fact that we readily ascribe pleasures to animals strongly suggests that this is not at all circular. But positive feeling takes in a very, very wide range of feelings, even though these are only those of our feelings that are "immediate," experienced *as such*, rather than mediated by thought or relations to various other things. And that is what makes them hard to compare if someone insists on comparisons. Some of Chopin's preludes are simply exquisite, perfect. I can also listen to one of John Philip Sousa's fine marches with pleasure. It would be hard to compare the pleasures of these two, even though both are musical experiences—already a pretty narrow genre, relative to the whole spectrum of possible experiences. Yet I have no hesitation in classifying the prelude as a better piece of music than the Sousa march, even though the latter might be a great march. But do I get "more" pleasure out of the prelude? I'm not sure I can even answer that. And that's where the problem begins for hedonism.

Pleasure, I am supposing, is positive feeling. But we can be positive about lots of things that are not feelings. Suppose one is an architect, and devotes much energy to some large building project, which won't be completed until after one's own death perhaps. We can contemplate the prospect of its completion with pleasure, to be sure. But are we to classify the entire endeavor in those terms? Or is it enough to say that this is going to be a great building, and that's all I need to give me a highly positive view of it?

The notion of pleasure is pretty flexible. Some things so called are easy to locate and rate the term 'pleasure' in an obvious and immediate way. By the same token, many other good things are not so easy to locate and rate. To save the strong thesis of hedonism, we could identify pleasure with *all* kinds of positive experience, including the experiences we have in simply contemplating or perceiving various things that we say are good. We can be very, very far from the taste of wine but still talk of pleasure in this way. The question is whether it is now worth doing. Or should we use the term 'pleasure' only for very specific, immediate thrills and leave other good things for other sectors of the evaluative vocabulary?

We much earlier cited a view that pleasure should be replaced by *enjoyment* as the central hedonist concept. This has the advantage that we do say that we enjoy a huge range of things that do not obviously supply us with the sort of immediate sensations that pleasure is generally identified with. It also leaves us with hedonism as a rather plausible doctrine about what is ultimately good. But while it is plausible, it is so in large part because it is so very unhelpful. We cannot learn that enjoyment is the good and then go out and know what to do in life—seek enjoyment! What we will enjoy is a matter of ultimate fact, hard to predict, impossible to quantify.

Ideals

We should not be left with the impression that the good in life is all mundane and domestic. People have ideals, and prominent among them are conceptions of how things could be better for many other people, perhaps all people. The business of thinking about the good is an important one; I have neglected it not because it is unimportant, but rather, because what moral philosophy can discover about it is precious little. Life experience is what is needed here.

On the other hand, it has to be appreciated that on the view here provided, morality is also not an intrinsic good. The good of morals lies in its enabling us to live well in whatever ways we conceive there are to live well, rather than in telling us how to do it—except in its own modest but by no means insignificant quarter. We live well in part by being honest, trustworthy, nonviolent, well-mannered, considerate, fair, and generally sympathetic, as well as by achievement in business, sport, science, education, the arts, or whatever. But notice that one cannot set forth in life simply to display all the moral virtues. You are only honest by engaging in activities honestly. None of those activities is simply the activity of being honest. They are, rather, activities involving exchanges of information or other goods. There is no "activity" of refraining from murder, rape, violence: to refrain is precisely not to engage in a certain activity, and thus to carry on one's other activities in such a way as not to include in them any of those morally proscribed activities.

A moral ideal is, I suggest, an ideal that is supported by distinctively moral considerations. A moral ideal is an ideal whose status as an ideal is that it is in the universal interest of people to encourage it. Such, I suggest, is the virtue of charity. Insofar as it is a virtue, it is upheld by the argument that charitable activities make for the good of someone at the expense of no one. (Note that government "charity" is for this reason an oxymoron.) Any activity that promotes someone's good, as seen by the person whose good is in question, and which does so without causing harm to anyone, is one which everyone should approve, though they need not join in. Charity, as we ordinarily think and as this explication makes clear, is precisely not an enforceable duty. We may put the matter in terms that will make sense to the contemporary university student: charity is not a required course but a recommended option. What is a duty is to approve of charity, if not to practice it oneself. By contrast, it is a duty to refrain from murder, cheating, lying, and in general visiting evil on others—it is not merely recommended that one approve of others refraining.

It is possible to devote a life to good works for people in general. But whether you should actually do that with your life is for you to decide. General morals can hardly require this. Even if we accept the utilitarian view, it would not be required. We do not know whether do-gooders actually do more good than ordinary people going about their self-interested businesses. But it is quite clear that if everyone were to do this, it would be quite indemonstrable that everyone would be better off from that, and quite clearly implausible to think so if most of those who did so did so under duress.

"What is the good life?" is the wrong question, then. "What is the best life for you?" is the right question—and it is *your* question. Perhaps only you can answer it; but more importantly, it is you to whom it matters, you who in some sense must answer it. A book about moral philosophy in the narrow sense employed here is intended to show how and whether certain restrictions must be put on the range of acceptable answers to this question; but no mere philosophical book can actually answer it for you. You have to do that yourself.

Happiness

We can now turn to the subject of happiness. Is happiness essentially a *feeling*? We certainly talk of feeling happy, feelings of happiness, and the like. But then we get to difficult cases such as Beethoven's. Here was a man of great genius, many frustrations, and much pain. Was he, despite all that, happy? Some of us are tempted to say that if we could compose music like Beethoven's, we would account ourselves happy no matter how much physical pain we felt in the process.

Or do we say that Beethoven lived a *great* life, but not a particularly *happy* one? We would, I think, understand this claim. But people who know, for example, the late quartets of this composer may find it difficult to believe that their creator was not a happy man. How, we can ask, could someone write the alternative finale of Op. 130, Beethoven's last and one of his happiest creations, even though he was suffering from his final illness at the time and was not to live another six months, without himself knowing and feeling the joy so wonderfully expressed in that music?

We have no difficulty appreciating that Beethoven was positive about life, however sick, deaf, disappointed in love, and messed up in his various personal circumstances he may have been. The same can happen in concentration camps, ghettos, and many other humanly terrible circumstances. This is often said to be a testimony to the resiliency of the human spirit, and I can't think of an improvement on that characterization—except that it is a tribute to the resiliency of *some* human spirits, for humans there are who have not loved life and have given up trying. Should you and I look to the former, or the latter? If we have our choice, surely, the former. Those people do better and live better lives. If we can emulate them, we should.

But can we? That is much less clear. For one thing, we have no choice about being ourselves. We simply are ourselves, and we aren't any of those other folks out there. Nor does it make clear sense to imagine that we could be. Suppose that I could choose to be you, and I do? What then? If I succeed in "becoming" you, what I would now be is you, not me. If "I" suddenly took on your history and memories, what "I" would remember is everything that you now remember, and nothing else—since I am now you. And at this point, the hypothesis has ceased to make sense.

Emulating others is something we can do, no doubt—but not very much. People sometimes imitate others in certain useful ways: the child may learn to ride a bike thus. Full-time imitation of someone else might be somewhat interesting, but not if the point is self-improvement. Sometimes we learn by imitating. In other cases, we waste our time or become ridiculous. Whatever, it is well to bear in mind that each of us is a distinct individual, and borrowed values and ideas are unlikely to suit.

What there is to the idea of self-realization, self-development, and related notions, is that our various powers are most likely to be well used when they are used in the service of interests we really have. Since there is a huge range of interests we might have, the net purport of this as an instruction is very little. But as an answer to what constitutes a good life, it's perhaps pretty good.

The hedonic view of happiness has more going for it than that: it tells us to select from among this wide range of options those that pay off in terms we will understand, namely because we actually feel them. But while it tells us that, it doesn't tell us, as such, when to conclude that a certain present pleasure is too costly in terms of future ones, and when not. Nor is it clear on the matter of "quality" of pleasure. Almost anyone will think that some pleasures are better than others, even while not obviously more "intense" in any measurable way. But what makes them better? The purport of earlier parts of this book is that there is no use in answering this by invoking intuition. That will be a label for the fact that we just don't in general know the answer to that, rather than itself a helpful answer.

However, that we don't in general know the answer to that can be regarded as a blessing rather than a curse. Life is interesting in considerable part because we don't quite know what's coming next, and we can't reduce its living to an exact science. It is, we may well think, a part of wisdom to settle for that.

Challenges

The general outlook of the kind of very thin hedonism suggested above can easily be supposed to imply that the best life would be one of unalloyed pleasure, uniform and reliable. But that can be met with a variant of another remark of Aristotle's, who lays it down that no one would want to live the life of a child on into adulthood, however happy the child in question.[11] To this we can add that adversity is itself a source of interest. Even considerable adversity, involving much pain and sorrow, can be regarded as a contribution to life that makes it more valuable on the whole rather than less. It is important to be able to cope with it, to overcome it—to win rather than to lose the game of life, as we might put it. But if we do that, we may also think that the resultant life is better. John Stuart Mill, despite his official hedonism, tells us, as a description of the views of many philosophers, that

> The happiness which they meant was not a life of rapture; but moments of such, in an existence made up of few and transitory pains, many and various pleasures, with a decided predominance of the active over the passive, and having as the foundation of the whole, not to expect more from life than it is capable of bestowing. A life thus composed, to those who have been fortunate enough to obtain it, has always appeared worthy of the name of happiness.[12]

---

[11] Aristotle, *Nichomachean Ethics*, bk. X, ch. 3: "And no one would choose to live with the intellect of a child throughout his life, however much he were to be pleased at the things that children are pleased at . . ."

[12] John Stuart Mill, *Utilitarianism*, ch. 2.

Mill does not go so far as to tell us what he thinks about Beethoven, let alone Helen Keller and any number of others. The usual idea of hedonism, though, is either too unclear to decide on these cases, or clear enough that it calls into question its claims. My much "thinner" idea, however, has no basic problem with any of these cases. Outsiders can understand, to a degree, what it was like to be Beethoven, and can conclude, if they like, that his was a type of life they would want to lead if they could. One's estimate of that will surely be influenced by the importance we attach to the sort of product that Beethoven so successfully aimed at—great music. But that we can attach so much importance to it as to prefer a life devoted to producing it despite many problems, ailments, and frustrations, tells us volumes. No superficial account will do.

A Final Word

Human life is finite. Indeed, it is vanishingly short compared to the durations of galaxies, say, and very short compared to giant redwoods, for that matter. Should we think its finiteness a terrible shortcoming? Discussion on that point will lead to no ways of rectifying it if it is one; so far as we know, human life will remain short, on the order of perhaps ninety years as the lot even of the fortunate. It can be argued that infinite life would also be infinitely boring, and not a kind of thing that sensible people should crave. But whatever we say about that, an interesting question here is whether the very last stages of life have special philosophical interest. Suppose that Jones can look back on her life with satisfaction: she has accomplished much that she thinks worth accomplishing, made not too many too devastating mistakes, and had many joys and not too many sorrows. Smith, by contrast, has had quite a boring and not very productive life, or been considerably frustrated and perhaps impoverished. He can't look back on his life with much satisfaction. Does this matter?

There are two things to say here, I think. The first is that it does if what we are looking for is a criterion of a good life, in the sense of a good completed life. Ms. Jones, in our example, has clearly had a better life than Mr. Smith. But the second question is: well—so what? What does it really matter, anyway? I am not sure this second is an answerable question if its answer is not identical with that to the first question. But I am not sure it is identical. Is it?

It seems difficult to escape the conclusion that the person to whom it most essentially matters is the very person in question, and that it matters to that person exactly as much as it seems to matter, neither more nor less. We will go to our graves either satisfied or not, but it will make no difference to the outcome in either case. At that point, there is nothing to be gained by either, in terms of strategies for the future, since at that point there is no future. It is the rest of us, contemplating any particular life lived, who may benefit from the contemplation. We will, of course, prefer to have lived the better life if we can, and to be as happy as we can with what we have had, whatever it is. If a final word is in order, that's it.

*   *   *

The question in this section is: what is the good life? Again some ideas from the past are explored. Is the good life one that "realizes" the self? The problem is whether such a formula actually has any content—it rather looks as if it doesn't. Is the good life the life of virtue? This can be made true redundantly, but it is otherwise rather short on content. Is the good life one of maximum *pleasure*? This has an obvious appeal, but only if the notion of pleasure is diluted so that it covers a good deal more than it usually means in ordinary speech. The life of accomplishments—scientific, artistic, athletic, and many others—is likewise immensely plausible. So is having ideals of various kinds—if constrained by moral considerations, of course. Is all this usefully described as the life of happiness? That is also unclear, but plausible. We must, in the end, wonder whether the good life doesn't defy general formulation—and note that, after all, people are immensely diverse, so why shouldn't it? Thus we conclude on an inconclusive note, with the thought that perhaps that is no bad thing.

General Bibliography

[The literature on ethics is endless; this is a very small and somewhat idiosyncratic selection. The list includes all the works cited in the text, plus several others.]

Anscombe, G.E.M. *Intention*. Oxford: Blackwell, 1957.

———. Anscombe, G.E.M. "Modern Moral Philosophy." In *20th Century Ethical Theory*, edited by Cahn and Haber, 351–64.

Aristotle. *Nichomachean Ethics*. Translated by W. D. Ross. In *Basic Works of Aristotle*, 927–1112. New York: Random House, 1941.

Ayer, A. J. "Critique of Ethics." In *Language, Truth and Logic*. London: Gollancz, 1936.

Baier, Kurt. *The Moral Point of View*. Ithaca: Cornell University Press, 1958.

Bayles, Michael. "Intuitions in Ethics." *Dialogue* 23 (1984): 439–55

Belliotti, Raymond. *Happiness Is Overrated*. Lanham, MD: Rowman and Littlefield, 2003.

Bentham, Jeremy. *Principles of Morals and Legislation*. 1789.

Binmore, Ken. *Game Theory and the Social Contract*. 2 vols. Cambridge, MA: MIT Press, 1994–1998.

Blanshard, Brand. "The New Subjectivism in Ethics." In *20th Century Ethical Theory*, edited by Cahn and Haber, 183–88. Originally published in *Philosophy and Phenomenological Research* 9 (1949).

Bond, E. J. *Ethics and Human Well-Being*. Oxford: Blackwell, 1996.

———. *Reason and Value*. Cambridge: Cambridge University Press, 1983.

Brandt, Richard A. *Ethical Theory*. Englewood Cliffs, NJ: Prentice-Hall, 1959.

———. *Theory of the Good and the Right*. Oxford: Oxford University Press, 1979.

Broad, C. D. *Five Types of Ethical Theory*. London: Routledge, 1930.

Butchvarov, Panayot. *Skepticism in Ethics*. Bloomington: Indiana University Press, 1989.

Cahn, Steven M., and Haber, Joram G, eds. *20th Century Ethical Theory*. Englewood Cliffs, NJ: Prentice-Hall, 1995.

Crisp, Roger. *Reasons and The Good*. New York: Oxford University Press, 2006.

Dancy, Jonathan. *Ethics without Principles*. Oxford: Clarendon Press, 2004.

———. *Moral Reasons*. Oxford: Blackwell, 1993.

Danielson, Peter. *Artificial Morality—Virtual Games for Virtuous Robots*. New York: Routledge, 1992.

Darwall, Stephen. *Impartial Reason*. Ithaca: Cornell University Press, 1983.

Edwards, Paul. *The Logic of Moral Discourse*. New York: Free Press, 1955.

Ellin, Joseph. *Morality and the Meaning of Life*. Ft. Worth, TX: Harcourt, Brace, 1994.

Ewin, R. E. *Co-operation and Human Values*. New York: St. Martin's Press, 1981.

Falk, W. D. "Goading and Guiding." *Mind* 62 (April 1953): 145–71.

———. *Ought, Reasons, and Morality*. Ithaca, NY: Cornell University Press, 1986.

Finnis, John. *Fundamentals of Ethics*. Washington, DC: Georgetown University Press, 1983.

———. *Natural Law and Natural Rights*. Oxford: Clarendon Press, 1980. An outstanding presentation of a sort of neo-Scholastic point of view.

Flew, Antony. "On Not Deriving 'Ought' from 'Is'." *Analysis* 25, no. 2 (December 1964): 25–31. Reprinted in *The Is-Ought Question*, edited by W. D. Hudson. London: Macmillan Press, 1969, 135–43.

Foot, Philippa. "Moral Beliefs." In *20th Century Ethical Theory*, edited by Cahn and Haber, 365–77.

———. *Natural Goodness*. Oxford: Oxford University Press, 2003.

———. *Virtues and Vices*. Berkeley: University of California Press, 1978.

Gauthier, David. *Morals by Agreement*. New York: Oxford University Press, 1987.

Gert, Bernard, *Morality*. New York: Oxford University Press, 1988.

Gewirth, Alan. "The 'Is-Ought' Problem Resolved." In *20th Century Ethical Theory*, edited by Cahn and Haber, 500–518. Originally delivered as the Presidential Address to the Western Division of the American Philosophical Association, 1974.

———. *Reason and Morality*. Chicago: University of Chicago, 1978.

Hampshire, Stuart, ed. *Public and Private Morality*. Cambridge: Cambridge University Press, 1978.

Hardin, Russell. *Morality within the Limits of Reason*. Chicago: University of Chicago Press, 1988.

———. *Trust*. Cambridge: Polity Press, 2006.

Hare, R. M. *Freedom and Reason*. Oxford: Oxford University Press, 1963.

———. *The Language of Morals*. Oxford: Oxford University Press, 1951.

———. *Moral Thinking*. Oxford: Oxford University Press, 1981.

Harman, Gilbert. *The Nature of Morality*. New York: Oxford University Press, 1977.

Hastings, Rashdall. *The Theory of Good and Evil*. Oxford: Clarendon Press, 1907.

Huemer, Michael. *Ethical Intuitionism*. London: Palgrave Macmillon, 2005.

Hume, David. *Enquiry Concerning the Principles of Morals*. (London, 1751).

———. *A Treatise of Human Nature*. Edited by L. A. Selby-Bigge. Oxford: Clarendon Press, 1955.

Hurka, Thomas. *Virtue, Vice, and Value*. Oxford: Oxford University Press, 2001.

Hursthouse, Rosalind. *On Virtue Ethics*. Oxford: Oxford University Press, 1999.

Kant. *Foundations of the Metaphysics of Morals*. Translated by Lewis White Beck. Indianapolis: Bobbs-Merrill, 1959.

Lewis, C. I. *An Analysis of Knowledge and Valuation.* La Salle, IL: Open Court, 1946.

MacIntyre, Alasdair. "The Nature of the Virtures." In *20th Century Ethical Theory*, edited by Cahn and Haber, 617–33.

——. *Whose Justice? Which Rationality?* Notre Dame: University of Notre Dame Press, 1988.

Mackie, J. L. *Ethics: Inventing Right from Wrong.* London: Penguin, 1977.

Medlin, Brian. "Ultimate Principles and Ethical Egoism." *Australasian Journal of Philosophy* 35 (1957): 111–18. Reprinted in *20th Century Ethical Theory*, edited by Cahn and Haber, 316–21.

Mill, John Stuart. *Utilitarianism.* 1863.

Moore, G. E. "The Conception of Intrinsic Goodness." In his *Philosophical Studies.* London: Routledge, 1922, essay 8.

——. *Ethics.* London: Hutchinson University Library, 1912.

——. *Principia Ethica.* Cambridge: Cambridge University Press, 1903. Reprinted by Hackett Publishing Co., Indiana.

——. "Reply to My Critics. In *The Philosophy of G. E. Moore*, edited by P. A. Schilpp. Library of Living Philosophers, vol. 4. Chicago: Open Court, 1942.

Nagel, Thomas. *The Possibility of Altruism.* Oxford: Clarendon Press, 1970.

Nakhnikian, George. "On the Naturalistic Fallacy." In *Morality and the Language of Conduct*, edited by H.-N. Castañeda and George Nakhnikian, 145–58. Detroit: Wayne University Press, 1963.

Narveson, Jan. "Formalism and Utilitarianism." *Australasian Journal of Philosophy* (May 1965): 58–71. Reprinted in *Respecting Persons in Theory and Practice*, ch. 1.

——. *The Libertarian Idea.* Philadelphia: Temple University Press, 1989.

——. *Morality and Utility.* Baltimore: Johns Hopkins Press, 1967.

——. *Moral Matters.* 2nd ed. Peterborough, Ontario: Broadview Press, 1999.

——. "A Puzzle about Economic Justice in Rawls' Theory." *Social Theory and Practice* 4, no. 1 (Fall 1976): 1–28. Reprinted in his *Respecting Persons in Theory and Practice*, ch. 2.

——. "Rawls and Utilitarianism." In *The Limits of Utilitarianism*, edited by H. Miller and W. Williams, 128–43. Minneapolis: University of Minnesota Press, 1982.

——. *Respecting Persons in Theory and Practice.* Lanham, MD: Rowman and Littlefield, 2003.

——. *You and the State: A Short Introduction to Political Philosophy.* Lanham, MD: Rowman and Littlefield, 2008.

Nielsen, Kai. *Equality and Liberty.* Totowa, NJ: Rowman and Littlefield, 1985.

——. "Why Should I Be Moral?" In *Contemporary Ethics, Selected Readings*, edited by James Sterba, 98–105. Englewood Cliffs, NJ: Prentice-Hall, 1985

Nowell-Smith, P. H. *Ethics.* Harmondsworth: Penguin Books, 1954.

Nozick, Robert. *Anarchy, State and Utopia.* New York: Basic Books, 1974.

Olen, Jeffrey. *Moral Freedom.* Philadelphia: Temple University Press, 1989.

Parfit, Derek. *Reasons and Persons.* Oxford: Oxford Unviersity Press, 1986.

Parker, Dewitt H. *The Principles of Aesthetics.* New York: Appleton-Century-Croft, 1946.

Popper, Karl. *The Open Society and Its Enemies*. 5th ed. Princeton: Princeton University Press, 1966.

Prichard, H. A. "Does Philosophy Rest on a Moral Mistake?" In *Moral Obligation* by Prichard, 1–17.

———. *Moral Obligation: Essays and Lectures*. Oxford: Clarendon Press, 1949.

Rachels, James. "Active and Passive Euthanasia." *New England Journal of Medicine* 292 (1975): 78–80.

———. *The Elements of Moral Philosophy*. 2nd ed. NewYork: McGraw-Hill, 1993.

Rand, Ayn. *The Virtue of Selfishness*. New York: Signet Books, 1964.

Rashdall, Hastings. *The Theory of Good and Evil*. 2 vols. Oxford: Clarendon Press, 1907.

Rawls, John. "Outline of a Decision Procedure for Ethics." *Philosophical Review* 60, no. 2 (April 1951): 177–97. Reprinted in *20th Century Ethical Theory*, edited by Cahn and Haber.

———. *A Theory of Justice*. Cambridge, MA: Harvard University Press, 1971.

Raz, Joseph. *The Morality of Freedom*. New York: Oxford University Press, 1986.

Ross, W. David. *The Foundations of Ethics*. Oxford: Oxford University Press, 1936.

———. "The Meaning of 'Right'." In *The Foundations of Ethics*.

———. *The Right and the Good*. Oxford: Oxford University Press, 1930.

———. "What Makes Right Acts Right?" In *The Right and the Good*, ch. 2. Reprinted in *20th Century Ethical Theory*, edited by Cahn and Haber, 87–105.

Santayana, George. *The Life of Reason: Reason in Religion*. New York: Scribner's, 1905.

Schmidtz, David. *Rational Choice and Moral Agency*. Princeton, NJ: Princeton University Press, 1995.

Searle, John. "How to Derive an 'Ought' from an 'Is'. *Philosophical Review* 73 (1964): 43–58.

Sidgwick, Henry. *The Methods of Ethics*. 7th ed. Cambridge: Cambridge University Press, 1907.

Singer, Marcus George. *Generalizations in Ethics*. New York: Alfred Knopf, 1961.

Sparshott, F. E. "Disputed Evaluations." *American Philosophical Quarterly* 7, no. 2 (1970): 131–42.

———. *An Enquiry into Goodness*. Chicago: University of Chicago Press, 1958.

Stevenson, Charles. "The Emotive Meaning of Ethical Terms." In *Facts and Values*, 10–31. Originally published in *Mind*, New Series 46, no. 181 (Jan. 1937): 14–31.

Stevenson, Charles. *Ethics and Language*. New Haven, CT: Yale University Press, 1944.

———. *Facts and Values*. New Haven, CT: Yale University Press, 1963.

———. "Retrospective Comments." In *Facts and Values*, 186–232.

Stocker, Michael. "The Schizophrenia of Modern Ethical Theories." In *20th Century Ethical Theory*, edited by Cahn and Haber, 531–40.

Taylor, Michael. *The Possibility of Cooperation*. New York: Cambridge University Press, 1987.

Toulmin, Stephen. *An Examination of the Place of Reason in Ethics*. Cambridge: Cambridge University Press, 1950. Republished as *Reason in Ethics*. Cambridge: Cambridge University Press, 1964.

Urmson, J. O. *The Emotive Theory of Ethics*. Oxford: Hutchinson University Library, 1968.

Wiggins, David. *Needs, Values and Truth: Essays in the Philosophy of Value*. 3rd ed. Oxford: Clarendon Press, 1998.

———. "Truth, Invention, and the Meaning of Life." In *20th Century Ethical Theory*, edited by Cahn and Haber, 541–72.

Williams, Bernard. *Ethics and the Limits of Philosophy*. Cambridge, MA: Harvard University Press, 1985.

———. *Moral Luck*. Cambridge: Cambridge University Press, 1981.

Index

aesthetic value, 7–8, 29, 33, 48, 64, 95, 102, 104, 132,150, 256, 262–63
Aquinas, Thomas, 7, 120,154, 199, 100
Aristotle
  on free will, 13
  on uses of 'good', 28
  on means and ends, 29, 39, 133, 260
  on subject matter of ethics, 31
  on practical reason, 66–67, 69
  on happiness, 94, 123, 270
  on nature of man, 99, 255
  on a central idea of morals, 112
  on virtue theory, 149–51, 236, 240
  vs. Kant on justice, 238

Belliotti, Raymond, 249n
Blanshard, Brand, 73–77, 106
Butler, Joseph, 52
  his crucial distinction, 144–45
  his Conscience Theory, 156–57

coercion, 203, 231
  re terrorism 221
common good, 120–24, 199–200, 236
  re virtue, 155
conscience, 61, 156–58, 192, 208

consequences, 54, 87, 118, 132. 183–85, 242
consequentialism, 27, 50,
convention(s), 158–60, 192, 210
culture 113,
  and relativism 139–40,

Dancy, Jonathan, 8–9, 54,
  and particularism, 172–74
definition
  and meaning, 20
  types of, 21–25
  and analysis, 26
descriptions and evaluations, 94, 116,130–31, 183–84, 270

egalitarianism vi, 230–36
egoism, 143–48, 192–93, 199
  defined 143
  analyzed re universalizability, 169, 199, 206
  re Hobbes, 201–2
elitism, 164–66
emotions
  and intuition, 46
  and emotivism, 63, 75,
  moral, 76, 77
  relation to cognitive, 76
  as part of the soul,149–50

and religion, 263
emotivism, 71–80
emotive meaning, 70–71, 75–77
ends, 27–29, 40, 95–100 passim,
    110–11, 145–6, 152, 167, 184,
    257
enforcement of morals
    the carrot and the stick, 225–26
equality, 190–92, 230–36
"Error" theory, 15, 131–32
ethics
    as distinct from morals, ix, 4,
    reason and, 3
    applied vs. theoretical, 3, 138,
evolutionary ethics, 132–33, 175, 259
"Existential" factor, 242–43

fact and value, 6–7, 109
Facts and Values (Stevenson), 61, 74
Finnis, John, 104–6
force,
    and reason, 142
    and coercion, 203
fuzziness
    inevitable in rules, 240–41

Gauthier, David, ix, 204–10, 219
good, common. *See* common good
goodness, 11, 22, 28, 33–36, 44–51,
    66–69
    and rightness, 27–31
    meaning of, 110
    and knowability, 92
    and preference, 93
    criteria open, 93
    Sparshott's analysis, 106–11
    concluding thoughts on, 110–11, 134
    in re theological ethics, 152–53
    authority theories of, 193
    and self-realization, 249–57, 269

Hare, R. M., 79–87, 181
hedonism, vii, 40, 50, 53, 249–50,
    264–70

Hobbes
    his "Law of Nature," 220–22
Hume, David
    fact and value, 5–8
    on analytical phenomenology,
        34–36
    influence on Stevenson , 66
    on moral sentiment, 79, 174, 228
    on egalitarianism, 235
    on promises, 91
    on social rules, 125
    and universalizability, 199
    on virtue, 237–41 passim
hypocrisy 93, 122, 129

impartiality, 177, 230, 234–35
innate reasons, 166, 193, 201
intrinsic value, 39–41, 44–47, 50, 57,
    100, 105, 111, 123, 127, 180,
    239,
    vs. inherent, 40
    vs. instrumental, 41
    and desire, 53
    experiences the only intrinsically
    valuable things, 102–4
    and Finnis (see Finnis)
    health an example, 254
intuitionism, 10–12
    rejected, 57
    methodological, 59
    theoretical, 59–63
intuitions
    linguistic, 22, 26,
    metaethical, 32–80 passim
    philosophical (Sidgwick), 52–53

Kant, Immanuel, 8
    and definition of morals, 31
    and rigorism, 54, 170
    and universalizability, 82, 198–99
    re happiness, 94
    and status of moral reason,
        166–72, 192–93
    his "Categorical Imperative,"
        167–68

and substantive morality, 229
morals and good will, 238
and the personal factor, 243

law, 4
  in Finnis, 104
  re John Stuart Mill, 119
  Natural law, 163–64
Legalism, 160–64
Locke, John, 36
logic and ethics, 11, 19, 25, 29, 41,
    43, 54, 58, 63–5, 71, 82, 84,
    184, 219
  and emotivism, 78–85
  re Searle's argument, 90–92
  re criteria of goodness, 93–94
  and relativism, 115
  role in substantive theorizing, 137
  and egoism, 144
  and theological ethics, 153–55
  in Gewirth, 212
  and egalitarianism, 234
  in virtue theory, 238–40, 256

Mackie, J. L., 69, 106
means and ends, 39–40, 45, 95,
    110–11, 260
metaethics
  re Brand Blanshard's argument
    72
  dist. between it and substantive, 3,
    4, 137
  defined, 19, 137,
  and various distinctions, 133
metaphysics
  and denial of free will, 13–14
  connection to metaethics, 45, 58,
    61, 109
  and moral realism, 130
  in Kant's ethics, 167
Mill, John Stuart
  and free will, 14
  on the idea of justice 119
monism, ethical. *See* pluralism
Moore, G. E., 11, 25, 32–51, 54–73

passim, 80–82, 93, 103–4, 109, 134,
    180, 126
  and intuitionism, 32–82 passim
  and utilitarianism, 180–82
  and noncognitive views, 80
  and prescriptivism, 80
moral
  definition of 'moral', 8, 111,
  diversity re use of, 31–32
  denial that there are nonderivative
    moral judgments, 57
  moral beliefs, 92
moral "administration," 119
moral complexity, 229–30
moral experts, 22, 26
moral luck, 241–42
moral relativism, 115–18
moral virtue(s), 148–49, 237, 240,
    256–57, 267
motivation
  and consequentialist/nonconse-
    quentialist distinction, 183
  and desire, 253
  and intuitionism, 49, 109, 198
  moral, 166–68
  and utilitarianism, 193
mutual aid, 226–28
  and children 244

naturalism
  ancient sense of, 250
  defined, 32
  and emotivism 65
  Moore and, 37–38, 60, 63–64
  naturalistic fallacy, 41–44, 133–34
  revival of, 91–109
  senses of, 38
negative rights. *See* rights, negative
Nielsen, Kai
  and egalitarianism, 231–35
  on moral motivation, 210–16,
    222–24
nonnatural properties, 11, 38–41,
    46–47, 59, 61–63, 67–70
nonnaturalism, 44
Nowell-Smith, Patrick, 62, 68

and multifunctionalism, 80
Nozick, Robert, 103, 188

objective, objectivity, 46–47, 73, 96.
    129–32, 149, 166, 225, 254
objectivism in ethics, 69
objectivity, 46–47, 106
ostension, 35–36

partiality. *See* impartiality
particularism, 55, 172–73, 192–93,
    236
personal concerns and morals,
    243
personal obligations, unchosen,
    244
Plato, 2, 38, 61, 92, 99, 151, 165,
    199, 224, 256, 265
pluralism, ethical, 52
politics, political, iv, vi, 142, 201,
    219
    morals and, 236
prescriptivism, 62–79 passim,
    82–87
Prichard, H. A., 51–60 passim
prima facie rightness (wrongness), or
    duties, 54–56, 89–90, 171–2, 190.
    192
prisoner's dilemma, 204–8

Rashdall, Hastings, 58, 65
rationality
    and morals, 222
Rawls, John, 59n, 185–93 passim
    re separateness of persons, 114
reasons in ethics, 77–79
rigorism, 170–72
Ross, Sir W. D. 7, 9, 51–68 passim,
    88, 171–72, 192, 230
rules
    role in morals, 244
    for the group, the central subject
    of morals, 256
    and virtues, 239–41

Searle, John, 87–91
self-evidence, 51–57 passim,
    in Finnis, 104–6
self-interest, 143–48
    as a potential basis of ethics,
    121
    as a theory of rational action,
    145
    potentially self-defeating, 206,
    208
selfishness
    as a vice, 146
self-realization, 249–57, 269
sense data, 59
sentiment, 5, 46, 79, 119, 174–75,
    192–93. *See also* emotion
Sidgwick, Henry, 51, n. 65
    and intuitionism, 52–53, 56, 60
    and universalizability, 55
social contract, vi, 124, 184–88,
    200–204, 208
    and Alan Gewirth, 211–20
    Hobbesian premise, 215–16
Sparshott, F. E., 106–11, 128, 131
Stevenson, Charles, 61, 64–71
    and truth, 74
    and reasons in ethics, 78
subjective, subjectivism, 46, 63–65,
    "new" subjectivism, 72–73
    re Kant, 166–68
supervenience, 48–49

Tarski truth paradigm, 74
theology and ethics
    theoretical problems, 151–55
    practical problems, 155–56
theory
    role of in ethics, 5
truth
    Stevenson's account, 74

universality, 81, 193, 200, 220–21,
    230
universalizability, 199, 214
    in Sidgwick, 51

Utilitarianism, 50–52, 114, 175–200, 204n
  foundational problems, 182–85
  intuitive discussions of, 179–80

weakness, moral, 92–93
will, freedom of the, 12–15
Williams, Bernard, 187n, 243